BOUNDARIES *of the* SELF

BOUNDARIES
of the
SELF

Gender, Culture, Fiction

Roberta Rubenstein

UNIVERSITY OF ILLINOIS
Urbana and Chicago

© 1987 by the Board of Trustees of the University of Illinois
Manufactured in the United States of America
C 5 4 3 2 1

This book is printed on acid-free paper.

Library of Congress Cataloging-in-Publication Data

Rubenstein, Roberta, 1944–
   Boundaries of the self.

   Bibliography: p.
   Includes index.
   1. American fiction—Women authors—History and
criticism. 2. Feminism and literature. 3. Sex role
in literature. 4. Self in literature. 5. Ethnicity
in literature. 6. English fiction—Women authors—
History and criticism. 7. American fiction—20th
century—History and criticism. 8. Women and literature.
9. Minority women in literature. I. Title.
PS374.F45R8   1987   813′.54′099287   86-11252
ISBN 0-252-01355-7

For Chuck, especially,
and
for Vanessa and Joshua
and
for my mother, Sarah

Contents

Acknowledgments ix

Introduction 3

PART 1
Boundaries of Relationship

Confinements of the Self: Penelope Mortimer 15
Escape Artists and Split Personalities: Margaret Atwood 63

PART 2
Boundaries of Cultural Identity

Pariahs and Community: Toni Morrison 125
Bridging Two Cultures: Maxine Hong Kingston 164
Boundaries of the Cosmos: Leslie Silko 190

PART 3
Reformulating Boundaries

Transformations of the Ordinary: Marilynne Robinson 211

Conclusion: Boundaries of the Self 231

Bibliography 241

Index 251

Acknowledgments

Among those who have contributed to the ultimate shape of this book, I appreciate the support of Carolyn Heilbrun, Paula Gilbert Lewis, and Frank Turaj during the early stage of the project. My colleagues and friends, Kay Mussell, Laura Tracy, and Linda Osborne, have been both exemplary readers and incisive critics. Annis Pratt and Blanche Gelfant read the manuscript in its entirety and made invaluable recommendations during its revision. Shirley Rosenstock and the Interlibrary Loan staff at The American University Library were particularly helpful during my research. I began this book with support from the National Endowment for the Humanities Senior Research Fellowships and completed it with the support of an American University Summer Research Grant, for both of which I am grateful.

My thinking on the subject of boundaries owes an immeasurable part of its inspiration to my family, through whom I have discovered the richest meanings of attachments. This book is dedicated to them.

BOUNDARIES *of the* SELF

Introduction

While anatomy may no longer be unquestioningly associated with women's destiny, it remains a powerful reference for understanding female (and male) experience. As Catherine F. Smith has phrased it, "Anatomy is part of epiphany. Our bodies, our visions[,] is one of the aesthetic implications of feminist thought."[1] In this sense, texts written by women necessarily mirror, comment upon, or explore this mode of relation to the world. Hélène Cixous argues that female texts exemplify the correspondences between language and body, dramatizing multiplicity and process rather than resolution:

> A feminine textual body is recognized by the fact that it is always endless, without ending: there's no closure, it doesn't stop. . . . [A] feminine [editor's note: read "female"] text goes on and on and at a certain moment the volume comes to an end but the writing continues and for the reader this means being thrust into the void. These are texts that work on the beginning but not on the origin. The origin is a masculine myth: I always want to know where I come from. . . . [It is] the manner of beginning . . . that marks a feminine writing. A feminine text starts on all sides, all at once, starts twenty times, thirty times, over.[2]

American feminist scholars are still deliberating whether in fact there are distinctly female literary forms, as Cixous insists. The very terms of debate in feminist literary criticism pivot on the issue of women's relation to language. While American critics implicitly view the language of female texts as a neutral tool, our French counterparts are "concerned more with the gender of the text than with the gender of the writer."[3] Few critics of either persuasion have considered the relationship between the gender of the writer and her characters: what kinds of meanings emerge from texts written by women in which the protagonist or central subject is male?

Since the constructs of the body and its parts are a function of materiality as well as language, it is virtually impossible to separate the images of corporeality from their figurative or existential ramifications. As Mary Douglas has pertinently observed, "The social body constrains the way the physical body is perceived. The physical experience of the body, always modified by the social categories through which it is known, sustains a particular view of society. There is a continual exchange of meanings between the two kinds of bodily experience so that each reinforces the categories of the other."[4]

The body is thus a template for figurative expressions of experience. In narratives by women writers, spatial constructs in particular are, as several recent feminist analyses have demonstrated, analogues for the female protagonists' existential condition.[5] Sandra Gilbert and Susan Gubar connect this ubiquitous trope in nineteenth-century novels by women to the writers' own experience of entrapment in patriarchy, declaring that "dramatizations of imprisonment and escape are so all-pervasive" that they represent "a uniquely female tradition in this period."[6]

Yet, despite Gilbert and Gubar's eloquent exploration of these metaphorical correspondences, the literary representation of spatial enclosure is not unique to the female gender—as works by authors as dissimilar as Fyodor Dostoevsky, Franz Kafka, Jean-Paul Sartre, Bernard Malamud, and others suggest. In his phenomenological analysis of metaphors of "intimate being," Gaston Bachelard proposes that such structures as rooms and houses are "psychological diagrams that guide writers and poets in their analysis of intimacy."[7] Images of the deepest personal experiences and memories derive from "the values of inhabited space, of the non-I that protects the I."[8]

Thus, the categories of "inside" and "outside," and the delineations of the boundary that determines them, are expressions of our common biological reality as discrete entities. The very notion of interiority is a reciprocal process mediated across these originally corporeal boundaries. As Jean Starobinski has written, individuality develops through "our relationship with the *outside,* with that which we have never been, or with that which we have ceased to be."[9] Furthermore,

> an inside comes into being the moment a form asserts itself by setting its own boundaries. A living organism exists only by virtue of the margin . . . through which it determines, defines and opposes itself, becoming individual: limit, finiteness, individuality, the struggle waged against the outside— all these are correlative. No inside is conceivable, therefore, without the complicity of an outside on which it relies. . . . No outside would be conceivable without an inside fending it off, resisting it, "reacting" to it.[10]

If in this generic sense the experience of biological boundary transcends gender, in another manifestation it expresses gender as well as the cultural interpretations that gender differences have acquired. In contrast to males, females have a physical marker of virginity in the membrane of the hymen; upon its rupture countless women's fates have been decided. Maternity itself is another potent image of boundary. In addition to the obvious physiological changes, the first-time mother crosses a dramatic psychological threshhold and acquires a new, irreversible social role as a mother; the last stage of labor, termed "transition," is suggestive beyond its physiological context. Additionally, in procreation a woman is privileged to experience through her own body both ends, as it were, of the umbilical cord.

Our material experiences of union and separation operate in the psychological sphere as well: boundaries constitute a person's sense of self as distinct from other people. According to psychoanalytic theorists of the object-relations school, initially the newborn infant exists in symbiosis with its mother, experiencing itself as continuous with her; there is no distinction between "inner" and "outer." Only gradually do the needs of mother and child become incongruent enough for the infant to discover the difference between "me" and "not-me." The formation of selfhood occurs through the child's recognition of the shifting shape of the emotional fields that interaction with the mother and others produces.

The development of consciousness is thus in an important sense the definition of a psychic geography: personal boundaries mapped in relation to the emotional fields of other people. In the "psychological birth of the human infant"[11] that occurs between birth and the age of three, a child gradually discovers and creates the boundaries that both separate it from and identify it with the mother. Through the fluctuation between opposing needs for dependency and autonomy, most children eventually achieve an integration that reflects the growing sense of ego separateness, along with its vulnerabilities. As Margaret Mahler describes this universal process, "Consciousness of self and absorption without awareness of self are the two polarities within which we move, with varying ease and with varying degrees of alternation or simultaneity. . . . As is the case with any intrapsychic process, this one reverberates throughout the life cycle."[12]

Feminist reconsideration of the course of ego development has focused on the unexamined gender distinctions that operate in this universal process. Both Nancy Chodorow and Dorothy Dinnerstein have influentially argued that the very asymmetry of parenting arrangements—with females fulfilling the primary nurturing role in nearly all cultures—necessarily contributes to gender-different paths in the organization of experience and, ultimately, of culture.[13] As Chodorow posits, boys acquire gender identity by progressively differentiating themselves from their mothers and modeling their identities on their fathers, a process that is corroborated by the mother's lesser identification with her male child. By contrast, girls continue to identify with their same-sex parent for a considerably longer time and may, in fact, never entirely separate psychologically from her. This dynamic is corroborated by the mother, who unconsciously sees her daughter as an extension of her own identity and is also drawn to recapitulate some of her own identifications with her female parent through her female child.

Though perhaps slighting the influence of other factors in the process of female personality development, Chodorow's thesis is particularly valuable for its focus on the gender differences in the formation of ego boundaries. A female's separation from her mother is characterized, Chodorow argues, by greater ambivalence and confusion over ego boundaries than is the parallel process for a male. "Because of their mothering by women, girls come to experience themselves as less separate than boys, as having more permeable ego boundaries. Girls come to define themselves more in relation to others."[14] Furthermore, the processes of separation and individuation "remain particularly female developmental issues. . . . [T]here is a tendency in women toward boundary confusion and a lack of sense of separateness from the world."[15]

Interpersonal boundaries mirror and are mirrored in the larger social body (or bodies). Beginning with what D. W. Winnicott terms the psychic "membrane" in each individual across which the dialectic between inner and outer reality occurs,[16] social organization and culture are the result of innumerable individual and collective mediations of boundary. Thus, identity can be understood as a dynamic interplay among the fluid layerings of experience: materiality and the body; intrapsychic and interpersonal processes; and the substructure of ethnic, national, or political forces acting upon the individual.

In addition to the obvious groupings created by national boundaries, there are heterogeneous ethnic and religious groups within a given geographical or political entity. Like ego boundaries, ethnic boundaries are figurative but powerful demarcations that, in the latter case, distinguish group from group. In effect, there are two "sides" to the demarcation between ethnic groups, as Anya Peterson Royce suggests:

> the boundary maintained from within, and the boundary imposed from outside, which results from the process of interaction with others. Individuals enclosed by the inner boundary share a common cultural knowledge; hence, their interaction may be varied and complex and tolerate a great deal of ambiguity. Interaction across the outer boundary is much more limited because of the lack of shared knowledge. If all cultural knowledge were the property of all groups, boundaries would be blurred and eventually disappear. Where these boundaries exist, groups tend to limit the circumstances in which they are willing to interact to those that do not threaten their cultural integrity.[17]

Yet the constructs of culture itself—whether our own or others'—often reflect unconscious bias in the assumptions about the dominant values within a particular group. Anthropology as the "study of man" quite literally reflects a perceptual asymmetry in the very descriptions of social organization. As recorded by (generally male) ethnologists, male informants provide descriptions that reflect the values of their own gender group as expressed through the dominant discourse; thus they unintentionally minimize or distort the often different values of their female peers. Hence, as Edwin Ardener theorizes, because women are "not in the male world-position," their perspective remains unarticulated; they are "'muted.'"[18] Ardener focuses on what he terms the "bounding" problem "presented by women in a situation in which the 'bounds' of 'society' are themselves defined by men."[19]

In Ardener's sense, the mutedness of women in a given culture or social group is a function of their subordinate position within it, which is in turn manifest in the form of discourse: the nature of what can be articulated as well as who speaks it. The effort to alter the "gender" of language, which too often reinforces the status quo, is a frequent if implicit dimension of the narratives discussed in the pages that follow. As the nameless narrator in Margaret Atwood's *Surfacing* phrases it, "Language divides us into fragments, I wanted to be whole."[20]

If women are typically muted within their own culture even when they constitute a demographic majority, then women of ethnic minority groups are doubly muted. Both gender and ethnic status render them "speechless" in patriarchy. In the following discussion, I explore the manner in which writers who may be considered "muted" because of either gender or ethnic identification, or both, articulate those very issues within and through their fictions. To the extent that women—as both authors and characters—have internalized models of selfhood that overlap along the axis of gender and may diverge along the axes of national and ethnic origin, their narrative representations of the world express their diverse experiences of boundary in both psychological and cultural senses.

Paradoxically, then, the very concept of boundary itself is fluid. In the most general sense, it indicates the figurative line that divides, defines, distinguishes between two or more contiguous areas. When these areas are conceived as metaphorical rather than literal, the possibilities of meaning extend into diverse aspects of experience. To address the issues of boundary and metaphorical space is to confront a series of questions: in what ways do the experiences of gender, as well as differences of ethnic or national origin and class, combine in the unique personality, as artistically represented in narratives by women? Or, stated another way, how might these dimensions of the writer's experience of "inside" and "outside"—of space, place, and location as material, psychological, and social constructs—be understood through her representations of boundary? In turn, how do language and literary form both mediate and articulate these experiences?

In this study I consider a series of contexts for diverse representations of boundary in contemporary narratives written by women, as artistic expressions of psychological, social, and cultural experience. I am mindful that my own circumstances may limit my full comprehension of ethnic and cultural realities in relation to which I am necessarily an outsider. Yet in several instances the writers included here address this very problem, as if to cross those boundaries and extend our understanding of plurality and diversity.

The analyses that follow focus on six contemporary writers whose narratives reflect varied expressions of the metaphors of boundary and spatiality: the experiences of the body; the formation of psychological boundaries; the crucial effects of attachment, union, separation, and loss as processes within primary emotional relationships—particularly between mothers (or mother-figures) and daughters; political or cultural conflicts between dissimilar groups or values; and the shape or narrative boundaries of each literary work.

The scope is necessarily selective rather than comprehensive. The authors discussed here are not meant to be "representative," though by chance they do reflect diverse geographical, national, ethnic, and recent historical contexts. Three of the writers I consider—Margaret Atwood, Toni Morrison, and Maxine Hong Kingston—have been the subjects of current critical attention by both feminists and other literary critics; the other three—Penelope Mortimer, Leslie Silko, and Marilynne Robinson—have received little if any critical consideration. In the former case, my hope is to bring a new perspective to well-known writers; in the latter, to give these undeservedly neglected or new writers the attention they merit. Within each chapter, I discuss an author's fictional canon through central themes and images that illuminate the concept of boundary in its psychological, cultural, and formal contexts. The boundaries of the narrative form itself are extended in several instances, as autobiography, fantasy, and legend are interwoven with the more traditional features of the genre. In the discussions of the less well-known authors or texts, I include somewhat more commentary on the narratives to orient the reader.

In part 1, "Boundaries of Relationship," I consider the fictional canons of Penelope Mortimer and Margaret Atwood. Mortimer, a British writer who is a generation older than the other writers included in this study, offers powerful representations of female constriction within, or without, the institution of marriage during the decades that predate the contemporary renewal of feminism in England and America. In a motif that recurs throughout her fiction as well as in the narratives of each of the other writers included here, Mortimer portrays women who are literally and/or psychically wounded by their experiences. Atwood dramatizes various dimensions of her female characters' experiences of attachment and separation, division and union, as fundamental to their discovery or recovery of selfhood and, in several instances, as expressions of Atwood's own strong national consciousness as a Canadian.

The mediation between gender and ideological or cultural boundaries is particularly central in the fiction of ethnic minority writers. In part 2, "Boundaries of Cultural Identity," I discuss three writers who portray the conflicts of values and the struggle for self-definition for characters of both genders who belong to minority ethnic groups within American society. Toni Morrison's dramatizations of people trying to survive as "outsiders" or of lovers defending different conceptions of authenticity, Maxine Hong Kingston's efforts to reconcile her anti-female Chinese tradition with her American experiences, and Leslie Silko's portrayal of a mixed-blood Indian man caught between two cultures are all expressions, in diverse literary forms, of the interplay of separateness and union on both individual and collective levels. In several of these narratives, additional resonances of meaning occur in the relationship between the author and her male protagonist, whose dilemma highlights the complex intersections of gender and ethnicity.

In part 3, "Transcending Boundaries," I analyze the single novel to date of Marilynne Robinson as an evocative narrative of female quest that strips away many of the presumptions of selfhood, and of the construct of boundary itself, through the use of mythic imagery and paradox. In the final chapter, I attempt to draw some conclusions about the meanings of boundary in narratives by women.

Virginia Woolf remarked that "books continue each other, in spite of our habit of judging them separately."[21] Though she was referring to fiction, her observation applies equally to works of criticism. I hope that this study of female boundaries will continue the dialogue and extend some of the stimulating ideas recently generated by scholars of literature and other disciplines. My aim is to illuminate the correspondences between the "shapes" of psychological and cultural female experience and their narrative expression, envisioned by each of these writers as a discovery or redefinition of the boundaries of selfhood.

NOTES

1. Catherine F. Smith, "Jane Lead Mysticism and the Woman Cloathed with the Sun," in *Shakespeare's Sisters: Feminist Essays on Women Poets,* ed. Sandra M. Gilbert and Susan Gubar (Bloomington: Indiana University Press, 1979), p. 18.

2. Hélène Cixous, "Castration or Decapitation," trans. Annette Kuhn, *Signs,* Vol. 7, No. 1 (Autumn 1981), p. 53.

3. Margaret Homans, "'Her Very Own Howl': The Ambiguities of Representation in Recent Women's Fiction," *Signs,* Vol. 9, No. 2 (Winter 1983), p. 187.

4. Mary Douglas, *Natural Symbols: Explorations in Cosmology* (New York: Pantheon, 1970), p. 65.

5. Shirley Ardener, ed. *Women and Space: Ground Rules and Social Maps* (New York: St. Martin's Press, 1981); Nina Baym, *Women's Fiction: A Guide to Novels by and about Women in America, 1820–1870* (Ithaca: Cornell University Press, 1978); Sandra Gilbert and Susan Gubar, *The Madwoman in the Attic: The Woman Writer and the Nineteenth-Century Literary Imagination* (New Haven: Yale University Press, 1979), pp. 83–88 and passim; Ellen Moers, *Literary Women: The Great Writers* (New York: Doubleday, 1976), esp. pp. 252–64; Annis Pratt, *Archetypal Patterns in Women's Fiction* (Bloomington: Indiana University Press, 1981), esp. pp. 45–54; Nancy Regan, "A Home of One's Own: Women's Bodies in Recent Women's Fiction," *Journal of Popular Culture,* Vol. 11 (Spring 1978), pp. 772–88; Roberta Rubenstein, "The Room of the Self: Psychic Geography in Doris Lessing's Fiction," *Perspectives on Contemporary Literature,* Vol. 5 (1979), pp. 69–78; Elaine Showalter, *A Literature of their Own: British Women Novelists from Bronte to Lessing* (Princeton: Princeton University Press, 1977).

6. Gilbert and Gubar, *The Madwoman in the Attic,* p. 85. Nina Baym, writing about popular fiction by nineteenth-century American women writers, suggests that "woman's fiction necessarily develops as its chief organizing metaphor the closed and structured social space. Within that space is yet a smaller space, the room of her own that is the heroine's particular territory, identified with her self. . . . The attachment to space is not by any means a gender-specific quality; but in the nineteenth century it seems that the major male writers were engaged in the process of trying to overcome the attachment to a particular space in favor of a loose commitment, while the women (belatedly, perhaps, or more realistically) were becoming increasingly insistent on the right to a defined space." *Women's Fiction,* p. 188.

7. Gaston Bachelard, *The Poetics of Space,* trans. Maria Jolas (New York: The Orion Press, 1964), p. 38.

8. Ibid., p. 5.

9. Jean Starobinski, "The Inside and the Outside," trans. Frederick Brown, *The Hudson Review,* Vol. 28, No. 3 (Autumn 1975), p. 335, emphasis in original.

10. Ibid., p. 342.

11. Margaret S. Mahler, Fred Pine, and Anni Bergman, *The Psychological Birth of the Human Infant: Symbiosis and Individuation* (New York: Basic Books, 1975).

12. Margaret S. Mahler, "On the First Three Subphases of the Separation-Individuation Process," in *Selected Papers of Margaret S. Mahler,* Vol. 2 (New York: Jason Aronson, 1979), p. 120.

13. Nancy Chodorow, *The Reproduction of Mothering: Psychoanalysis and the Sociology of Gender* (Berkeley: University of California Press, 1978); Dorothy Dinnerstein, *The Mermaid and the Minotaur: Sexual Arrangements and Human Malaise* (rpt. New York: Harper and Row, 1977).

14. Ibid., p. 93.

15. Ibid., p. 110. Elsewhere, Chodorow emphasizes that "the more secure the central self, or ego core, the less one has to define one's self through separateness from others. Separateness becomes, then, a more rigid, defensive, rather fragile, secondary criterion of the strength of the self and of the 'success' of individuation. . . . *Differentiation is not distinctness and separateness, but a particular way of being connected to others.* This connection to others, based on early incorporation, in turn enables us to feel that empathy and confidence that are basic to the recognition of the other as a self." Chodorow, "Gender, Relation, and Difference in Psychoanalytic Perspective," in *The Future of Difference,* ed. Hester Eisenstein and Alice Jardine (Boston: G. K. Hall, 1980), pp. 10–11 (emphasis in original).

16. As D. W. Winnicott describes the eventual bounded structure of the developed ego, inner psychic reality is "the personal property of each individual in so far as a degree of mature integration has been reached which includes the establishment of a unit self, with the implied existence of an inside and an outside, and a limiting membrane." *Playing and Reality* (New York: Basic Books, 1971), p. 106.

17. Anya Peterson Royce, *Ethnic Identity: Strategies of Diversity* (Bloomington: Indiana University Press, 1982), p. 29.

18. Edwin Ardener, "The 'Problem' Revisited," in *Perceiving Women,* ed. Shirley Ardener (New York: John Wiley and Sons, 1975), pp. 21–22.

19. Ibid., p. 23.

20. Margaret Atwood, *Surfacing* (rpt. New York: Popular Library, 1972), p. 172.

21. Virginia Woolf, *A Room of One's Own* (rpt. New York: Harcourt Brace Jovanovich, 1957), p. 84.

PART 1

Boundaries of Relationship

Confinements of the Self

Penelope Mortimer

In the past decade, feminist literary criticism has advanced in a number of fruitful directions, including redefinition of the historical canon through the discovery of neglected women writers. Remarkably, Penelope Mortimer, a contemporary of Doris Lessing in age and of the early Lessing as well as of Margaret Drabble in subject, has to date been overlooked in these important reconsiderations.[1] Yet at least several of her nine narratives deserve to be included among those of her more widely read and critically analyzed peers who fictively explore the lives of women in marriage, domesticity, and motherhood.

Though Mortimer's narratives are for the most part traditional in both structure and characterization, they sensitively and artfully explore many of the problems of women in patriarchy that have since become central issues in feminist thinking. In fact, she gave narrative form to "the problem that has no name" a decade or more before Betty Friedan diagnosed the condition in 1962.[2] Her fiction is of contemporary interest for several reasons. Although certain of the assumptions that permeate her novels of the fifties and sixties are dated—the absolute economic and emotional dependence of her female characters on fathers or husbands and the sense of female subordination to unquestioned patriarchal values—other dimensions of her fiction have resonance today, not only for the historical perspective they provide, but for their depiction of perennial psychological aspects of experiences that have recently become the subject of feminist inquiry. The most important of these are the effect of the original emotional dynamics of the mother-daughter and father-daughter bonds

15

on the adult female's self-image and on related issues of separation, sexuality, and autonomy; the correspondences between physical environments—rooms and spaces—and psychic realities; and the dynamics of female roles and self-realization, particularly when they embody contradictory or untenable expectations.

Like the rediscovered work of Jean Rhys, the fiction of Penelope Mortimer describes a world of women who confront limit and negation, partly because of their own natures, partly because of the nature of the world in which they live. Through their narratives, a contemporary reader gains access to social realities for women of earlier decades and alternative visions of female possibility. Mortimer, an ironist with a moral vision of female experience in a world of male entitlement, addresses the nature of relationships between the sexes and between generations, between self and other, self and sexuality; and—her most persistent theme—the often irreconcilable conflict between erotic and domestic fulfillment.

These issues are narratively expressed through images that resonate throughout Mortimer's fiction, connecting her work to the female literary tradition: mirrors and reflections, confinement and imprisonment, houses and homes, and other metaphorical structures through which social and psychological life are expressed. Frequently, the titles signify or imply the centrality of such structures: villa, prison, cave, home, "bulletproof," "long distance." Of her nine narratives to date, the most artistically successful and psychologically meaningful for contemporary readers, for reasons I will elucidate in due course, are *Cave of Ice, The Pumpkin Eater, The Home,* and *Long Distance.*

In Mortimer's narrative representations of the lives of women, certain patterns predominate in her characters' domestic circumstances: if married, they are emotionally and economically dependent upon roving, unfaithful husbands; if single, they are lonely and anxious about their attractiveness to men. In several instances they suffer either physical or psychic injuries that impair their self-esteem so seriously that they are depicted in crisis. Several psychological issues underscore these dilemmas, particularly in the later fiction, though they are adumbrated from the beginning: female emotional dependency and the accompanying anxiety about separation from or loss of loved ones; anxiety about death (both psychological and physical); and the tendency to repeat destructive emotional patterns.

Moreover, in virtually all of Mortimer's narratives, a crucial social distinction between men and women is the latter's responsibility for children while they are at the same time economically and emotionally dependent on men. (Only Muriel Rowbridge of *My Friend Says It's Bulletproof* is single, childless, and employed.) As in most conventional marriages, the mothers in these stories take far more responsibility for their children than the fathers and consequently are more restricted by their emotional ties and domestic obligations. In the author's early novels, the wife temporarily flees those commitments and the husband is placed in circumstances in which he must assume an unaccustomed and unwelcome responsibility for his offspring. Marriage and motherhood are dramatized not simply as the female characters' sole access to identity but also as the emotional frameworks within which earlier patterns of relationship (generally with one or the other parent) are repeated and, only rarely, resolved.

Mortimer's early novels—*Johanna* (1947) and *A Villa in Summer* (1954)—are dense, talky narratives whose main interest is their anticipation of forms of female experience that recur and evolve throughout the author's later works. Conventional in narrative structure, these novels, including the more economically written and artistically satisfying *The Bright Prison* (1957), depend on the external machinations of plot rather than the inward exploration of character. The three novels belong, with qualifications for the first one, to the species of domestic romance, complete with scrambled and then reunited couples. Since the couples are already married, romance is envisioned as the beckoning temptation of a new erotic partner.

As is typical of the romance form, the trajectory of these narratives is, like the image of imprisonment that characterizes the respective marital relationships, a closing circle: in two of the three novels the partners' reconciliation at the end is signified by their reunions in their respective domiciles, rejoined but sobered by their new insights into the mutual act of faith upon which marriage depends.

Thus, a central theme in Mortimer's early narratives is the nature of the boundaries of the matrimonial relationship, while the later novels explore the consequences of its failure or the difficulty for a woman who lacks other expectations for herself to survive outside such boundaries. Marriage begins as a cocoon of exclusivity created by the lovers to shelter their mutual desire in privacy and gradually hardens into a prison of habit and obligation from which one or both spouses may feel compelled to escape. The imagery of literally bounded spaces expresses the domestic and emotional imprisonment of most of Mortimer's female characters. *The Pumpkin Eater* (1962) brings the exploration of the boundaries of marriage to its most artistically accomplished culmination.

In several others of Mortimer's novels, the issue of boundary expresses different aspects of female experience: the dynamics of the mother-daughter relationship and the idea of the literally or psychically wounded female self. In *Cave of Ice* (1959) the merging of identity between mother and daughter results in a literal repetition of experience that both must confront; in *My Friend Says It's Bulletproof* (1967) a woman's self-image is threatened as a result of the radical alteration of her body boundaries from an operation for breast cancer. *The Home* (1971) and *The Handyman* (1985) are Mortimer's most explicit explorations of issues of psychological and emotional boundary, attachment, union, separation, and loss. *Long Distance* (1974), an experimental reprise of her oeuvre, brings a new narrative and psychological perspective to the issues of emotional imprisonment and loss.

As a way of considering Mortimer's novels, most of which will be unfamiliar to contemporary readers, I have grouped them partly by publishing chronology and partly by their expression of different (though sometimes overlapping) aspects of the boundary issues that I have suggested: first, the cluster of issues and images emerging out of the marital relationship and its transgression—enclosure, infidelity, and imprisonment or confinement, the latter with its additional connotation of maternity; second, the extension of these ideas into the issues and imagery of merged ego boundaries (between wife and husband and between mother and daughter), female wounding, and the emotionally resonant idea of "home"; and, finally, the effects of memory, time, and loss on the boundaries of the self.

Lacking the psychological complexity of her later fiction, Mortimer's early works nonetheless anticipate the author's moral seriousness in their focus on the conflict between domestic fidelity and erotic license. Each narrative focuses on a young married couple with a child or children. Additionally, each explores the conflict between the security of marriage and the limitations it imposes on desire or, in moral terms, the opposition between duty and freedom. Chance events subject apparently stable relationships to new temptations and force the married pair to examine the terms of their emotional contract. One or both spouses find themselves drawn to sample the freedom that seems to be available for the asking outside the figurative boundaries of what Annis Pratt has termed the "archetypal enclosure" of marriage.[3] Antonia Painton of *The Bright Prison* expresses this discovery in terms of the opposition between security and desire: "It was as though a door she had thought permanently sealed, nailed up for comfort and protection against the outside world, had begun to swing open, not far enough for her to see what lay beyond but far enough to suggest the curious idea of escape."[4]

In *Johanna*, the marriage of Johanna and Peter Freund is tested against (and destroyed by) both personal failures and the larger pressures of politics and ideology; the action alternates between London and Vienna on the eve of Hitler's rise to power. Johanna projects her sense of insecure boundary into her immediate environment. At one point, she feels strange walking alone, experiencing "an unprotected feeling, as though one was open to assault from the side."[5] Later, when her eventual lover visits her for the first time, she feels that they are sealed together in a "square, lighted box" (*J*, p. 67). At times she experiences her loneliness as "life imprisonment" (*J*, p. 114) and "solitary confinement" (*J*, p. 132).

Emily and Andrew Addams of *A Villa in Summer* move from their secure—and crowded—London flat to a more spacious borrowed house in the country for the summer and are catapulted into threats to their relationship for which the relocation of their dwelling space is the analogue. Similarly, in *The Bright Prison* the Paintons' house is the correlative of the temporary boundary confusions experienced by its adult occupants. When Antonia Painton is emotionally most distanced from her husband, she regards their house—like their marriage—as "a myth in which, disillusioned but without rancour, she no longer believed. She thought of it only as a receptacle for the shrilling telephone, a small, black, palpitating heart alive in the dead and dusty wreckage of walls and landings" (*BP*, p. 143). Mark Painton, seeking his wife for solace after a series of disorienting events, finds only an "empty, uncared-for house"— the sign of "a positive deprivation, a tearing from him of something he owned, part of his life" (*BP*, p. 127).

Antonia, leaving the house that is equated with both literal security and the "reliable authority in herself . . ." (*BP*, p. 109), gets off a bus "obediently" at a nearby park, "for this was the perimeter of her world and to go beyond it did not yet seem necessary" (*BP*, p. 108). As this and equivalent passages in other novels suggest, several of Mortimer's female characters suffer from a form of agoraphobia. Described by Robert Seidenberg and Karen DeCrow as a problem far more common in women than in men, the condition is characterized by the sufferer's experience of acute anxiety when away from familiar surroundings. In what resembles Antonia Painton's self-chosen geographical restriction, they describe the "tether phenomenon"—the agoraphobic's reluctance to leave certain safe, known parameters or boundaries.[6] Mortimer's Antonia Painton confronts the fragility of her selfhood apart from the images reflected back to her by her family and the married couples who form their social network. "Supposing . . . that she was, away from her reflections, nothing . . . no more than a reflection, possessing no separate heart?" (*BP*, p. 110).

In *Cave of Ice,* Ruth Whiting's house is a bounded space where "the walls, built for protection, had become barriers surrounding pits of solitude." To that place her children come—"breaking in on a fragile state of anxiety"—and go—"leaving the door open for an inrush of silence."[7] Mrs. Armitage of *The Pumpkin Eater* tries to flee from the problems of her deteriorating marriage by going to the couple's "tower" in the country. There, she compares herself to a prisoner whose body is "an uninhabited house and the outside walls are the last to crumble."[8]

Eleanor Strathearn of the resonantly titled novel *The Home* is equally entrapped, even after her separation from her husband of twenty-six years. Though her grown children's presences temporarily turn the house to which she moves into an emotionally full space, more often Eleanor feels herself radically alone and psychically numb. After a "life sentence of marriage" she feels "as strange to the world as a released prisoner."[9] She has a recurrent dream of being in her original house, "which was decomposing, floors rotting, ceilings collapsing, unmanageable chaos everywhere. She couldn't make up her quarrel with Graham [her husband] *because he wasn't there*—a total conviction of his absence . . ." (*H*, p. 137, emphasis in original). The images are transparent reflections of Eleanor's waking anxieties. Her marriage *has* rotted and collapsed; for years her husband has been emotionally absent, though she cannot come to terms with the absence of love. When she is alone in her house, it becomes a "house of death" (*H*, p. 146).

Like several other male spouses in Mortimer's fiction, Eleanor Strathearn's husband has left her for another (younger) woman. Infidelity is, if not the central event of most of the author's novels, a crucial catalyst for the unfolding of the plot or a comment on the fragility of domestic order. Tony Tanner, in his study of adultery as "the main, if undescribed topic" of the nineteenth-century "bourgeois" novel, describes marital transgression in terms that are instructive for Mortimer's more contemporary narratives as well. As he observes, "If society depends for its existence on certain rules governing what may be combined and what should be kept separate, then adultery, by bringing the wrong things together in the wrong places (or the wrong people in the wrong beds), offers an attack on those rules, revealing them to be arbitrary rather than absolute. In this way, the adulterous woman becomes the 'gap' in society that gradually extends through it."[10]

Moreover, in such erotic triangles the adulterous partner ultimately discovers that it may become impossible to "participate in two different patterns . . . without mediation." As a result, Tanner continues, something must "give. . . . For without anything or anyone necessarily having changed place or roles (in social terms), the action of adultery portends the possible breakdown of all the mediations on which society itself depends, and demonstrates the latent impossibility of participating in the interrelated patterns that comprise its structure."[11]

In twentieth-century novels of adultery, and in Mortimer's novels in particular, transgression of mutually exclusive boundaries of relationship remains a central issue, though the threat is less to the fabric of the social order than to the emotional equilibrium of the weaker (or faithful) spouse. Through the imagery of boundary, Mortimer elaborates the changes that occur in the relationship of the central married pair.

In *Johanna,* Mortimer explores the emotional destructiveness unleashed when an intelligent and ambitious woman is confined, even if originally by her own choices, in a role that denies her an outlet for her talents as well as her passions. Images of imprisonment and explosion punctuate the narrative, underscoring both the personal suffocation and political violence operating beneath the surface of the characters' lives.

The novel anticipates the author's preoccupation with the problems faced by women who are unable to find a way to "be": unable, because of their internalization of the attitudes and norms of their times, to identify themselves or exercise their talents apart from their men. Johanna Freund, sexually estranged from her husband since the birth of their son, feels herself reduced to "nothing . . . but a wife and a mother. Sober, incapable, impotent . . . merely mov[ing] between a child and husband as between two poles setting the boundaries of a world" (*J*, p. 63). As a young woman who leaves her small child and a moribund relationship with her husband for an erotically irresistible man, Johanna resembles one of her most famous predecessors in adultery, Anna Karenina; the extended debates about the nature of happiness and "how to live" betray Mortimer's incompletely assimilated indebtedness to other nineteenth-century writers, particularly Dostoevsky, Schopenhauer, Nietzsche, and Marx.

In the less ideologically ambitious *A Villa in Summer,* women—except for a seductive married schoolmistress—are circumscribed by matrimony and motherhood, typically dependent on their husbands for their identities and economic security if not their sexual fulfillment. Emily Addams's very sense of herself is contingent on that fact: "if, one morning, she woke up and found that she no longer loved [Andrew] it would be like waking to find that she was someone else; she wouldn't know what to do, how to behave; she would be frightened." [12] By contrast, men are characterized as sexually polygamous; in the words of one of Andrew Addams's cynical acquaintances, "'Women are one thing, your wife's another'" (*VS*, p. 270). [13]

Mortimer's first novel initially seems to suggest an alternative to such mutually exclusive sexual presumptions. Johanna Freund admires friends of both sexes who eschew personal happiness in their almost religious commitment to political activism. Yet she is erotically attracted to a soldier who appears to her as the Nietzschean "Superman" (*J*, p. 56). Though he awakens Johanna to the Dionysian dimension, he does not offer her true freedom, erotic or otherwise, for he too exhibits the typical attitude of his time and gender, and of Mortimer's male characters: he assumes that Johanna wants a man to "'take care of [her] all day and make love to [her] all night'" (*J*, p. 81).

Johanna is torn between erotic desire and a more abstract desire to affect the course of public events. Choosing her lover, she is denied the clearest route to personal happiness, for he is killed in a freak accident. A political friend who functions as a moral critic reminds her that she is "'still perfectly free to choose [her] own political or social prison; to decide which form of slavery's most congenial'" (*J*, p. 246). Indeed, Johanna's self-abnegation does seal the door of her private prison. At the end of the narrative, even though lover, husband, and son are lost to her, she is still bound by marriage, though not by love, unable to claim an identity apart from her conventional roles as wife and mother. Broken in spirit and spent of all forms of desire, she would "sooner die than live alone" (*J*, p. 276).

Reminiscent of some of Doris Lessing's early works,[14] *Johanna* suggests the conflict between individual conscience and the collective good, as well as the power of social expectations to shape and inhibit female self-determination. Johanna Freund's sole "power" is the capacity to destroy someone else (and herself) through self-denial. She is the first of Mortimer's lonely and alienated women who do not know who they are apart from their men and yet who are often imprisoned in the very relationships that provide them with identity and security.

In the more confined setting of *A Villa in Summer,* Mortimer reverses the roles and softens the consequences of marital transgression. As Andrew Addams (ironically, a divorce lawyer) commutes between London and a borrowed villa in the country, he similarly oscillates between fidelity to his wife and the imperative need to "explore something new, to add, in some way, to himself . . . . If [Emily] loved him, she should . . . understand that a man had to investigate, experiment, widen his horizons beyond the small, familiar limits of his wife's body. It didn't mean that he loved her any less. It simply meant that he wanted something else as well" (*VS*, p. 185).

Emily, stunned by her husband's desire to stray from fidelity, wonders "what it would be like to live alone, without Andrew. Of course they loved each other. Nevertheless, she felt suddenly that it would be as wonderful, as unthinkable, to be without him as it would [be] to be without some part of you that hurt . . ." (*VS*, p. 156). The prospect of both the exhilaration and the anxiety of freedom from monogamy and domesticity is the paradoxical dilemma facing Mortimer's couples. The phrase "Of course they loved each other" recurs like a refrain, emphasizing that the taken-for-granted quality of the marital bond is precisely what weakens it and makes it vulnerable to outside temptations.

Through a series of interrelated developments on the theme of adultery, Mortimer brings her troubled couple together at the end. Even as

Andrew Addams confronts the unhappiness he has created by his extra-marital flirtation, Emily, determined to escape further hurt, leaves the villa and her children as Andrew's responsibility and returns to their London flat alone. Predictably, once Andrew realizes that Emily has left him, he feels a resurgence of his temporarily misplaced love for her. He needs her not only because he loves her but because she maintains the domestic order that makes it possible for him to function. Exhausted by his search for her and dismayed by his discovery of his own dependence, Andrew goes to their London flat with their two children and—in a fitting finale to the couple's circular journey—finds that Emily has arrived there first.

Beneath the dense narrative details of *Johanna* and *A Villa in Summer* is the outline of a moral dilemma that plagues many of Mortimer's characters. Each narrative explores the apparently mutually exclusive possibilities of relationship between men and women as the characters court varying degrees of disillusionment along with their erotic digressions. Mortimer is careful to show that, while infidelity is a prerogative not restricted to men, women have far more to lose, both socially and emotionally, regardless of their position in the erotic triangle.

The Bright Prison illustrates the ways in which matrimony is indeed the tie that binds. As Antonia Painton phrases it, thinking back to her wedding day, "Certainly [then] she hadn't thought of these years, these children, this fortress, which, though containing change and growth in itself, had been built to last, unaltered as they grew older, until they diminished inside its strong walls; until, at last, they died" (*BP*, p. 9). Moreover, the prison includes children, whose presence becomes a central element in the challenge to domestic equilibrium. The intrusion of their needs and dependencies into the adults' lives thwarts the parents' hunger for freedom, forming an almost comic counterpoint to the solemn encounters between the sexes.

Like her counterparts in the earlier novels, Antonia Painton does not so much seek as stumble into erotic temptation. Flattered by the attentions of an attractive widower, she discovers new possibilities in herself that domestic habit has obscured. Yet, with greater insight than that of Mortimer's earlier protagonists, she recognizes that she is literally suspended on the boundary between fidelity and adultery, "balancing on a tightrope; the slightest movement and she would be lost" (*BP*, p. 137). Ironically, the temptation of eros is sabotaged by the very family responsibilities from which the would–be lovers attempt to flee; inevitably, children interrupt at moments of ripening passion.

Through a series of rather contrived plot coincidences, the Paintons are reunited at a party, each unable to clarify for the other the reality behind the appearance of duplicity. Antonia, recognizing that erotic desire is inevitably displaced by the often banal pressures of domesticity, confronts the "bright prison" of her marriage and the true perimeters of her world:

> [S]he seemed to have come a long way, as though through a maze in which, though the distance is short, one can walk the circumference of the earth. . . . She was astonished that having been travelling so long, so far, she should again find herself in this familiar place, in the doorway of a crowded room, with a child in her arms. The centre of the room, among the outwardly staring strangers, was the place she had been trying to reach: to get there seemed impossible. (*BP*, p. 160).

Although the Paintons are ultimately reunited in their own darkened house, *The Bright Prison* ends irresolutely; Mortimer leaves the reader to judge whether, as a result of their parallel indiscretions, the "bright prison" of their marriage has been unlocked or secured even more completely.

The Pumpkin Eater, one of Mortimer's most complex and accomplished novels, is the author's culminating exploration of the conflict between erotic and domestic fulfillment for a woman. One of her two departures from linear narrative form (the other is *Long Distance*), the nonchronological narrative is told in the first person and retrospectively; the narrator is the protagonist rather than an omniscient voice outside the action. The frame, a monologue "spoken" by Mrs. Armitage to a psychiatrist–like doctor, occurs in the narrative present, within which she recounts key events from her life. Narratively, then, the past is framed by the present, as the narrator selects the details of her history for their bearing on her recent depression and emotional stasis. Because plot is subordinate to the changes in perception it generates—in the reader if not in the central character—and because the focus is less on the circumstantial than the psychological reality of the female protagonist, the novel is one of Mortimer's most unsettling and powerful works.

The Pumpkin Eater is also of historical interest for contemporary feminist readers, as a virtual case study in fiction of Betty Friedan's later-diagnosed "problem that has no name."[15] Mrs. Armitage, the veteran of four marriages (twice divorced, once widowed, and currently married to a philandering playwright), is the mother of a numberless, genderless brood of children who justify her identity and her marriages. When the validity of these derivative claims to identity is radically threatened, her entire world collapses.

Like the young couples of Mortimer's earlier novels of marital discord, Mrs. Armitage is both bound by and dependent on the structures of matrimony and motherhood. Her first name is never given in the narrative—a revealing indicator of her auxiliary identity as an extension of her husband.[16] (In an unintentional irony that reveals the presumptions of the author's own Zeitgeist, the jacket copy for the first American edition of *The Pumpkin Eater* reads, "Penelope Mortimer is the wife of John Mortimer, the playwright and novelist. The mother of a large family, she finds time to review fiction as well as write it herself.")

Mrs. Armitage's history recapitulates the history of women in patriarchy: the daughter of a remote father who hoped for a son instead, she has never successfully dealt with his rejection. While making her feel insignificant, her father asserts his patriarchal right to "give" his daughter in marriage to another man, despite her much-married state. Not coincidentally, Mrs. Armitage's last pregnancy occurs literally as her father lies dying. Speculating that the fetus might be male, she placates her husband, Jake, as if he were her father finally acquiring the son for whom he had longed in her place.

The powerful but unloving father is a central image in the novel. Both Jake and Mrs. Armitage are only children of emotionally distant fathers, both of whom die during the course of the story. When Mrs. Armitage's father dies, she feels that the only time he has ever needed her is at the moment of his death, when she holds his hands. Further, as she reflects, "Although he has no use for Freud . . . Jake would unhesitatingly say that I longed all my life for a husband like my father: practical, positive, a man with a work bench, reliable. But then, my father was not like this. His reliability was invented by Jake" (*PE,* p. 66).

Though Jake may be mistaken about his father-in-law's character, he is right about his wife's psychology; in fact, each of Mrs. Armitage's marriages is, in a sense, a search for a more suitable father—or, psychologically, an attempt to escape from, while continuing, the unfinished business of her relationship with him. Her father is the first of the powerful men in her life who make decisions to which she repeatedly acquiesces even though they are against her interests. He not only subsidizes her marriage to Jake financially by purchasing the lease on their house; more crucially, he persuades her to send her three oldest children to boarding school rather than keeping them with her in her new marriage. Failing to challenge this pressure, she is also unable to face her own rage at being thus cruelly manipulated. Instead, she "burn[s] with anger, but dully. Anger against whom, against what? It was all for the best . . ." (*PE*, p. 26).

Mrs. Armitage's inability to locate the object of her anger is one of the recurrent instances of her estrangement from her legitimate feelings as well as one of Mortimer's central representations of the destructive consequences of unquestioning female submission to male authority. As Johanna Freund of Mortimer's first novel phrases the problem of dependency, "One's life should never be filled with one thing, one person . . . because when that person went away, or was hanged and dropped in the bottom of a well, there was nothing left; nothing more to live for. It would always be necessary to keep something back, otherwise one would be lost" (*J*, p. 46).

In *The Pumpkin Eater,* Mrs. Armitage initially lacks this central insight, repeatedly attaching herself to men who are as dominating and emotionally inadequate as her father. Jake Armitage is the least sufficient of them all. Motherless from childhood and attracted to the images of domesticity and maternity, he fell in love with the eventual Mrs. Armitage when she was married to another man and seven months pregnant. Inevitably the Armitage marriage falters because neither partner can adequately fulfill the emotional role of the lost parent.

Moreover, for most of her adult life Mrs. Armitage identifies herself through her own parental role. Maternity, if not children, provides a source of being that is absent from her relationship with her husband(s). Except for the eldest, the children are anonymous, known primarily through their collective clamor—suggesting that they are less important to Mrs. Armitage than the procreative function itself. The doctor she eventually sees at her husband's prompting suggests that her compulsive desire to be pregnant conceals a fear of nonprocreative sexuality—an unconscious strategy for neutralizing her fear of adult intimacy. Ironically, this very compulsion jeopardizes her marriage and indeed binds her to nurturance.

By contrast, her husband is more interested in eros; his continuing history of infidelity began early in their marriage. Significantly, he builds a "tower" in the country for his wife and family—an apt image of sexual domination and female imprisonment in male structures. Mrs. Armitage, despite evidence to the contrary, persists in believing in her husband's faithfulness, though she is plagued by anxiety. Rather than confronting him and perhaps losing him, she swallows her own anger as she did with her father—an emotional repression that leads to a progressive "failure of [her] will" (*PE*, p. 44).

When Mrs. Armitage is forced to recognize that her husband is drifting away (caught in his own repetitive emotional pattern, Jake is involved in yet another adulterous relationship), she carelessly abstains from using birth control and becomes pregnant. Procreation is her sole defense and her means of self-confirmation. As she ironically phrases it, "It's not that I've forgotten [how to live]. It's that I never knew. A womb isn't all that important. It's only the seat of life, something that drags the moon down from the sky like a kite and draws the sea in and out, in and out, the world's breathing" (*PE*, p. 148).

Jake emphatically rejects the possibility of another child and persuades his wife to have both an abortion and sterilization. Repeating the pattern of acquiescence to male authority, Mrs. Armitage represses her legitimate anger and consents to these physically and psychically invasive procedures. Pointedly, she also longs for the male figure who first shaped her universe—her father. That her mother is, to her, an insignificant figure in this emotional constellation is revealed in her admission, "I wanted to go home, but now my father was dead there was no home to go to, only a house where my mother mourned and thanked goodness that I had at last seen reason" (*PE*, p. 173).

Psychoanalytic theory suggests that a daughter's intense bond with her father in fact represents a negative identification with and rejection of her mother, whose internalized image still powerfully influences the nature of the daughter's primary emotional interactions. As Nancy Chodorow has summarized this eventuality in a girl's emotional development during the oedipal phase, the daughter's "turn to her father is both an attack on her mother and an expression of love for her."[17]

Though Mrs. Armitage's mother is a shadowy figure in Mortimer's narrative, she is suggestively associated with her daughter's confused attitude toward her own sexuality. In an extended flashback, Mrs. Armitage describes an emotionally central sequence of events from her adolescence. After being jilted by a boy whom she loved chastely, she had impulsively arranged to meet one of her father's Rotary Club colleagues. Unintentionally leading him to expect a sexual encounter, she had been shocked and disgusted by his groping advances. Failing to acknowledge her sexual desires (or her ambivalent attraction to a stand-in for her father), she had felt instead a sense of sin—reinforced by her mother's shocked insistence that the incident be concealed from her father.

The episode crystallizes the splits between love and sex, innocence and guilt, that disturb Mrs. Armitage's subsequent relationships. She views the adolescent sexual incident in moral terms that continue to shape her perceptions of men: "The nervous boy, whom I loved, was good. Mr. Simpkin was evil. I wanted to be delivered from evil by love, and never to touch it again for the rest of my life" (*PE*, p. 97). Mr. Simpkin—and by implication her own sexuality—was "the first thing [she] hated" (*PE*, p. 13).

Through Mrs. Armitage's dilemma, Mortimer extends her exploration of the boundaries of both female selfhood and the marriage relationship. Mrs. Armitage's despair escalates as a response to her husband's success in his career and their increasing material comfort. As their circumstances improve, the care of the children, the house, and the garden are all delegated to paid servants. She is thus stripped of the domestic role through which she has identified herself.

The deliberately nameless (and thus representative) doctor she sees at her husband's prompting offers the conventional explanations for her depression, calling it her "will to self-destruction" (*PE*, p. 100), and prescribes tranquilizers for her chronic weeping rather than recognizing it as a symptom of her deeper injury. While the doctor regards Mrs. Armitage as a neurotic housewife, the reader sees her illness as something outside of the doctor's limited comprehension. As psychoanalyst Alice Miller has sensitively observed, what "doctors refer to curtly as depression" is more accurately "the painful feeling of being separated from [one's] true self" and can be understood as "a denial of one's own emotional reactions and feelings." [18]

If Mortimer's earlier protagonists are confined in literal houses and suffer a kind of agoraphobia, Mrs. Armitage is not only literally but emotionally confined and may be said to suffer from "existential agoraphobia."[19] The crucial feature of this condition is a limbo of "eventlessness" in which the repetitive quality of domestic life results in "submission to authority, absence of choice, and a general exclusion and isolation from the significant stimuli of life."[20] In *The Pumpkin Eater*, Mrs. Armitage's fruitless dialogues with the doctor reveal to us, if not to him, the nature of her malady. To him she asserts that she will try to be honest, though "'I suppose really what you're more interested in is my not being honest'" (*PE*, p. 9). As Mortimer implies, Mrs. Armitage cannot expect insight into or sympathy for her real condition from a doctor steeped in the patriarchal assumptions of the time about women's "adjustment" to marriage and motherhood.

As Mrs. Armitage later admits to Giles, one of her former husbands, and to herself, "'There must come a time in your life, mustn't there, when the most important thing to do is to find out who you really are, what you're really like. That doctor I went to . . . he made me angry, he wanted me to change. You know, he wanted to sterilize my . . . *attitude* to everything. All right, it was an idiotic attitude—that you have a kind of duty to avoid . . . evil. I couldn't even tell him what I meant by evil. I kept on talking about the dust . . .'" (*PE*, p. 191, emphasis and ellipses in original). Ironically, the doctor's patriarchal blindness has one salutary result: it enables Mrs. Armitage to recover her repressed anger.

Giles, like a benevolent father (the figure she so desperately seeks), takes her home and cares for her; his very solicitousness exposes her confused emotional needs and moral position. Giving in to a kind of retaliatory adultery, she makes love to her former husband while thinking of her present one, amazed that her body offers no resistance to this compromised act: "My skin grew no spurs, barbs, thorns, briers to protect it, I had no shell to shrink into—why, when the rest of me was speared like a battlefield?" (*PE*, p. 202). The language reinforces the sense of Mrs. Armitage's anxiety about the vulnerable boundaries of her body and psyche. She has at last lost her innocence—for, since Mr. Simpkin, she has unconsciously associated her sexuality with evil and death, unless it is justified by maternity. But because her perceptions are thus polarized, she feels that she has corrupted herself absolutely. "'Avoid evil? There's nothing else. . . . Nothing else in me'" (*PE*, p. 204).

Fleeing to the tower in the country, Mrs. Armitage takes refuge in the "cell of brick and glass" (*PE,* p. 212). In fact, she merely exchanges one kind of empty cell or shell for another, even comparing herself to a (male) prisoner (*PE,* p. 215). Indeed "confinement," with its multiple connotations of imprisonment, mental incarceration, and maternity, is the perfect expression of Mrs. Armitage's condition: she is literally a prisoner in the phallic tower of patriarchy. As Phyllis Chesler has observed in her study of women and madness, confinement in the clinical sense is both "an expression of female powerlessness and an unsuccessful attempt to reject and overcome this fate."[21] The image in Mortimer's novel also suggests the protagonist-narrator's fear of non-being as her reproductive function abruptly ceases. Procreation is the only means Mrs. Armitage feels she has had to participate in life rather than death, the only state in which she feels alive.

Jake, the "pumpkin eater," may have "put her in a shell," as the nursery rhyme has it, but Mrs. Armitage has acquiesced to live in the empty shell of herself. Mortimer makes her protagonist's struggle to fill that shell not only an emotional crisis but "a moral tale" (*PE,* p. 172). In retelling her story, Mrs. Armitage ultimately understands that blaming someone else for her circumstances does not entirely absolve her of responsibility for choices she has made—or failed to make—that have resulted in her experience of powerlessness and emptiness. In yielding responsibility for her identity to male figures of authority, she has never developed an autonomous self capable of action rather than reaction. Through her substitution of maternity for sexuality, she has become an unintentional complicitor in her own imprisonment in the phallic tower of oppressive female roles.

At the same time Mortimer's narrative suggests that the traditional patriarchal arrangement between male and female, originating in the relationship between father and daughter and in the daughter's unconscious choice of marriage to a man like her father, dictates against female autonomy and affirmation of selfhood. As Friedan later phrased it, "[T]he core of the problem for women today is not sexual but a problem of identity— a stunting or evasion of growth. . . . [O]ur culture does not permit women to accept or gratify their basic need to grow and fulfill their potentialities as human beings, a need which is not solely defined by their sexual role."[22]

Once Mortimer's Mrs. Armitage admits that her husband's history of infidelity is at least partly a reaction to her own passivity and her fear of sexuality without procreation, she is less able to cling to a vision of her innocence. Having determined that their relationship has been based on the patriarchal imperatives of "fear, and anger, and sexual necessity" (*PE*, p. 218), she vows that she will no longer be bound to her husband by these destructive needs. The narrative concludes with Mrs. Armitage re-iterating her initial disclaimer of "honesty," but this time with a new sense of entitlement to her own perceptions. As she asserts, "Some of these things happened, and some were dreams. They are all true, as I understood truth. They are all real, as I understood reality" (*PE*, p. 222).

In affirming the radical subjectivity of perception as well as the diffi-culty of articulating the true story of female imprisonment in patriarchy, Mortimer abstains from providing more than an equivocal resolution. The power of *The Pumpkin Eater,* particularly for contemporary readers, is the way in which, through Mrs. Armitage's story, the author gives the lie to the prevailing assumptions of her day which promised women ful-fillment solely through marriage and children. The claustrophobically narrow boundaries of the "pumpkin shell" are the creation not of Jake Armitage but of patriarchy itself; the nursery tale of the pumpkin eater does not have a happy ending from the wife's point of view.

As her female protagonists reflect an increasing dissatisfaction with the marital arrangement, Mortimer's interest shifts from the exploration of the matrimonial enclosure to that of the boundaries of individual female selfhood; the subject of unhappy marriage leaves a legacy of vulnerable women who are emotionally and often literally wounded. The equation between psychological or ideological and material dimensions of expe-rience is adumbrated in the author's first novel. Johanna Freund, whose hand is seriously injured by Nazi soldiers, discovers that "it's only when an idea goes mad and makes your nose bleed that you begin to take it seriously" (*J*, p. 190).

In Mortimer's later fiction, the ideology in question is not Fascism but patriarchy—the circumstance of being female in a male-defined world, in which even the female body is subject to patriarchal rules. Three of Mortimer's women undergo "female" operations (abortion, sterilization, mastectomy), two of which are clearly performed at the discretion of male doctors or spouses. Dr. Fickstein, the doctor who performs an abortion for Angela Whiting in *Cave of Ice,* is representative of Mortimer's acid satire of the patronizing medical profession:

> Whether he delivered a living child or removed an embryo he always, afterwards, sent them flowers, bushes of thornless roses for the sad, soft, pretty creatures who had been disfigured by men. He persuaded them not to feed their babies, hating to see a breast misused; when he could, he tied their little Fallopian tubes into knots so that they need never suffer again. . . . Women were his pets, to be protected against the ravages of childbirth and all ugliness. The sexual act itself was to him only tolerable when performed with so much technique, so much consideration and application to the right zones and climates and meridians that it resembled a safari rather than a necessary expression of love. (*CI,* p. 190)

In *The Pumpkin Eater,* Mrs. Armitage's inner wounding is expressed first figuratively and then literally in her body. Feeling utterly helpless and useless in her roles of wife and mother, she finds herself one day flooded with tears, "a kind of haemorrhage of grief. . . . I wondered if I was going out of my mind. Was this how it began, with this terrible sense of loss, as though everyone had died?" (*PE,* p. 49). Pertinently in this context, Julia Kristeva cites Freud's discussion of melancholy in terms of "'wound,'" "'internal hemorrhage,'" and "'a hole in the psyche,'" and adds that "the erotization of abjection . . . is an attempt at stopping the hemorrhage: a threshold before death, a halt or a respite?"[23] For Mortimer's Mrs. Armitage, it is the abjection and loss of her own selfhood that consumes her, as virtually every aspect of her life is removed from her power to direct or influence. Her feeling that she is "dying of grief" (*PE,* p. 51) is an accurate description of her existential state.

After the abortion and sterilization, she senses the fragility of her selfhood through her altered body: "To be cut open and sewn up makes one realize how much is contained inside skin and muscle: we're only stuffed with life, and can easily burst open" (*PE,* p. 151). Though she feels sexually and emotionally liberated by the operation, she is quickly punished for her faith when she discovers her husband's betrayal. The violation of her psychic boundaries is mirrored in the flesh: her wound opens, as though it were "laughing" at her (*PE,* p. 160). Tellingly, once she confirms the fact of her husband's adultery, the wound "would not heal. . . . The idea that I was in some way monstrous grew unchecked, except by the feeble attacks of my own reason" (*PE,* pp. 172–73).

Simone de Beauvoir's observations on abortion precisely describe Mrs. Armitage's dilemma in both psychic and existential terms that have changed less in three decades than feminists would wish. As she wrote in *The Second Sex,*

> When man, the better to succeed in filling his destiny as man, asks woman to sacrifice her reproductive possibilities, he is exposing the hypocrisy of the masculine moral code. Men universally forbid abortion, but individually they accept it as a convenient solution of a problem; they are able to contradict themselves with careless cynicism. But woman feels these contradictions in her wounded flesh; she is as a rule too timid for open revolt against masculine bad faith; she regards herself as the victim of an injustice that makes her a criminal against her will, and at the same time she feels soiled and humiliated.[24]

In Mortimer's *The Home* and *The Handyman*, the female wound is envisioned in psychic terms; the loss of the security of marriage, no matter how destructive it may have been, leaves Eleanor Strathearn and Phyllis Muspratt emotionally maimed. Eleanor regards the death of her sexual life as "a secret disfigurement, a hidden wound that stabbed her without warning in daylight" (*H,* p. 7); since her husband stopped touching her, she has perceived herself as "untouchable, a leper" (*H,* p. 72). Her life-long emotional dependency becomes a "widening wound" (*H,* p. 103). Similarly, the hole that Phyllis Muspratt discovers in the floor of her house corresponds to the hole in her emotional life created by her husband's sudden death.

Though a slighter novel than either *The Pumpkin Eater* or *The Home,* *My Friend Says It's Bulletproof* is interesting for its exploration of the correspondences between physical and emotional boundaries. The "housewife's disease" of the earlier novels becomes literal disease: the novel's protagonist, Muriel Rowbridge, feels herself diminished and undesirable because of her disfiguring loss of a breast to cancer. Because she is single, childless, and afraid that she is permanently barred from the intimacies of erotic mutuality and motherhood, she experiences her altered body as a death sentence for the possibility of personal happiness.

Much of Muriel's anxiety about her disease and its resultant disfigurement can be understood through cultural attitudes toward both the female body and cancer. Men worship the female breast and women internalize the male overvaluation of this aspect of their anatomy. Because it is also associated with the actual and symbolic qualities of nurturance, the loss of a breast affects a woman's sense of her procreative capabilities.

Moreover, cancer itself is the most dreaded affliction of the twentieth century. In *Illness as Metaphor*, Susan Sontag has observed, "Nobody conceives of cancer the way TB was thought of—as a decorative, often lyrical death. Cancer is a rare and still scandalous subject for poetry; and it seems unimaginable to aestheticize the disease." [25] It is intrepid for Mortimer—and Margaret Atwood, in *Bodily Harm,* published fourteen years later [26]—to use it so centrally in a fictive context, articulating and exploring a fear that is perceived as threatening to one's very sense of identity.

In fact, the two novels bear a remarkable number of parallels. The protagonists of *Bulletproof* and *Bodily Harm* have each lost part or all of a breast through surgery just before the respective narratives commence, resulting in each woman's experience of a radical threat to her ego and body boundaries and her self-image. Both women are single journalists who write for women's magazines: Mortimer's Muriel Rowbridge writes about "how [women] live, what they wear" [27]; Atwood's Rennie Wilford writes about "'what people wear, what they eat.'" [28] Both take journeys by air to other countries and, while away from home, confront their anger, sense of loss, and fear of intimacy in their disfigured state. Both are aided in their recovery of a new and positive self-image by men who, though unsuitable as permanent lovers, accept them as they are. Finally, both return to their home countries significantly altered by their experiences abroad.

While Atwood symbolically links the condition of her protagonist's body to the body politic, Mortimer focuses in a more limited way on her female character's redefinition of selfhood following her experience of physical and psychic alteration. The only never-married protagonist in Mortimer's canon, Muriel Rowbridge erroneously believes that the cure for her alienated state is loss of herself in physical union with another: "The only true contact with reality is being joined with another body; then you are lost, free, alone at last. . . . You might say it's easier for women—the umbilical cord is threaded straight through them, mother on one end, child on the other. . . . But men—what about men? Sliced off, tied up, sewn up, sealed, their only remaining apertures intended for giving out some inexhaustible supply of good or evil" (*FB,* p. 10). These

35

images do not describe mutuality, as Muriel thinks, but loss of the self in symbiotic connection and dependency (for females), or separation and isolation (for males).

In this novel, as throughout Mortimer's fiction, correspondences between inner and outer worlds are often signified through a cluster of images that refer to both boundary and perception. In *The Bright Prison*, for example, people do not really see one another; they see through or past one another, or seek their own images in mirrors or in reflection from one another. Much of the action occurs during fog or darkness, which function as obstructing mediums, blanketing or concealing emotional matters as well as external objects. At one point Antonia Painton peers into the fog and feels as if "out there . . . she would be nothing, she would have no existence" (*BP*, p. 35). Fog also suggests the blurred state in which the inner authority of self is in abeyance.

Mirrors are in a sense the "opposite" of fog and blindness, given their capacity to confirm (but also to distort) the image of the self. In *My Friend Says It's Bulletproof*, the tropes of vision and mirroring metaphorically express female self-perception and cultural perception of females. Before leaving England for a press tour of the United States, Muriel Rowbridge had turned the mirror in her flat over so that she would not have to face her image there; instead, its decaying back had reminded her all the more forcefully of her disease. Her lover, Ramsay, gave her a new mirror which distorted their reflections into "bulbous [shapes], our legs like little growths" (*FB*, p. 13)—figuratively reflecting the distortions of disease as well as of their relationship. In the United States, Muriel's liaison with Robert Schumann begins with glances exchanged through the rear-view mirror of his car. (The novel's awkward title, a comment about Robert's Bentley by an admiring youth, implicitly refers to the prosthetic breast that symbolizes Muriel's vulnerability and disfigurement.) Muriel frequently examines herself in the mirrors of her hotel rooms or in her facial compact; they reflect the state of her feelings about herself.

The cluster of images of mirrors, reflections, and vision is central to Muriel's eventual insight into herself. The child of a blind father, she often experiences herself as "unseen," a condition compounded by her present disfigurement. That absence of confirmation of one's self by others creates a kind of solipsistic isolation. As the narrator phrases it, "When you aren't seen, hidden within a protective shell, you live always in secret, alone; the world's eyes give back no reflection. You have only your own knowledge of your existence to keep you alive, and even that may be illusory" (*FB,* p. 161).

In another country and continent, Muriel feels herself uniquely without past or future, alternately overwhelmed by loneliness and exhilarated by the opportunity she has to recreate herself. The most important of the three men who contribute in various ways to her exploration and recovery of herself is Robert Schumann, a company lawyer whom Muriel meets at a reception. Robert is too good to be true—a man who from the first moment of their meeting is tender, solicitous, affectionate, loving. The erotic relationship that develops between them forces Muriel to acknowledge her fear of sexual intimacy as well as her anger at her condition. Discounting his affectionate acceptance of her, she feels that her missing breast creates an ineradicable boundary between her and any man she might care for, "a one-way insuperable barrier against which they could mourn for the rest of their lives, but never again touch. This was the need she felt could never be satisfied, the sense of forced separation, the wilderness in which one way was as pointless as another, since none of them led through the barrier, and home" (*FB,* pp. 111–12). Here, as elsewhere in Mortimer's fiction, the boundaries of the body are congruent with the experience of the self, and "home" is not simply a physical place but a psychic space—located in the past or the future, but rarely in the present—where one might be entirely oneself and emotionally at peace.

Robert does succeed in breaking through Muriel's loneliness and self-pity, persuading her not to wear her prosthetic breast because, as he tells her, "'I prefer you as you are'" (*FB,* p. 160). His unqualified acceptance releases Muriel into a true rebirth: "The sensation was unknown to her. . . . It had the appearance of a bird breaking slowly out of its shell, a chrysalis crumbling, a snake moving deliberately but thoughtlessly out of its skin. Like the bird, the butterfly, the snake, she did not know what was happening to her. . . . She was materializing, becoming reembodied. She was visible. She could be seen" (*FB,* pp. 160–61). The language suggests her recovery of her selfhood through the affirmation of her body; she is "reembodied." But Muriel's feelings toward the man who has "brought her to life again" (*FB,* p. 194) are composed too much of gratitude and affection and too little of real passion. The real love she discovers through him is love for herself.

Having found a path "through the wilderness, away from the barrier

. . ." (*FB*, p. 194), Muriel chooses to return to England rather than to accept Robert's marriage proposal. Their final embrace is emblematic of their entire relationship: "She gave in, clinging to him as though she were drowning; but after a moment he detached himself and made her stand alone" (*FB*, p. 207). Although the narrative concludes with Muriel airborne and en route back to England, the "home" to which she returns is not the one she has left at the beginning of the novel. Newly self-defined as a whole woman, she has arrived at a renewed capacity for life; precisely because Robert has given her a future, she must leave him to pursue it on her own.

In Mortimer's later novels, the images of female wounding and death are both literal and emotional threats; Ruth Whiting of *Cave of Ice*, Mrs. Armitage of *The Pumpkin Eater,* and Eleanor Strathearn of *The Home* are emotionally eviscerated by dying or dead marriages. In *The Handyman,* Phyllis Muspratt, forced to adjust to the sudden death of her husband of forty-five years, is periodically "attacked by mourning," a condition that ends only with her own equally sudden death late in the novel.[29]

Mrs. Armitage of *The Pumpkin Eater* describes her anxiety about dust, the repeated image of which brilliantly links the "housewife's disease" to the death of the self. The image is also one of several references to death and dying that punctuate the narrative. Mrs. Armitage implicitly regards as dead her three oldest children who were sent away, referring to those who remain with her as the "surviving" children (*PE*, p. 25). The Armitages' tower in the country is likened to a "sepulchre" (*PE*, p. 174), while their house in the city is, like their marriage, "dying" (*PE*, p. 174). At a party at the Armitages' house, "dying"—with its additional sexual connotation—is the underlying theme.

In *Cave of Ice*, emptiness—the steady state of most of the characters— is signified by empty beds, rooms, houses, and a number of other objects or locations. Not only Ruth Whiting but virtually all the other characters in the novel are emotionally frigid and spiritually dead. The miscellaneous objects of ordinary experience are described as dead or dying; time itself is "killed" (*CI*, p. 118), and the postures of sleep imitate death (*CI*, p. 121). Recurring like a dirge to alienation, these images reach a crescendo in Ruth's unsuccessful efforts at "disciplining emptiness" (*CI*, p. 75) and her return at the conclusion of the novel to an "empty world" (*CI*, p. 252).

The domestic crises that form the plots of Mortimer's early novels and *The Pumpkin Eater* are presumed as past history in both *Cave of Ice* and *The Home*. Furthermore, in both novels, a troubled marriage is not foreground but background to the exploration of another central relationship in a woman's life: that between mother and daughter. As astute depictions of the complex dynamics of the mother–daughter bond and the corollary psychological issues of ego boundary, attachment, dependency, separation, and loss, Mortimer's narratives deserve a wider audience among contemporary readers and should acquire their rightful place among the literary treatments of a vital theme in female experience.

In *Cave of Ice*, Ruth and Rex Whiting occupy the empty shell of their marriage by habit and without love, caught in "a long war in which attack, if not happening, was always imminent . . ." (*CI*, p. 11). Their emotional estrangement is mirrored in the living arrangements of their peers: the husbands, successful professionals, live in London during the week and spend weekends with their families, who live on "the Common" in an affluent but sterile country village. The wives are like "little icebergs, each keep[ing] a bright and shining face above water; below the surface, submerged in fathoms of leisure, each keeps her own isolated personality. . . . [A] few have talent, as useless to them as a paralysed limb" (*CI*, p. 40).

The Whitings have three children, eighteen-year-old Angela and two younger sons. Angela, who was conceived out of wedlock, in fact was the reason for her parents' marriage as well as a major excuse for its failure. Rex, a self-preoccupied and infantile man, quickly came to resent the child that shifted his wife's attention away from him. Unconsciously blaming both his wife and daughter for his feeling of entrapment, he engages, in the characteristic polygamous pattern of Mortimer's male characters, in shallow affairs with younger women. Ruth, in marrying because she was pregnant, also lost the affection of her own mother, whom she has never seen again.

The Whitings' contemporaries blithely discuss the difficulties of rearing daughters and their concern to save them from "a fate worse than death" (*CI*, p. 52)—Ruth's own fate. Yet the sexual anxieties of the parents are fulfilled in their daughters' carelessness. For Angela Whiting, intimacy with a young man is the outlet for her longing for the affection her parents, and particularly her mother, withhold from her. The event that shifts the balance within the mother–daughter relationship is Angela's discovery that she is pregnant by a young man "exactly like Daddy" (*CI*, p. 61), whom she does not love and has no desire to marry.

Ruth understands her daughter's predicament, for it replicates her own hunger for love: it is the desire of an insecure, unformed female to merge with and be defined by a dominating male. Now older and wiser, she imagines Angela's future unhappiness—if she were to marry the father of the child—in language that in fact describes her own marriage (and echoes Virginia Woolf's classic comment[30]): "To love him would be to hold up a heavy mirror month after month, year after year, in which he could see his own manliness reflected; to grow, behind it, older and weaker[,] and certainly, in the end, to give way. He would drive his wife mad" (*CI*, pp. 60–61).

The daughter completes the portrait of women's subordinate position in a patriarchal world. Uncertain of herself, Angela wonders, "What does my self look like? I mean, who am I? . . . What shall I do with myself all my life?" (*CI*, pp. 122–23). She answers herself with an almost liturgical description from an imaginary "answer book" that prescribes the traditional submissive female role—as exemplified by her own mother and the women of her parents' milieu—including self-control, self-sacrifice, and self-abnegation (*CI*, p. 123).

Without realizing the irony of her condition, Angela Whiting is caught in a literal repetition of events through which her mother relives the painful emotions surrounding her own sexuality, marriage, and motherhood. It is as if the mother's guilt manifests itself in the daughter's unconscious duplication of events from her mother's life. Though this doubled pattern may initially seem to be a narrative contrivance, it is in fact convincingly anchored in psychological reality. As Alice Miller describes such repetitions from one generation to the next, "Every mother carries with her a bit of her 'unmastered past,' which she unconsciously hands on to her child. Each mother can only react empathically to the extent that she has become free of her own childhood, and she is forced to react without empathy to the extent that, by denying the vicissitudes of her early life, she wears invisible chains."[31]

During the difficult series of steps leading to an illegal abortion for Angela Whiting (convincingly represented in this novel of the fifties), Ruth relives her resentments and partially acknowledges her part in her daughter's predicament. Some of these feelings are dramatized through other characters in the novel. For example, the Whitings' neighbor, Jane

Tanner, illustrates a recurrent view in Mortimer's fiction, that the birth of a child is the death of a marriage.[32] Conversely, the women's pre-occupation with their children is a response to their husbands' actual and emotional absence. Jane Tanner is a self-chosen slave to her two-year-old daughter, upon whom she projects sadistic fantasies: "'I'm sure . . . she's dreaming of stretching me on the rack or putting lighted matches under my fingernails'" (*CI,* p. 51).

Observing Jane's smothering attention her small daughter, Ruth Whiting feels "drawn into a cult . . . in which adult people were no longer required to stand alone, but were supported by their children. How can we move, think, breathe, they groaned, when impeded by these living crutches? But without them, life would be too dangerous; an emptiness in which, the most fearful thing of all, there would be no time, no landmarks" (*CI,* p. 181). This and other images of figuratively shared boundaries, symbiotic connection, emptiness, and death underscore Mortimer's representations of the death of the female self in patriarchal marriage, with its suffocating assumptions about sexuality and motherhood.

Additionally—and of particular interest to contemporary readers—beneath the realistic psychological details of Mortimer's story is the outline of the classical mother-daughter relationship symbolized by Demeter and Persephone. *Cave of Ice* begins in autumn and ends in winter; the cycle of reunion is left incomplete, for the relationship between mother and daughter is frozen at the point of their separation. As Adrienne Rich has written in her examination of motherhood in patriarchy, "The loss of the daughter to the mother, the mother to the daughter, is the essential female tragedy."[33] In Mortimer's novel, the daughter is symbolically lost to the mother, whether by choice or carelessness, through her sexual loss of innocence. In a passage that alludes to the mourning Demeter, Ruth is described as "in a dream, an absentee, noticing nothing. Her eyes . . . had become great shadows in a face as small and wavering as a reflection in water. . . . She was wearing dead brown, the colour and texture of dried leaves; and this only because her black dress, the obvious, was now too big for her" (*CI,* p. 155).

In arranging for the abortion for her daughter, Ruth feels she is in some way killing the unwanted fetus of long ago; Angela, unaware of the irony of her situation, is alternately grateful for and resentful of her mother's aid. Her self-pity and anger against herself are internalizations of her mother's similar state; she dramatizes the unresolved feelings that have psychologically eroded Ruth Whiting. Nancy Chodorow has summarized such typically ambivalent feelings in mother-daughter relationships, observing that "a girl alternates between total rejection of a mother who represents infantile dependence and attachment to her, between identification with any one other than her mother and feeling herself her mother's double and extension. Her mother often mirrors her preoccupations."[34]

Ruth's "mirroring" of these feelings is intensified by her own, but not her daughter's, knowledge of the repetition of accidental pregnancy. In effect, each invests the fetus Angela carries with her own fears, desires, and unmet emotional needs: "Angela carried the child in her body; Ruth carried it in her imagination. To Angela it was a useless growth, already dead. To Ruth it was an image, unformed, folded and wrapped in itself, concerned only with survival. Her imagination built protective walls round her idea of the child. She dreamed about it. . . . These dreams disgusted her, because in them the child was her's [sic] and Angela did not exist" (*CI,* pp. 199–200).

Angela's unwanted baby represents not only the perennial problem for women in the years before they acquired control over reproductive decisions but the crux of unresolved psychological matters between mother and daughter. For Ruth, it embodies her guilt for her failure in mothering and her fantasy of undoing the mistake of her past; for Angela, it embodies the need to remain a child herself, to be loved and mothered.

The stress of the identification between mother and daughter is registered in their very flesh, suggesting the merged boundaries between them. Once Ruth takes charge, her daughter feels "light and free" (*CI,* p. 96) while she "seem[s] to stagger, give way, the exact motion of trying to carry something far too heavy" (*CI,* p. 97). Later, as Angela gains weight, Ruth loses it. The Whiting house registers the tense state of its occupants: "With all its doors except Angela's open, [it] had a startled look, gaping with shock" (*CI,* p. 217). This and other references to "gaping" resonate with the "cave" of the title, suggesting female sexuality and the impending medical procedure as well as violation, wounding, and emptiness. In the Homeric hymn of Demeter and Persephone, the earth begins to "gape" open just before Persephone is forcibly taken to the underworld.[35] The more obvious allusion to Coleridge's "sunny pleasure-dome with caves of ice"—quoted on the novel's frontispiece—is clearly ironic.

The reality of her daughter's abortion finally forces Ruth to face a buried memory that anchors her guilt about Angela, not only for the circumstances of her birth but for their later ambivalent attachment. When Angela was six years old, she had gone to a nearby home for what would now be called day-care. One day, Ruth had sent Angela to walk there by herself across a vacant lot. Then, guiltily following at a distance, she had become an unintentional accomplice in her daughter's misery: "The child, thinking she was alone, had started to cry. . . . She's all right, [Ruth] told herself. . . . But she couldn't leave her. Neither could she call out. She walked behind, useless, witnessing an enormous agony. There, but not known to be there. And so, as far as Angela was concerned, not there at all" (*CI,* p. 234).

Ruth's painfully recovered memory vividly evokes the merged ego boundaries between mother and daughter as well as the ambivalence of separation: the mother desiring both to hold on and to let go, the daughter feeling abandoned and desperate without the mother's support. The sense of being "there, but not known to be there" is exactly the position Ruth has since held in her daughter's life. As Rich has written of the classical story to which Mortimer's narrative alludes,

> The separation of Demeter and Kore is an unwilling one; it is neither a question of the daughter's rebellion against the mother, nor the mother's rejection of the daughter. . . . Each daughter, even in the millennia before Christ, must have longed for a mother whose love for her and whose power were so great as to undo rape and bring her back from death. And every mother must have longed for the power of Demeter, the efficacy of her anger, the reconciliation with her lost self.[36]

In Mortimer's narrative, Ruth attempts to effect that reconciliation with her lost self by confessing to Angela the circumstances of her birth, thereby removing the wedge of dishonesty that has prevented any mutuality between them. Yet, though the initiating circumstances may be parallel, their outcome is not. Ruth's newly kindled love comes too late for both of them; the abortion, rather than drawing them closer as Ruth expects, releases Angela, but not her, from their negative attachment. The daughter's different resolution of the identical female dilemma is a rejection of the passive choice the mother had made years before. Angela responds to her release from the grip of her mother's guilt by quietly leaving home, as if "leaving a hotel in which she had spent a long night of childhood" (*CI,* p. 252).

Angela is the pivot for Ruth's fragile sense of her own existence; when she leaves, "there [is] nowhere to put a belated love, a small, painfully achieved humanity" (*CI,* p. 252). In a dialogue with the two sides of herself—the trapped woman who long ago capitulated to an empty life and the woman who, through Angela, has glimpsed freedom—Ruth considers the possibility of escape. But, too long habituated to a sterile but secure dependency on her husband, she is unable to act upon the possibilities and new insight opened to her through the mutual act of courage that she and her daughter have shared. Feeling herself "inadequate, commonplace, no longer young, she found the burden of consequence too heavy. It crushed her" (*CI,* pp. 253–54). The cave of ice is the image of her irrevocably frozen inner life.

Throughout Mortimer's fiction, "home" is a resonant image of psychic as well as physical location and boundary. In the early novels, the young couples leave their respective homes in order to rediscover the terms of their marriages; their return home at each novel's end signifies a new emotional compact. Ruth Whiting in *Cave of Ice* is a passive prisoner of marriage who, by the end of the narrative, returns home to her husband because she lacks the courage to leave an empty relationship. With greater insight, the dependent and despondent Mrs. Armitage of *The Pumpkin Eater* precipitates a change in her marriage by moving from her husband's house—though to an equally imprisoning tower in the country. Muriel Rowbridge of *My Friend Says It's Bulletproof* travels a circular route from home and, after facing loss and the fear of death, returns there with a newly recovered sense of herself. In *The Handyman,* the recently widowed Phyllis Muspratt leaves the London house of her long years of marriage for a run-down house in the country; there she unwillingly settles into a disillusionment that concludes with her own accidental death.

Of Mortimer's nine novels, *The Home* focuses most explicitly on the issues of female attachments, boundary, separation, and loss. Bringing together two of the author's recurrent subjects—a woman's connection to others through marriage and family, and the consequences of her submergence in these roles—the novel unfolds through a group of characters who express the psychic dilemma of the central female character.

If *The Pumpkin Eater* reveals the crucial roles played by patriarchal fathers in their respective children's emotional stunting, then *The Home* dramatizes the mothers' even more central role in keeping their children emotionally infantilized into adulthood, as they themselves have been as daughters and wives. In a comment that is both satirical and utterly serious, the narrator remarks early in the novel, "The reason for everything could be found in [the Strathearns'] mothers. . . . Mothers, first off the mark at birth, resolutely hanging on for years after the fathers die or disappear, constructing and manipulating, providers of food and love and never enough of either, guilty of appalling excesses and incredible meanness . . ." (*H*, p. 13).

This comment becomes the central psychological premise on which much of the action rests. Virtually all the characters in *The Home* are either emotionally bound to their mothers, want to be mothers, or *are* mothers. Expressed another way, the competing needs to mother and to be mothered are the powerful but ambivalent pressures in these characters' lives, often directly affecting—and interfering with—their capacity to maintain positive intimate relationships. Eleanor Strathearn occupies a pivotal role within this cluster of needs as both mother of three daughters and two sons, and daughter (and only child) of the indomitable Mrs. Bennet.

The most powerful mothers in *The Home* are of the elder generation: the widowed female parents of the recently separated couple, Eleanor and Graham Strathearn. In particular, the morally upright Mrs. Bennet is an emotionally smothering woman who does not believe in "sex, machinery, or the independent, unrelated existence of her daughter" (*H*, p. 14). Eleanor has been "brainwashed by this formidable good woman from the moment she had first plucked at her stern nipple and felt, perhaps, her mother's distaste. . . . Life was like a room in which one hardly dared move for fear of tripping over rules, blundering into shibboleths, breaking some valuable regulation" (*H*, p. 14).

Even as an adult with a home and children of her own, Eleanor does not "really think of herself as having a separate identity" (*H*, p. 15). She has internalized Mrs. Bennet's values so completely that her husband regards her as the emotional equivalent of her (or his own) mother. Consequently, he resents her refusal to indulge his infidelities and eventually finds it impossible to make love to her. The woman for whom he leaves Eleanor enables him to feel "permissibly incestuous" (*H*, p. 16) while rebelling against the powerful mother figure who still shapes his emotional needs.

Inevitably, despite its passionate intensity and surprising duration (the separation occurs after twenty-six years of matrimony), the Strathearn marriage is consumed by the partners' mutual dependencies. Over time the "frail receptacle" (*H*, p. 12) has become a prison from which Graham periodically strays and within which Eleanor is both sheltered and trapped—financially dependent on the man who has cut her off emotionally. The novel traces Eleanor's unsuccessful attempt to separate not just legally but emotionally from her husband. Symbolically, because she takes most of the furniture of her marriage with her to her new home, she is never able to extricate herself from the emotional dependency of that relationship.

However, Eleanor's emotional crippling is less the result of her separation from her husband than the most recent casualty of her failure to have "left home"—to have successfully resolved her attachment to her dominating mother. As she half-consciously recognizes at one point, "The child inside herself . . . wanted love now, and to give love now, and to be with her proper parent, and to be reassured that no other child had taken her place. She wanted to be taken home; but this was her home" (*H*, p. 51). In psychoanalytic terms, she has failed to achieve individuation, the positive resolution of the earliest attachment between child and mother.[37] Marriage merely resulted in the transfer of her symbiotic needs to a husband on whom, ultimately, she could not lean because he sought the same emotional succor from her. Her husband has the benefit of society's double standard; he simply leaves the woman whom he unconsciously associates with "mother"—because she both indulges his infantile needs and inhibits his sexual freedom—tellingly, for another woman with the same name as his wife.

While Eleanor struggles painfully to establish a new emotional space for herself, she capably sustains the sense of home for her family; during the course of the narrative, all of her children and an assortment of other relatives and friends either visit or take up temporary residence in her home and receive sustenance from her. Yet she is excessively dependent on their good opinion of her. Because she so wants her daughters to feel "at home," she willingly overlooks the messes made by Jessica's unhousetrained puppy and condones Cressida's sexual involvement, which even-tually leads to pregnancy, with one of Eleanor's own former lovers.

Furthermore, the mother's unresolved dependencies inevitably influ-ence the daughters' emotional development. Cressida is obsessively pre-occupied with becoming a mother herself, for "until she could have a child, and find some function for her body, she was paralyzed" (*H*, p. 67). Similarly, Daphne seeks to lose herself in marriage, and eventually finds a willing partner. Jessica, the only one of Eleanor's daughters who has eluded the influence of Grandmother Bennet's values, is a carefree hippie who lives out of a knapsack, corresponding to the part of her mother that is "free and blameless" (*H*, p. 134).

Even Eleanor's relationships with her sons bear the mark of her merged boundaries with and suffocating attachment to her own mother. The eld-est, Marcus, reciprocates her affection to the exclusion of all other women in his life, living in Paris with his male lover. Philip, the youngest and only child still legally dependent, feels caught in a prison of mother-love, both drawn to and threatened by Eleanor's acute need for companionship.

With her daughters, Eleanor attempts to determine new emotional boundaries as a single woman. Her house becomes a female world, "a Bennet stronghold" (*H*, p. 67) where the women share their lives, loves, and disappointments. Eventually Eleanor acknowledges the engulfing repetitions of this domestic arrangement, regretting that

> in her own way, she was repeating the pattern of herself and Mrs. Bennet: depriving her children of responsibility, lying to them by making out that she was resistant and self-governing, limiting their ability to feel and to act freely from their feelings. She thought that she was encouraging their in-dependence; but by her remoteness, her brave face, the no-nonsense voice she put on when her heart was breaking, she bound them to her by worry and uneasiness and, worst, the suspicion that she was being dishonest with them. (*H*, p. 147)

Gradually all her children depart from her, leaving Eleanor emotionally bereft and isolated in "no man's land" (*H*, p. 133).

In fact, Eleanor's life of incompletely resolved separations and loss of attachments has left her—like Mrs. Armitage of Mortimer's *The Pump-kin Eater*—dying of grief. She recognizes, but is never able to overcome, her vulnerability to the pain of separation, what she terms "parting." An extended reflection on loss, precipitated by Eleanor's recollection of a childhood picture book of female anatomy, is a central passage in the novel's psychological subtext. The association with the female body underscores the link between gender and the attachment to and loss of love objects:

> Some original, buried parting which she would never remember—the banishment, perhaps, from Mrs. Bennet's womb?—followed by an endless series of partings, her dying father (why did she so seldom think of him?), her school friends, her few childhood sweethearts; then, one by one, her children, her lovers, Graham—and what was to come? Thirty more years of life at least; a parting lurking in each one of them? Was there to be no approaching, coming together; never a union? . . . [T]here was a questioning in her mind that was flavored by . . . the taste of a continual goodbye. (*H*, p. 129)

When Mrs. Bennet volunteers to stay with her in the new house, Eleanor is ambivalently both gratified and defeated. With her mother in residence, her own personality is figuratively reabsorbed: "The crust of [her] identity seemed to crumble. . . . She had collapsed against Mrs. Bennet's strength; she had become, as she had always become with her mother, emasculated" (*H*, p. 109). In classic psychoanalytic terms, the smothering mother emasculates her son, not her daughter, who, technically, cannot be castrated.[38] The term nonetheless suggests the extent to which Eleanor's symbiotic tie to her mother inhibits her adult sexuality and autonomy.

The women in Eleanor's life create an emotional center through the primary mother–daughter bond and within the locus of traditional female experience, the home; the men embody her experience of "parting." The "homelessness" (*H*, p. 202) that Eleanor experiences during a European trip, with her sons as traveling companions, is prelude to the shattering event that occurs during her absence: her mother's sudden death. This ultimate separation is the true death of possibility for Eleanor. When the dominant partner in a symbiotic relationship dies, the dependent one is left emotionally amputated; the death of Mrs. Bennet is the death of the part of Eleanor that is still merged with her mother. Her death strips her daughter of "her last few illusions that she could be solitary, independent and autonomous" (*H*, p. 215).

In *The Handyman*, Phyllis Muspratt struggles painfully to adjust to her sudden widowhood. As she begins to feel increasingly superfluous, she leans on her grown son and daughter. However, both are so preoccupied with the disarray of their own affairs that they are incapable of seeing their mother as a person with needs of her own. Phyllis's acute loneliness and dependency make her vulnerable to a "handyman" who cynically exploits her circumstances. Demanding payment for his household repairs in either excessive sums of money or sexual favors, he erodes Phyllis's tenuous grip on her life. Her oblivious children fail to see, until it is too late, her gradual slippage "over the edge of her life" (*HM,* p. 150).

In both *The Home* and *The Handyman,* Mortimer powerfully dramatizes what happens to an emotionally dependent woman whose love attachments depart and leave her unable to survive these losses psychologically: her husband as the locus of her sexual identity; her children as the locus of her social role and her capacity to give and "serve"; and, in Eleanor Strathearn's case, her mother as the source of her long-standing symbiotic dependency. As Ernest Becker has described in existential terms the ambiguous bind of such attachments, "We enter symbiotic relationships in order to get the security we need, in order to get relief from our anxieties, our aloneness and helplessness; but these relationships also bind us, they enslave us even further because they support the lie we have fashioned." [39]

Although Mortimer's Eleanor Strathearn recognizes her crippling dependency, she can find no way to break that emotional stranglehold, even after her mother's death. Similarly, Phyllis Muspratt, despite her efforts at literal and emotional relocation, never overcomes her experience of incompleteness and loss. Pessimistically, Mortimer implies that such patterns may become so deeply embedded in the personality that they can scarcely be altered by external events. Home is, as the dictionary definitions from the frontispiece to *The Home* suggest, both a dwelling place and an "institution of refuge and rest for destitute or infirm persons. . . ." At the end of *The Handyman,* Phyllis Muspratt is dead from a household accident caused by carelessness and neglect; at the conclusion of *The Home,* Eleanor Strathearn remains in a helpless, afflicted state, knowing that "Graham was dead. Her mother, all mothers, were dead" (*H,* p. 252), but still struggling to be born into her own life.

Through unconscious repetition of deeply rooted emotional patterns, not only Eleanor Strathearn and Phyllis Muspratt but many of Mortimer's female characters are circumscribed by past events that continue to affect and constrict their capacity to act in the present. The author's only experimental fiction, *Long Distance,* takes as a structural principle one of the psychological principles of the preceding novels. In this novel, repetition is not only a central theme but an aspect of its narrative organization. As the epigraph by George Santayana states, "Those who cannot remember the past are condemned to repeat it." The protagonist-narrator of *Long Distance* discovers that her "task" is literally "to repeat experience until it is remembered"—that is, to escape from the imprisonment of repetition.[40] In directly engaging the dynamic of repetition, she confronts the nature of boundary as both objective and subjective framework for the shaping of self and experience.

Mortimer's autobiography of her early years is entitled *About Time:*[41] *Long Distance,* a narrative in which autobiographical events are transposed into fiction and in which time is ostensibly absent, is also "about time." Time, in this sense, is a particularly suggestive aspect of boundary: by the segments of hours, days, and years, one comes to delineate experience and to achieve identity based upon a history of significant events and relationships.

The unconscious, according to psychoanalytic theory, is without time parameters; only the conscious ego imposes such demarcations.[42] In the ostensibly timeless world of *Long Distance,* the narrator's repressed past—the domain of the unconscious—unfolds as a kind of psychodrama occurring in the narrative present. Deprived of the organizing framework of chronology, the protagonist cannot determine whether these experiences occur uniquely or recur in an endless cycle: whether "the part I know is over or whether it is yet to come" (*LD,* p. 23). She inhabits a kind of existential nightmare—"freedom" without "free will" (*LD,* p. 19).

Long Distance is unique in Mortimer's canon. Rather than being situated in an easily identifiable reality, the narrative is surreal in setting and time; events are linked not by the logic of plot, character development, or chronology but by an inner logic originating in the psychological reality of the nameless narrator. It reproduces the narrator's chaotic and multi-layered experience: the order of events, narrated in the present tense, is apparently random. Gradually, as certain themes, people, and locations reappear, the protagonist-narrator (and the reader) begins to see their emphasis, although it is difficult to establish definitive meanings for these suggestive occurrences. At times the obscurities seem narratively unjustified; certain details seem to refer to images from the author's life that resist literary interpretation, while others lend themselves to multiple readings, both autobiographical and fictitious.

Among these images are psychological issues carried forward like an unpaid balance from Mortimer's previous narratives, particularly those concerning dependency, female sexuality, parent-child relationships, the significance of "home," the inevitability of loss. Additionally, the narrator confronts the levels of emotional desire or possibility that lie—in both senses—beneath the socialized self: the potentialities for incest (both father–daughter and mother–son relationships are inferred), promiscuous sexuality, murder, treachery, and other morally questionable acts or desires that might well be hidden from consciousness. Like Doris Lessing's *The Memoirs of a Survivor, Long Distance* is a "literary biography," a reprise of the author's fictional preoccupations combined with veiled details from her own life.

The novel's narrator finds herself in a curious domain: a large white mansion and its environs, whose precise function is never disclosed. She feels as if she "can't stop travelling" (*LD*, p. 6), but this movement clearly occurs in the dimension of memory rather than place, involving different phases of her past self. Watches are removed from arriving residents, and clocks are absent, as if to annihilate chronological orientation. The narrator experiences a state of simultaneous motion and paralysis, "being moved forward, sometimes at really fantastic speed—but staying in the same place. . . . Bits of me keep getting stripped off and thrown out of the window, into the rushing wind" (*LD*, p. 6). The tone and setting recall the surreal experiences of Kafka's Joseph K of *The Trial* and K of *The Castle* or the characters in Robbe-Grillet's novel and film, *Last Year at Marienbad,* who struggle in dream landscapes, forever approaching but never arriving at a clear destination or explanation.

While the dimension of time is problematic in *Long Distance,* space and place are given definite, if also ambiguous, boundaries in a metaphorical topography. The narrative is divided into six sections that correspond to locations the narrator occupies at various stages of her journey through the domain of the mansion or, figuratively, the unconscious.[43] Her odyssey begins with her arrival through a side door and entry through a dark passage, images suggesting birth or entry into the unconscious. Her eventual room has four doors, but "only one way out" (*LD*, p. 10). Situated at the symbolic nexus of time and space, it exists exclusively in the present or "'now'; if only it were 'then' I would know it better," the narrator determines (*LD,* p. 10).

Eventually even "mental travel" ceases as the narrator declares, "I am literally no longer myself. I have no past, but am doing everything for the first time. This is where I begin. Memory, if it ever existed, is irretrievably drowned" (*LD,* p. 43). Ego-consciousness—that figurative dimension through which the self is anchored in personal history—is dissipated. In the "imaginary climate" of the mansion, the narrator explores the "boundaries of [her] horizon" of consciousness, eventually confronting the Other or "unconscious type" (*LD,* pp. 7–8) within herself.

Mortimer's psychodrama is populated by a cast of characters who, as is true of dreams and other artifacts of the unconscious, function in multiple and overlapping roles. The most important of these protean figures is the oddly-named Gondzik, who is alternately (and even simultaneously) authority figure, father figure, lover, tormenter, betrayer, and betrayed. Gondzik's room, unlike the narrator's spartan one, evokes religious associations: painted "virgin white" (*LD,* p. 38), it resembles a chapel, complete with altar screen and papal chair. Scarcely suiting its occupant, it obliquely recalls the environment of the narrator's (and the author's) own father, a joyless, sexually obsessed Church of England minister who is associated with the narrator's (and Mortimer's[44]) feelings of guilt and incestuous violation, succor and betrayal. As the narrator moves through this reified topography of memory, Gondzik is an ambiguous guide, introducing her to the domains of the mansion and both supporting and criticizing her reactions.

One of these domains is a garden—a highly allusive location, suggesting the satisfaction of appetite as well as the biblical loss of innocence. The gardener is specifically associated with the protagonist's (and the author's) father, not only by his clerical collar, but by the emotions he elicits. First he offers her a tomato and then sexually fondles her. She passively allows his violations, then flees from his shame and her own disgust by plunging into a nearby pool. Somehow, she realizes, the father who had sung to her as a child is connected to the man whose hands fumbled illicitly in her body, an acutely distressing memory that she has repressed: "Now I know what to expect from the place, that it is full of traps and snares, one must be continually wary. . . . Slowly, very very slowly, I lay the memory to rest. It leaves me, sinking fathom after fathom into darkness" (*LD,* p. 36).

During her sojourn, the figure of the father appears in multiple and conflicting images for the daughter: as sexual being (both aggressor and object), source of solace, and, ultimately, betrayer. As with most of the other events of the novel, the narrator confronts her past—whether as memories or desires—as if it could be recovered with all of the originally censored feelings made conscious.

Another cluster of experiences connected with the themes of merged emotional boundaries occurs in the "West Wing" of the mansion. There, in a place that resembles a psychiatric hospital, the narrator is erotically involved with a young man named Simon, whose filial relationship to her is implied. She is later treated with electric shock and other measures, either to fulfill her attraction to pain and suffering or to cure her of it. She is subjected to tests of physical endurance; a doctor examines her internal female anatomy in an assaultive manner; even Simon participates in her sexual torment. These events dramatize reifications of guilt and psychic pain associated with female sexuality or repressed erotic desires.

Like the figures of father and son, the mother-figure in *Long Distance* is in part a composite of details from Mortimer's earlier fiction as well as from recollections of the author's own mother.[45] Images suggestively associated with the domestic role occur in a chaotic, disorganized house to which the narrator is taken as "punishment" for her inappropriate emotional reactions to other events at the mansion. The episode is an ironic enactment of "putting one's house in order," a particularly telling activity in Mortimer's narratives in which houses and homes figure so centrally as metaphors for a dependent female's imprisonment. The chaotic house is a stunning image of the layering of time, as if successive moments of the past and the inexorable accumulation of objects could be superimposed.

The house is also populated with an assortment of children (recalling Mrs. Armitage's brood in *The Pumpkin Eater*). Leaving them to fend for themselves, the narrator occupies herself with "the baby" and with fruitless efforts to subdue disorder. Yet, confronted with her maternal responsibilities, she feels intense conflict: "If the baby is still crying at twenty-five to three I will kill it. What a relief that at twenty-eight minutes to three everything is quiet" (*LD,* p. 73).

The narrator's domestic dismay also reflects in almost comic exaggeration the cyclical, unremitting, and unrewarding task of housekeeping: "I confront the problem. But it refuses to be confronted. Where . . . do I begin? If I start with the shoes—a day's work at least—the kitchen will become uninhabitable. If I start with the kitchen, the mattresses will never get aired, the laundry will never get done. If I do the laundry, when shall I decide what they are going to eat? But then again, how can I cook with all that washing up waiting to be done?" (*LD*, p. 71).

Like Psyche faced with the overwhelming task of sorting disparate items, the narrator longs for aid, imagining that her mother could master the disorganized nightmare "in a jiffy. It really is too bad of them to put me here without my mother. And too bad of my mother to allow it" (*LD*, p. 72). These and other passages illustrate the linkages between domestic order and the mother, the figure who first contributes to the child's (particularly the daughter's) sense of boundary and demarcation of inner and outer worlds. Presiding over the child's image of "home," she represents the original locus of emotions about the self and relationship.

The chaotic house of *Long Distance* conveys the emotional tone of the narrator's experiences as both a daughter and an overwhelmed mother and housekeeper. In a remark that expresses the domestic reality of most of Mortimer's female characters, she comments, "It's not the hard labour, quite honestly, that's so exhausting: it's the loneliness, the guilt, and the unendurable exercise of loving" (*LD*, p. 76). Mortimer articulates the ironic bind of domestic obligation: her female protagonist reenacts her complicity by acquiescing to, and even coming to enjoy, her domestic oppression.

In another part of the mansion's domains, the narrator meets an old woman in the woods and, like a small child, begs, "'Tell me a story'" (*LD*, p. 93). The old woman obliges, describing a little girl who loved stories so much that "'she believed everything she was told!'" (*LD*, p. 94). According to the old woman, the girl "'grew up and had a great many babies and grew old and died'" (*LD*, p. 95). This stark oversimplification of a woman's life in patriarchy—reminiscent of the lives of Mortimer's other fictive women—horrifies the narrator, who later comes to regard the "domain of women" (*LD*, p. 142) as an endless round of domestic tasks, obstetrical illnesses, and empty gossip. The figure of the gardener/father promises liberation from this prison of domesticity. As he assures her, "'Marriage is the coffin of love! . . . Sex is a great and glorious experience, it can't survive behind bars'" (*LD*, p. 98).[46]

The narrator's unsatisfactory attempts to find both erotic fulfillment and reciprocation of affection reflect a central theme of her unconscious repetitions, that of loss or—as Eleanor Strathearn of *The Home* terms it—"parting." In her dreams, a series of attractive men evoke her affections and then disappear. Each time she merges with the male partner, "slip[ping] into him . . . forever. Then he gets up and walks easily away" (*LD*, p. 101). The men's casual disregard for her feelings convinces her that "the gardener is inevitable in the end; that my original meeting with him is the only solace I can remember" (*LD*, pp. 101–2). In psychological terms, she is driven back to the original but forbidden incestuous attachment to the father—the daughter's first sexual object. But he too both tempts and rejects her. These multiple betrayals and losses push the narrator to the extreme of self-alienation, "that imperceptible separation from myself which, when completed, will be permanent" (*LD*, p. 141).

A "shred" of the narrator's "dividing self" (*LD*, p. 144) splits off from her; the two selves "separate and lead their contradictory lives in freedom" (*LD*, p. 146). In a passage that applies not only to the narrator of this novel but to others of Mortimer's diminished women, R. D. Laing has described the "divided self" or schizoid personality as

> an individual the totality of whose experience is split in two main ways: . . . there is a rent in his relation with his world and . . . a disruption of his relation with himself. Such a person is not able to experience himself "together with" others or "at home in" the world. . . . [Instead], he experiences himself in despairing aloneness and isolation; moreover, he does not experience himself as a complete person but rather as "split" in various ways.

Once the division into "true" and "false" selves occurs, "the self is extremely aware of itself, and observes the false self, usually highly critically."[47]

In *Long Distance*, the narrator reenacts the themes of self-betrayal and loss through the split self. The amoral or false self engages in treachery and in promiscuous acts; the "innocent" narrator, observing and criticizing from a distance, concedes that she is implicated in these acts since they "share the same body" (*LD*, p. 166). Eventually, after the "other" self has accomplished the deflection of responsibility onto other people, she leaves the mansion. The narrator, strengthened by her recognition of their underlying identity, feels released from infinite repetition of the themes of her own psychic reality.

By the end of *Long Distance,* all four doors of the narrator's room in the mansion are open. Having integrated or exorcised the denied Other, who has been successively projected onto parents, children, lovers, and others, she finds order and freedom of movement in her inner reality. Following the model of the old woman in the woods, she consciously assumes the role of storyteller. Her new capacity suggests the form of truth she has discovered—or recovered—during her sojourn: that the deepest and most powerful emotional realities comprise a series of themes and images bounding the self. Although the characters and settings may change, the story repeats itself until it becomes "indelible," that is, until its themes are integrated into the conscious personality, which only then may be released from repetition.

The narrative does not conclude, as one might expect, with the narrator's departure from the mansion; rather, she hopes to live there "forever" (*LD,* p. 204). Psychologically, one cannot undo the past; one can only come to terms with it. The narrator, having achieved the figurative perspective of "long distance," takes responsibility for her own story and transforms the themes of her experience into fiction.

Mortimer, looking back on her country childhood, has written in her autobiography of her realization late in life that "all movements on this earth are circular, and that in the end I would begin to recognize the landscape again, the wall, the bushes, the long grass path."[48] In contrast to several of her earlier circular narratives, *Long Distance* concludes with a resolution in psychological as well as narrative terms: the female protagonist-narrator achieves a rare insight into her past experience and thus finds a door through which to exit from emotional imprisonment.

In one way or another, Penelope Mortimer's novels are about loss: of love and sexual fidelity; of parents, children, or spouses; of innocence; of self. In the early narratives, separation or loss (or both) are dramatized on the domestic and social level: a threat to the relationship between wife and husband is posed in terms of an erotic temptation that tests the moral and emotional terms of their marital contract. The opposition between freedom and commitment is explored through marriage—the central social institution through which women have traditionally achieved identity—and infidelity—the private and social transgression of its boundaries. In these narratives of women confined by domesticity, children are present less as developed characters in their own right (except for Angela Whiting of *Cave of Ice*) than as extensions of their mothers' anxieties and their parents' ambivalent relationships. Occupying far more central positions in their mothers' psychic equilibrium than in the fathers', they initially advance and eventually impede the erotic arrangement.

In the later novels, marriage either fails or fails to occur; the female protagonists are literally alone, either legally or emotionally "separated." These latter narratives focus on a woman's struggle to come to terms with her solitary state. The underlying implication is the isolation of human beings from one another regardless of their domestic and erotic arrangements. Union with another is, for Mortimer's women, both necessary and destructive. Thus, such physical and emotional events as pregnancy, abortion, mastectomy, divorce, or the death of a spouse challenge the most basic emotional commitments between women and men, while undermining the women's sense of "ontological autonomy."[49]

Furthermore, Mortimer's fictions are prescient and, in several instances, masterful explorations of the destructive consequences of the "feminine mystique": many of her women suffer from the later-named "housewife's disease." Antonia Painton of *The Bright Prison* describes her "grief" as "the despair of all women for something gone, never to come again—something never known, now never to be known" (*BP*, p. 138). Of Mortimer's female protagonists, only Muriel Rowbridge of *My Friend Says It's Bulletproof* is employed; in fact, she is the only one who does not derive her identity through marriage and motherhood, though she is not free from anxieties about their absence in her life.

As Betty Friedan argued in the early sixties, and as the married women of Mortimer's fictions (published beginning in the forties) illustrate, "The very condition of being a housewife can create a sense of emptiness, non-existence, nothingness, in women. There are aspects of the housewife role that make it almost impossible for a woman of adult intelligence to retain a sense of human identity, the firm core of self or 'I' without which a human being, man or woman, is not truly alive."[50] Mortimer's narratives artfully belie the stereotypical expectation of her generation, that "a woman's place is in the home": "home" in her fiction is the locus not only of security but of imprisonment. The imagery of boundary suggests an inescapable identity between gynecological and existential confinement.

NOTES

1. Apart from book reviews of her works, there is virtually no critical commentary on Mortimer. In a discussion of the failure of women writers to create autonomous female characters, Carolyn Heilbrun terms Mortimer "a fine and underesteemed novelist," though her novels support Heilbrun's argument in that "all her protagonists suffer a notable lack of selfhood. Only one has the single element that has preserved Mortimer's own life: her work." *Reinventing Womanhood* (New York: W. W. Norton, 1979), p. 83.

2. Betty Friedan, *The Feminine Mystique* (rpt. New York: Dell, 1963).

3. Annis Pratt suggests that "marriage as archetypal enclosure" is a recurrent pattern in fiction by women. See *Archetypal Patterns in Women's Fiction* (Bloomington: Indiana University Press, 1981), p. 45.

4. Penelope Mortimer, *The Bright Prison* (New York: Harcourt Brace, 1957), p. 90. All subsequent references are from this edition, indicated in the text by "BP" and parenthetical page numbers.

5. Penelope Dimont, *Johanna* (London: Secker and Warburg, 1947), p. 9. Published under her name in her first marriage, this is the author's only novel not published in the United States. All subsequent references, indicated in the text by "*J*" and parenthetical page numbers, are to this edition.

6. Robert Seidenberg and Karen DeCrow, *Women Who Marry Houses: Panic and Protest in Agoraphobia* (New York: McGraw Hill, 1983), p. 47. See also note 20 below. Sandra Gilbert and Susan Gubar observe that "agoraphobia and its complementary opposite, claustrophobia," are central images in narratives by nineteenth-century poets and novelists, expressing the writers' (if not their female characters') "feelings of social confinement and their yearning for spiritual escape." *The Madwoman in the Attic: The Woman Writer and the Nineteenth-Century Literary Imagination* (New Haven: Yale University Press, 1979), p. 86.

7. *Cave of Ice* (New York: Harcourt Brace, 1959), p. 74. All subsequent references in the text, indicated by "*CI*" and parenthetical page numbers, are to this edition.

8. Penelope Mortimer, *The Pumpkin Eater* (New York: McGraw Hill, 1962), p. 215. All subsequent references, indicated in the text by "*PE*" and parenthetical page numbers, are to this edition.

9. Penelope Mortimer, *The Home* (New York: Random House, 1971), p. 7. All subsequent references, indicated in the text by "*H*" and parenthetical page numbers, are to this edition.

10. Tony Tanner, *Adultery in the Novel: Contract and Transgression* (Baltimore: Johns Hopkins University Press, 1979), p. 17, p. 13.

11. Ibid., p. 17.

12. Penelope Mortimer, *A Villa in Summer* (New York: Harcourt Brace, 1954), p. 146. All subsequent references, indicated in the text by "*VS*" and parenthetical page numbers, are from this edition.

13. In analyzing the sexual double standard, Dorothy Dinnerstein suggests the source of such asymmetries in the original asymmetrical parenting arrangement. Men unconsciously seek both to avoid the unilateral power of the female, as originally vested in the mother, and to return to her through a variety of erotic mates. By contrast, women seek the security of a monogamous relationship as the framework for their muted erotic needs and their greater dependency upon a relationship that combines emotional and erotic objects. See *The Mermaid and the Minotaur: Sexual Arrangements and Human Malaise* (New York: Harper and Row, 1977), esp. chapter 4, "Higamous-Hogamous," pp. 38–75.

14. See particularly Doris Lessing, *Retreat to Innocence* (rpt. New York: Prometheus, 1959). In that novel, the characters debate ideological alternatives, and the female protagonist, Julia Barr, is in love with a Marxist radical whose political philosophy she is unable to appreciate.

15. Friedan, *The Feminine Mystique,* p. 11 and following. Friedan's book was published in the United States in 1963; Mortimer's *The Pumpkin Eater* was published in England in 1961. As Friedan described a distinctly female dilemma, "Since the human organism has an intrinsic urge to grow, a woman who evades her own growth by clinging to the childlike protection of the housewife role will—insofar as that role does not permit her own growth—suffer increasingly severe pathology, both physiological and emotional" (p. 279).

16. A minor character named Hilary Armitage appears in Mortimer's first novel, *Johanna* (see note 5 above), but she is not developed enough to establish that she is in fact the Mrs. Armitage of this novel.

17. Nancy Chodorow, *The Reproduction of Mothering: Psychoanalysis and the Sociology of Gender* (Berkeley: University of California Press, 1978), p. 126.

18. Alice Miller, *Prisoners of Childhood*, trans. Ruth Ward (New York: Basic Books, 1981), pp. 99 and 45. Miller's observations about depression are also instructive in this context. She writes, "Depression can be understood as a sign of the loss of the self and consists of a denial of one's own emotional reactions and feelings. This denial begins in the service of an absolutely essential adaptation during childhood, to avoid losing the object's love. Subsequently, it continues under the influence of the introjects. For this reason depression indicates a very early disturbance. Right at the beginning, in infancy, such persons have suffered from a deficiency in certain affective areas that are necessary for stable self-confidence. From the reconstructions available through analyses, I have gained the impression that there are children who have not been free to experience the very earliest feelings, such as discontent, anger, rage, pain, even hunger and, of course, enjoyment of their own bodies" (pp. 45–46).

19. Robert Seidenberg, "The Trauma of Eventlessness," in *Psychoanalysis and Women*, ed. Jean Baker Miller (rpt. Baltimore, Md.: Penguin Books, 1973), p. 352.

20. Seidenberg traces the root of the term 'agoraphobia,' noting that "the Greek word *agora* mainly referred to the popular political assemblage of a community. We also know that 'proper' women were excluded from this public domain; courtesans were the only women seen in this environment. Today, the term 'agoraphobia' connotes the fear of open spaces and is a symptom most commonly, although not exclusively, found among women. One then is faced with the paradox of a woman who was originally prohibited by law and custom from entering 'public areas' of activity, now diagnosed as 'phobic' when she becomes anxious there!" (Ibid., p. 350). From another angle, Enid Balint describes the condition of "being empty of oneself" as one in which the sufferer—more frequently female—feels as if her "presence [has] been taken away from [her], although [she] had once had it." "On Being Empty of Oneself," *International Journal of Psycho-Analysis,* Vol. 44, No. 4, pp. 470–80, quote on p. 471.

21. Phyllis Chesler, quoted by Pratt, *Archetypal Patterns in Women's Fiction*, p. 34.

22. Friedan, *The Feminine Mystique,* p. 69.

23. Julia Kristeva, *Powers of Horror: An Essay on Abjection*, trans. Leon S. Roudiez (New York: Columbia University Press, 1982), p. 55.

24. Simone de Beauvoir, *The Second Sex,* trans. H. M. Parshley (New York: Alfred A. Knopf, 1952), pp. 491–92.

25. Susan Sontag, *Illness as Metaphor* (New York: Farrar, Straus and Giroux, 1977), p. 20.

26. Margaret Atwood, *Bodily Harm* (Toronto: McClelland and Stewart, 1981). The only other novel of which I am aware that concerns a woman who has undergone a mastectomy is Joan Winthrop's *Underwater* (New York: G. P. Putnam's, 1974). Like Mortimer and Atwood, Winthrop uses her female protagonist's disfigurement to explore questions about female self-image and sexuality— but in this instance to explore the idea of bisexuality and androgyny. Kate Stevens, the unhappy wife of dull Harry and the mother of a baby daughter, finds her true sexuality in her first lesbian relationship. The flat side of her chest is, symbolically, her "male" side, an alter ego named Valery St. John, who "[drives] a yellow convertible, [keeps] gin in the dashboard, and [climbs] up the gutters of the snug dormitories and into the beds of exciting women" (p. 14).

27. Penelope Mortimer, *My Friend Says It's Bulletproof* (New York: Random House, 1967), p. 36. All subsequent references, indicated by *Bulletproof* or "*FB*" and parenthetical page numbers in the text, are to this edition.

28. Atwood, *Bodily Harm,* p. 136.

29. Penelope Mortimer, *The Handyman* (New York: St. Martin's/Joan Kahn,

1985), p. 125. Because the novel was published in the United States as this study went to press, I have included only a partial discussion of it here. Subsequent references, indicated by "*HM*" and parenthetical page numbers in the text, are to this edition.

30. The language recalls Virginia Woolf's observation in *A Room of One's Own*: "Women have served all these centuries as looking-glasses possessing the magic and delicious power of reflecting the figure of man at twice its natural size" (rpt. New York: Harcourt Brace Jovanovich, 1957), p. 35.

31. Miller, *Prisoners of Childhood,* p. 28.

32. The phrase echoes Hegel's claim, quoted by Simone de Beauvoir, that "the birth of children is the death of parents." *The Second Sex*, p. 497.

33. Adrienne Rich, *Of Woman Born: Motherhood as Experience and Institution* (rpt. New York: Bantam Books, 1977), p. 240.

34. Chodorow, *The Reproduction of Mothering*, p. 138.

35. See Karoly Kerenyi, *Eleusis: Archetypal Image of Mother and Daughter*, trans. Ralph Manheim (New York: Bollingen Foundation/Pantheon, 1967), p. 34. Mortimer's first novel adumbrates the emotional significance of the images: Johanna Freund remarks that "'shouting can't be helped inside a cave of ice. You say, "I'm cold"; it echoes, and all the sound comes back to you, draining back into your heart where the shouting comes from'" (*J*, pp. 25–26).

36. Rich, *Of Woman Born*, pp. 242–43.

37. Margaret Mahler writes, with respect to these psychological processes, "The intrapsychic process of separation and individuation runs on two intertwined, but not always synchronized[,] developmental tracks: one is *individuation*—the evolution of intrapsychic autonomy; the other is the intrapsychic *separation* process, which runs along the track of differentiation, distancing, boundary-structuring, and disengagement from mother." "A Study of the Separation-Individuation Process and Its Possible Application to Borderline Phenomena in the Psychoanalytic Situation," in *The Selected Papers of Margaret S. Mahler*, Vol. 2 (New York: Jason Aronson, 1979), p. 173, emphasis in original. Nancy Chodorow, in her analysis of the sources of ambivalence between mother and daughter, quotes Alice Balint: "'The mother's ambivalence . . . is apt to manifest itself partly by an exaggerated (because guilty) tenderness, and partly in open hostility. In either case the danger arises that the daughter, instead of finding the path away from mother towards men, remains tied to the mother. Coldness on the mother's part may, because of the child's unappeased love for her, prevent the requisite loosening of the bond between them.'" Alice Balint, *The Early Years of Life* (1954), p. 90, quoted by Chodorow in *The Reproduction of Mothering,* p. 135.

38. However, girls may have the *fantasy* of being castrated. As Margaret Mahler writes, "The girl's fantasy of being castrated and its influence on the ensuing ambivalence toward the mother seem to account for the greater frequency of the

early and later depressive responsiveness in the female." "Notes on the Development of Basic Moods: The Depressive Affect," in *Selected Papers,* 2: 75.

39. Ernest Becker, *The Denial of Death* (New York: The Free Press, 1973), p. 56.

40. Penelope Mortimer, *Long Distance* (Garden City, N.Y.: Doubleday, 1974), p. 83. All subsequent references, indicated in the text by *"LD"* and parenthetical references, are to this edition.

41. Penelope Mortimer, *About Time: An Aspect of Autobiography* (Garden City, N.Y.: Doubleday, 1979).

42. According to Freud, "In the id there is nothing corresponding to the idea of time, no recognition of the passage of time and . . . no alteration of mental processes by the passage of time. . . . [T]he repressed remains unaltered by the passage of time." *New Introductory Lectures on Psycho-Analysis,* trans. W. J. H. Sprott (New York: W. W. Norton, 1933), pp. 104–5.

43. In one of the most thoughtful reviews of this novel, Doris Grumbach proposes an eschatological interpretation, suggesting that the domain of the mansion is the "house of death" or the afterlife, "located in heaven or hell, it makes no difference. . . ." She adds, "Because it is the past [the narrator] is reliving, everything must end in death or disappearance as it does in life." Doris Grumbach, "Hail to a Distinguished Novel," *The New Republic,* September 28, 1974, p. 23.

44. Mortimer, *About Time,* pp. 85–87.

45. Ibid., pp. 39–49. A portrait of the author's mother appears in the autobiographical story, "The King of Kissingdom," in Penelope Mortimer, *Saturday Lunch with the Brownings* (New York: McGraw Hill, 1961), esp. p. 68.

46. These words also reflect autobiographical reality; in *About Time,* Mortimer describes her father's identical perorations to her. Trapped in a loveless marriage himself, he had advised his daughter to preserve her freedom by avoiding marriage. "[A]mong other things, he had told me that I must always be free, always kick against the pricks and try to demolish brick walls. . . . He told me that marriage was the coffin of love" and "always to follow the devices and desires of my own heart. . . ." (p. 151). But when she had attempted to apply these pronouncements literally by running away from boarding school, her father, outraged, had returned her to her school, where she was disciplined for the rest of the term.

47. R. D. Laing, *The Divided Self: An Existential Study in Sanity and Madness* (rpt. Harmondsworth, Middlesex, England: Penguin Books, 1965), pp. 17, 74.

48. Mortimer, *About Time,* p. 186.

49. Laing, *The Divided Self,* p. 56.

50. Friedan, *The Feminine Mystique,* p. 293.

Escape Artists and Split Personalities

Margaret Atwood

The oeuvre of Margaret Atwood is almost paradigmatic as a series of representations of boundary, union, and separation. In dramatizing diverse aspects of the nature of identity, Atwood's works also implicitly or explicitly comment on the nature of Canadian identity. Atwood has frequently noted the effects on Canadian consciousness of the country's border relationship with the United States. In one such remark, she observes that "There are boundaries and borders, spiritual as well as physical, and good fences make good neighbours. But there are values beyond national ones. Nobody owns the air; we all breathe it."[1]

The idea of boundary gains additional resonance in the context of issues that have for generations plagued Canada, a nation composed of two distinct linguistic and political groups, a country alternately irritated and intimidated by its geographically southern neighbor. While, as Marshall McLuhan observed, "Canada is a land of multiple borderlines, psychic, social, and geographic,"[2] Russell M. Brown suggests that the political boundary between Canada and the United States also "reifies" cultural differences between the two countries. Additionally, the Canadian population clusters along a one-hundred-mile-wide strip along the boundary, giving the more northerly country "a border-defined existence. Canada *is* a border land, and to live here is to experience a 'being between.'"[3]

Of the images in Atwood's work that embody this awareness of boundary, one of the most emblematic and recurrent is the figure of Siamese twins. Atwood has specifically commented that "Canada *is* a Siamese twin."[4] The image of joined twins is a brilliantly suggestive symbol for the paradoxical nature of attachment and separation, whether as an aspect of individual or national identity, or both. As Atwood has revealingly suggested in another context, "Writer and audience are Siamese twins. Kill one and you run the risk of killing the other. Try to separate them, and you may simply have two dead half-people."[5]

Images of joined or overlapping bodies or Siamese twins appear throughout Atwood's writing. In *The Edible Woman* (1969), Marian MacAlpin sees her reflection in the fixtures of her bathtub as three interconnected, distorted bodies, and in her mirror as two overlapping dolls.[6] In the same novel, a poster advertisement for women's underwear displays a young woman with three pairs of legs (*EW*, p. 95); Marian wonders if her pregnant friend, Clara, will produce a monster with three heads (*EW*, p. 117). Joan Delacourt Foster of *Lady Oracle* (1976) had visited the Freak Show at the Canadian National Exhibition as a child, where she had seen the remarkable twins "JOINED HEAD TO HEAD AND STILL ALIVE."[7] In *Life before Man* (1979), Lesje's lover, William, who is obsessed with environmental pollution, worries that radiation bombardment will cause Lesje to give birth to "a two-headed child" or a monster.[8] Elizabeth Schoenhof's monstrous stepmother, Auntie Muriel, is remembered at her funeral as "a phenomenon, like a two-headed calf or Niagara Falls" (*LBM*, p. 300), while Joan Delacourt of *Lady Oracle* is haunted by an image from childhood of her "three-headed" mother in a triple mirror.

The narrator of *Surfacing* (1972) sceptically regards marriage as a relationship in which she would "turn into part of a couple, two people linked together and balancing each other" and recalls her abortion as "a section of my own life, sliced off from me like a Siamese twin."[9] Her friend Anna reads her palm and asks, "'Do you have a twin? . . . because some of your lines are double'" (*S*, p. 10); later the narrator starts "seeing double" (*S*, p. 167). Rennie Wilford of *Bodily Harm* (1981) undergoes a transforming experience on Caribbean "Twin Islands In The Sun."[10] In Atwood's most recent novel, *The Handmaid's Tale* (1985), the narrator Offred thinks of herself and Ofglen, her partner for public errands, as "Siamese twins" moving "in tandem, travelling smoothly along our daily track."[11]

Though I shall discuss only Atwood's novels in the analyses that follow, I should mention that the image of joined twins also appears throughout her poetic oeuvre, along with frequent images of mirrors and doubles.

In one of her volumes of poetry, significantly entitled *Two-Headed Poems,* the title sequence begins, "The heads speak sometimes singly, some-times/ together, sometimes alternately within a poem./ Like all Siamese twins, they dream of separation."[12] Other poems within the sequence of twelve address variations of overlapping boundaries. It is indeed an apt image for dilemmas of symbiosis and separation and for confusion about ego boundaries and body image that preoccupy each of Atwood's pro-tagonists. Leslie Fiedler, in his study of freaks, has observed that Siamese twins "challenge our individuality, along with the distinction between self and other upon which that individuality depends; in other words, not the uniqueness of our bodies but of our consciousnesses, or what used to be called our souls."[13]

"Separatism," separation, and overlapping or ambiguous boundaries are thus simultaneously central unresolved national concerns of Canadian experience and metaphors for analogous issues within the individual psyche. Atwood's narratives clearly illustrate the relationship between female identity and boundary in diverse forms, including the parallels between a woman's inner psychological struggle for identity and the con-flicting images of national identity. Three of Atwood's fictional protag-onists travel either within Canada or outside the country; each ultimately achieves a new perspective on her inner dilemma from the different geo-graphical (and psychological) position. Moreover, of the author's six nov-els to date, five focus on a female protagonist who is confused about her selfhood; the remaining novel (*Life before Man*) concerns two women and one man who share the same predicament. Frequently the central female character regards her mother with ambivalence and is involved in a dis-turbed love relationship that repeats some of the same separation/identity problems.

In addition to the striking figure of Siamese twins, a number of other images in Atwood's fiction suggest preoccupation with issues of bound-ary. As I will elaborate in the following pages, most of her central char-acters experience themselves as internally divided, a feeling that may also be expressed in the way they perceive their bodies. Often, distorted im-ages of the self or the body are manifestations of crucial unresolved psy-chological issues. In several of the novels, the relationship between mother and daughter is revealed as a central aspect of the narrator's prob-lems with identity, self-image, and selfhood. These boundary issues in the mother–daughter relationship and other relationships are manifested as anxieties in connection with ingestion and/or maternity; fear of drowning or engulfment; the experiences of invasion, violation, and existential panic; and the desire for actual or psychological escape from these threatening experiences.

Finally, the concern with boundary issues broadens in Atwood's most recent fiction to emphasize the further correspondences between personal and political reality. Atwood has acknowledged her own increasingly explicit ideological focus, noting that there is a vital connection between the function of the novel as a "moral instrument," the responsibility of the writer to "bear witness," and politics. As she elaborates, "By 'political' I mean having to do with power: who's got it, who wants it, how it operates; in a word, who's allowed to do what to whom, who gets what from whom, who gets away with it and how."[14] In her fiction, the divisions within the female self or self-image eventually evolve into an encompassing metaphor for the difficult mediations between self and other, self and world.

In *The Edible Woman,* these concerns are demonstrated through the dilemma of the protagonist, Marian MacAlpin, who experiences a crisis of identity precipitated by confusion about selfhood, sexuality, and relationship. Images of stereotypical female roles surround her, from the "office virgins" and matronly women with whom she works to her eternally pregnant friend Clara, whom she regards as the victim of a body that "seemed somehow beyond her, going its own way without reference to any directions of hers" (*EW,* p. 36).

The implied loss of control of body boundaries characterizes Marian's own predicament; her perception of distorted images of her body mirrors her inner confusion. Agreeing desultorily to marry her steady boyfriend, Peter, without considering her motivations or feelings, she begins to experience her self as separate from her body. Eventually, her body "put[s] its foot down" (*EW,* p. 209) in resistance to food. As Marian finds herself involuntarily refusing to eat, she hopes that "her body might change its mind" (*EW,* p. 183).

The men in Marian's life are both contributors to and manifestations of her inner division. While Peter subtly tries to alter his new fiancee to conform to his conventional image of a wife, Marian becomes oddly attracted to Duncan, a sophomoric and "cadaverously thin" (*EW,* p. 48) graduate student who hangs out at the local laundromat. A kind of male double of Marian herself, with decidedly domestic fantasies, Duncan is also dissatisfied with the social expectations of his gender; mirroring Marian's boundary anxieties, he would prefer to be an amoeba, whose flexible shapelessness would be less complicated than being human.

Many of the altered body images in Atwood's narratives are literal reflections in mirrors, in people's eyes, in shiny surfaces. For example, Marian, early in her anxiety attack, observes her grotesque reflection in an eating utensil, "upside down, with a huge torso narrowing to a pin-head at the handle end. She tilted the spoon and her forehead swelled, then receded" (*EW,* p. 150). Some time later she sees her multiple reflections in the three fixtures of a bathtub as a "curiously-sprawling pink thing. . . . It was a moment before she recognized, in the bulging and distorted forms, her own waterlogged body. . . . [S]he swayed herself back and forth, watching the way in which the different bright silver parts of her body suddenly bloated or diminished" (*EW,* p. 224).

Marian's loss of boundary increases directly with her continuing liaison with Peter, becoming so acute that when he proposes a party in honor of their engagement, she fears "losing her shape, spreading out, not being able to contain herself any longer" (*EW,* p. 225). As she attires herself for the occasion, her attention is caught by two old childhood dolls; she views herself "in the mirror between them . . . as though she was inside them . . . the two overlapping images drawing further and further away from each other; the centre, . . . the thing that held them together, would soon be quite empty. By the strength of their separate visions they were trying to pull her apart" (*EW,* pp. 225–26).

Marian is both dolls, "overlapping" like Siamese twins, yet inwardly divided. Her resemblance to Lewis Carroll's fictitious Alice, whose literal alterations of shape and size are barely under her control, is underscored by Duncan's roommate Fischer's ingenious pseudo-Freudian interpretation of Carroll's story. "Fish," who is known for his obsessive preoccupation with womb imagery, observes that

"*Alice* is a sexual-identity-crisis book. . . . [T]his is the little girl descending into the very suggestive rabbit-burrow, becoming as it were pre-natal, trying to find her role . . . as a Woman. . . . One sexual role after another is presented to her but she seems unable to accept any of them. . . . She rejects Maternity when the baby she's been nursing turns into a pig, nor does she respond positively to the dominating-female role of the Queen and her castration cries of 'Off with his head!' And when the Duchess makes a cleverly concealed lesbian pass at her, sometimes you wonder how *conscious* old Lewis was. . . . [Then] she goes to talk with the Mock–Turtle, enclosed in his shell and his self-pity, a definitely pre-adolescent character; then there are those most suggestive scenes . . . one where her neck becomes elongated and she is accused of being a serpent, hostile to eggs . . . a rather destructively-phallic identity she indignantly rejects; and her negative reaction to the dictatorial Caterpillar, just six inches high [in Carroll's version it is *three* inches], importantly perched on the all-too-female mushroom which is perfectly round but which has the power to make you either smaller or larger than normal. . . . (*EW,* p. 199, emphasis in original)

Allusions to *Alice in Wonderland* recur throughout Atwood's fiction. Like Alice, several of her female characters, beginning with Marian MacAlpin, feel that their ability to master either circumstances or themselves is problematic; metamorphoses of body size or shape dramatize their preoccupation with boundary issues. In *Life before Man,* all of the principal characters subjectively experience occasional free falls through space. Lesje, the most obvious Alice figure (her name means Alice in English, according to her mother [LBM, p. 91]), is caught in a series of events that she regards as beyond her control. Wandering in the imaginary wonderland of the Pleistocene, she fantasizes naming a geological location after herself, regretting that she "couldn't call this place Aliceland" (*LBM,* p. 92). A related image appears in Elizabeth Schoenhof's recollection of her deceased lover, Chris, whom she fears might materialize if named as an accessory during her divorce trial, "fragmented, his head watching her with a Cheshire grin, his body still contorted in agony" (*LBM,* p. 261).

In the same novel, allusions to another children's classic, *The Wizard of Oz,* are woven through the narrative, with equally suggestive implications. In the Frank Baum story, Dorothy is literally (like Elizabeth Schoenhof figuratively) swept upwards into a vacuum in space created, in Dorothy's case, by a tornado; she is separated from the ambiguous Auntie Em (like Elizabeth's Auntie M: Auntie Muriel). Elizabeth puts herself to sleep with the scene in *Oz* in which Dorothy douses the Wicked Witch of the West with water and dissolves her. When Auntie Muriel literally shrivels up and dies like the bad witch of the story, Elizabeth recalls that "Dorothy was not jubilant when the witch turned into a puddle of brown sugar. She was terrified" (*LBM,* p. 279). Reviewing her feelings to an imaginary psychiatrist, Elizabeth thinks, "I've already been down this particular yellow brick road a couple of times, and what I found out mostly was that there's no Wizard of Oz" (*LBM*, p. 99). Nate Schoenhof suspects that deep down "he's patchwork, a tin man, his heart stuffed with sawdust" (*LBM*, p. 246).

The two children's stories share a concern with separation and boundary: Alice experiences dramatic alterations in her physical shape; Dorothy, involuntarily separated from her foster parents, presses through unknown lands with her dependent entourage, in pursuit of the powerful wizard, a figure of authority who proves to be a fraud. In place of the vivid scenery of Wonderland and Oz, *Life before Man* takes place in the more prosaic geography of Toronto and the museum, within whose symbolic walls the several characters try to resolve their troubled intimate relationships. That institution looms as a resonant symbol, suggesting both the void of separateness and absence and a place of refuge from that void. As Lesje describes this ambiguous womb/tomb in terms that recall the Wizard of Oz's palace of illusions, the museum is in one sense

> a palace built in the pursuit of truth, with inadequate air conditioning but still a palace. At other times it's a bandits' cave: the past has been vandalized and this is where the loot is stored. Whole chunks of time lie here, golden and frozen; she is one of the guardians . . . without her the whole edifice would melt like a jellyfish on the beach, there would be no past. She knows it's really the other way around, that without the past, she would not exist. (*LBM*, p. 308)

If Marian MacAlpin of *The Edible Woman* and Lesje Green of *Life before Man* recall Alice in Wonderland, the comic protagonist of *Lady Oracle* suggests Alice not only in Wonderland but Through the Looking Glass. Joan Delacourt Foster describes her visits with her Aunt Lou to the Freak Show at the Canadian National Exhibition, where the grotesque figures she witnesses externalize her own anxieties and fantasies. She is disturbed by the images of her altered body in the "distorting mirrors" of the Fun House "that stretched you and shrank you. . . . I didn't want to be fatter than I already was, and being thinner was impossible" (*LO*, p. 97). Though she never sees the Fat Lady, the image haunts her for years afterward.

Later, Joan describes her figurative journey through the looking-glass: in a trance state she "enters" through a triple mirror to the "other side," where she encounters an unhappy goddess who lives under the earth or in a cave and a man both good and evil. These displaced versions of her own parents also allude to several figures from literary tradition. The "unhappy goddess" suggests both Tennyson's "Lady of Shalott" and Persephone, Demeter's daughter, who was abducted by Hades. (The latter also recalls the paradoxically benign and sinister male figure in Joan Foster's own experience.) The multiple images of Joan's mother in the triple mirror also evoke the figure of the triple goddess of mythology, who symbolized three aspects of female being—crone, mother, and daughter. Hecate, the crone aspect who "lives in a cave at the entrance to the netherworld," traditionally completed the Demeter-Persephone relationship, catalyzing "the reunion with lost parts of the self" [15]

As Joan Foster reveals at the beginning of her narrative, her life has had "a tendency to spread, to get flabby, to scroll and festoon like the frame of a baroque mirror" (*LO*, p. 3). During the course of the novel, she describes at least five different "selves": one-time fat girl; presently successful popular poet; author of "costume Gothic" romances (themselves divided between the virtuous Charlotte and the sensuous Felicia, Joan's two alter egos); the mistress of a Polish count and later of an avant-garde artist; and wife of Arthur Foster, a political activist for lost causes.

Like Marian MacAlpin and Joan Foster, the unnamed narrator of *Surfacing* experiences herself as acutely self-divided, but the manifestations of her boundary anxieties are quite different. As she comments, "The trouble is all in the knob at the top of our bodies. I'm not against the body or the head either: only the neck, which creates the illusion that they are separate" (*S*, p. 91). Thus does she articulate a kind of mind-body problem: the rift between spirit and flesh that she tries to mend during the course of her narrative.

The narrative itself structurally reflects the narrator's inner division. The first and final sections of *Surfacing* are narrated in the present tense, the middle section in the past tense, all in the first-person voice of the detached female protagonist. These narrative shifts exemplify the original split and eventual fusion of the protagonist's past and present, mind and body, which have been radically severed as the result of experiences she is initially unable to acknowledge.

The friends with whom she travels to the backwoods of Quebec mirror her self-division. She repeatedly makes associations between her traveling companions and her own family; Anna, David, and Joe are in one sense stand-ins for important figures in her own fragmented past. Anna, who "could be me at sixteen," the narrator comments (*S,* p. 59), is an exaggerated embodiment of the narrator's false public self. She wears heavy make-up and never allows anyone (even her husband) to see beneath that mask; "her artificial face is the natural one" (*S,* pp. 50–51). Her husband, David, is a crude "pastiche" (*S,* p. 178) of superficial and stereotypical masculinity. Joe, the fourth member of the group, is a rather primitive man whose animal magnetism attracts the narrator despite her psychic numbness and distrust of love. Both men are overgrown boys, full of contempt for women, cartoon mannerisms, and sexual vulgarity.

Unlike others of Atwood's protagonists, the narrator of *Surfacing* had a "good childhood" (*S,* p. 21). However, her inner division has early roots: her father had "split" the family "between two anonymities, the city and the bush" (*S,* p. 68). Her family was different from those of her contemporaries, living as they did in the "border country" (*S,* p. 30) where two distinct cultures, religions, and languages overlapped; her views of God, religion, and sex were sharply set apart from those of her *Quebeçois* Catholic companions. Her botanist father, a rationalist and an atheist, instructed his son and daughter accordingly: "He said Jesus was a historical figure and God was a superstition. . . . If you tell your children God doesn't exist they will be forced to believe you are the god, but what happens when they find out you are human after all, you have to grow old and die?" (*S,* p. 124). Years later, the daughter still retains the infantile fantasy of her parents as gods.[16] Only when she dives to the bottom of the lake and, figuratively, her protective fantasy, does she mend her inner division and achieve an adult identity.

Like Penelope Mortimer's female characters, Atwood's women often collude unconsciously with the very forces that divide, victimize, or fragment them. Initially the narrator of *Surfacing* reveals that she was married and had a baby that, mysteriously, she left behind when she was divorced from her husband. The authentic version of events is disclosed much later: her love affair with a married man, a brief pregnancy terminated by an abortion that had made her feel brutalized and dehumanized despite her own acquiescence, and her termination of the relationship afterwards.

The narrator's "marriage," "baby," and "divorce" are central events in a defensive fantasy she has created to protect herself from pain, both self-created and unchosen, and to disguise the details of experiences she is loath to acknowledge. As she eventually explains her subterfuge, "I couldn't accept it, that mutilation, ruin I'd made, I needed a different version. I pieced it together the best way I could, . . . pasting over the wrong parts" (*S*, p. 169). Other images of wounding and mutilation punctuate the narrative: the narrator had experienced her divorce as an "amputation"—"you survive but there's less of you" (*S*, p. 49); she recalls a woman with only one hand and wonders if her own hand could "come off like that" (*S*, p. 31); she experiences her psychic numbness as a "pond freezing or a wound, shutting me into my head" (*S*, p. 126).

Her alterations of fact thus express her inner wounding, as her self-division is manifested in her "unreliability" to her self. Language itself is duplicitous; it can both falsify and articulate the truth. The narrative moves backward as it moves forward: its central character dialectically constructs and deconstructs her past as preamble to her recovery of authenticity. That process is also signified in her shift from the view of language as that which "divides us into fragments" (*S*, p. 172) to language as "everything you do" (*S*, p. 153). *Surfacing* almost could have been titled *Surfaces:* nothing is what it initially seems; everyone is in camouflage. Suggestive of the confusion over national identity that forms a subtext of the narrative, even the "Americans" who fish in the lake are later revealed to be Canadians.

Images of boundaries reflect the narrator's experience of inner division. In her parents' cabin, she discovers a family photo album with snapshots of herself, surrounded by "borders of blank paper . . . like small gray-and-white windows opening into a place I could no longer reach. I was in most of the pictures, shut in behind the paper; or not me but the missing part of me" (*S*, pp. 128–29).[17] She sees the sky meeting the lake in "absence of defining borders" (*S*, p. 100). By contrast, when she fights with Joe, she feels anxious and "want[s] a truce, the borders restored to where they'd been" (*S*, p. 110). At times, her companions' forms are literally split into sections by the trees that divide her visual field (*S*, pp. 158, 160). She is unable to see anything whole, so internally divided is she herself.

Yet, like Penelope Mortimer's Mrs. Armitage, who dissociates herself from evil and death and thus maintains a false vision of her own innocence, the narrator of *Surfacing* divorces herself from life. The termination of her pregnancy, like that of Mrs. Armitage, was a capitulation to the very forces of destruction she repudiates: "I'd allowed myself to be cut in two. . . . The other half, the one locked away, was the only one that could live; I was the wrong half, detached, terminal. I was nothing but a head, or, no, something minor like a severed thumb; numb" (*S,* p. 129). Her choice of comparisons underscores her conviction of insignificance; in a sense, she identifies with the aborted fetus.

Atwood has called *Surfacing* a "ghost story," the kind in which "the ghost that one sees is in fact a fragment of one's own self which has split off."[18] Her protagonist recovers her split-off self when she sees the images or "ghosts" of her "lost" parents and her lost (aborted) child. Thereafter, the figures of the parents recede, no longer supernatural entities, as she acknowledges that the deities (or ghosts) of childhood must be relinquished: "They dwindle, grow, become what they were, human. Something I never gave them credit for" (*S,* p. 221).

Through these visions, the narrator ultimately transforms her nostalgia for childhood dependency into a true reconciliation that allows for her own autonomy, by internalizing the dualisms of union and division, head and heart, that the parents represent. Atwood thus dramatizes the primary psychological task of integrating the ambivalent images of the parents in order to move beyond immaturity: to see the "lost gods" of childhood simultaneously as limited human beings and as enabling sources of power for the self.

The three central characters of *Life before Man* also manifest internal division and are preoccupied with boundary issues. Elizabeth Schoenhof experiences anxiety in place of grief over the suicide of her most recent (discarded) lover, Chris. (Indeed, half of the characters in the novel consider suicide, suggesting their emotional dislocation.) Feeling both numb and vulnerable, she describes herself as "a peeled snail. . . . I want that shell back, it took me long enough to make. . . . I want a shell like a sequined dress, made of silver nickels and dimes and dollars overlapping like the scales of an armadillo. Armored dildo. Impermeable; like a French raincoat" (*LBM,* p. 11).

The remote narrative voice describes Elizabeth as "somewhere between her body, which is lying sedately on the bed . . . and the ceiling with its hairline cracks. . . . She knows about the vacuum on the other side of the ceiling, which is not the same as the third floor where the tenants live. . . . Into the black vacuum the air is being sucked with a soft, barely audible whistle. She could be pulled up and into it like smoke" (*LBM,* p. 12).

The two "voices"—first and third person—dramatize Elizabeth's two different states, one in which she is very much in control, the other in which she is a helpless Dorothy of Oz, drawn upward into a black hole in space. The imagery also reflects Elizabeth's contradictory sense of herself as both powerful and dependent. The psychic boundaries she describes are both weapons and defenses, "armor" and "dildo," expressing her ambivalent need for both protection and sexual aggression. Though her lover, Chris, is dead by the beginning of the narrative, his very absence functions as a kind of presence. He is associated with mass, weight, gravity; in him Elizabeth had temporarily found a way to anchor herself against the void. After his suicide, she overeats without feeling hunger, as a way of "weighting herself down" (*LBM*, p. 13).

In an image that recalls the figure(s) elsewhere in Atwood's fiction of Siamese twins as an emblem of problematic boundaries and the anxieties of attachment, Elizabeth reads a children's riddle that characterizes her own divided condition: "Two bodies have I / Though both joined in one, / The stiller I stand / The quicker I run" (*LBM*, p. 89). Identifying with the hourglass, Elizabeth imagines herself filled with sand trickling down through her glass body. "When it's all gone she'll be dead. Buried alive" (*LBM*, p. 89). The image evokes the sensations of engulfment and suffocation that periodically plague her.

Elizabeth's husband, Nate, himself divided between law and toymaking, understands that "half of [Elizabeth] wants a sensitive, impoverished artist, the other half demands a forceful, aggressive lawyer" (*LBM*, p. 41). In the current time of the narrative, she wants neither of these. Earlier in their marriage, she had realized that Nate sought her because she provided a secure enclosure, "a door he could go through and shut behind him" (*LBM*, p. 162). Presently, she has "rearranged time and space" to avoid intimate contact with Nate (*LBM*, p. 100), stretching an "invisible thread" across the threshold of her room to keep him out (*LBM*, p. 13).

Nate bores Elizabeth because "she doesn't like boxes whose contents she can guess" (*LBM*, p. 213); she chose a "demon lover" like Chris because he penetrated her heavily defended but fragile psychological boundaries, luring her into an emotionally "dangerous country, swarming with ambushes and guerrillas, the center of a whirlpool" (*LBM*, p. 213). Both attracted to and threatened by that vortex, Elizabeth had eventually terminated the relationship and her lover had terminated his life.

Nate also feels himself pulled in contrary directions—by his pious mother and his manipulative wife. He sometimes regards himself as "a lump of putty, helplessly molded by the relentless demands and flinty disapprovals of the women he can't help being involved with. . . . He fails [to make them happy] not because of any intrinsic weakness or lack of will, but because their own desires are helplessly divided" (*LBM,* p. 41). Yet, by his own admission, his failures are intensified by his passivity in the face of these strong women's competing claims.

Nate's involvement with his mistress, Martha, is the direct result of these pressures. Initially he had been attracted to Martha's "lack of focus, an absence of edges that gave her a nebulous shimmer" (*LBM,* p. 34). This impression of diffuse boundaries and passivity—qualities notably lacking in his perception of his wife—ultimately attracts him to Lesje Green, who accurately regards herself as an "appeaser" (*LBM,* p. 62). Nate, a doting father to his two daughters despite the sterility of his relationship with Elizabeth, tries to shift domiciles imperceptibly to ease the pain of separation for all concerned: "He thought that by moving to Lesje's he could rid himself of the need to be in two places at once. . . . He should have two sets of clothes, two identities, one for each house; it's the lack of this extra costume or body that is cracking him apart. He knew in advance, in theory, that separation is painful; he did not know it would also be literal. He has been separated; he is separate. Dismembered. He is no longer a member" (*LBM,* p. 244).

Not surprisingly, Lesje Green also suffers from inner division. Perhaps she is the most self-aware of the central characters in *Life before Man* in viewing herself as "damaged beyond repair" (*LBM,* p. 196). Not just an only child but an only grandchild, Lesje is the fiercely contested granddaughter of two possessive women, a Christian Ukrainian and a Jewish Lithuanian. Regarding herself as an odd hybrid whose foreignness compounds her sense of exclusion, she aptly embodies in slightly disguised terms the religious and ethnic schisms of Canadian identity to which Atwood frequently alludes. Lesje sometimes imagines that "she was produced, not by her parents in the usual way, but by some unheard-of copulation between these two old ladies who never met. They'd existed in an odd parody of marriage, hating each other more than either hated the Germans, yet obsessed with each other; they'd even died within a year of each other, like an old devoted couple. They'd infested her parents' house in relays, fought over her as if she'd been a dress at a bargain" (*LBM,* p. 93).

Rennie Wilford of *Bodily Harm* is "dismembered" in another sense. Like Muriel Rowbridge of Penelope Mortimer's *My Friend Says It's Bulletproof,* she experiences herself as internally divided as the result of a literal alteration of her body through surgery for breast cancer. Besides suffering from diminished self-regard as a result of her disfigurement, she is alienated from her body, which she regards as a "sinister twin, taking its revenge for whatever crimes the mind was supposed to have committed on it" (*BH,* p. 82). When she first learned of her disease, she was outraged, as if "she'd been betrayed by a close friend. She'd given her body swimming twice a week, forbidden it junk food and cigarette smoke, allowed it a normal amount of sexual release. She'd trusted it. Why then had it turned against her?" (*BH,* p. 82).

Compounding her distrust of her body is the fact that conventional attitudes toward the female (and male) body are reinforced at every level of culture. Rennie herself both participates in and perpetuates these stereotypes. A commentator on "radical chic"—fads in fashion, new styles of ornamentation, and other trends of interest to readers of women's magazines—she writes articles that emphasize the traditional passive role for women. A projected article on "drain-chain jewelry" with its "slave-girl effect" hints at her unacknowledged complicity in female bondage.

Rennie's boundary anxiety is projected onto other people. Late in the novel, when she is in jail for her presumed involvement in political intrigue, she regards her cell mate Lora Lucas's fingernails bitten below the quick and is repulsed by the "sight of ravage, damage, the edge between inside and outside blurred like that" (*BH,* p. 86). Ironically, Rennie flees Canada to escape the overwhelming pressures on her physical and mental integrity: not only her sadistic lover, Jake, but also the intruder who forcibly entered her Toronto flat and the insidious disease she harbors in her body. Her journalistic pose is partly a pretext for travel, partly a neutral mask to provide anonymity and distance from whatever she might encounter.

Rennie is one of several of Atwood's female protagonists who are in emotional flight from some person, event, or image that severely threatens the integrity of the self. Each seeks, at least initially, some sort of escape from her body, her problems, or her past. Each regards herself, or might be regarded, as an "escape artist" (*S,* p. 83), though both the motivation for and method of escape vary. The narrator of *Surfacing,* who is in fact a commercial artist, selectively omits or alters details of her past experience and determines that her true talent is that of escape. A childhood drawing is an important catalyst for her confrontation with her repressed experience.

In *Lady Oracle,* Joan Delacourt is inspired to write escape fiction by her first lover, Paul, who, having also escaped from his past in war-time Poland, writes nurse romances under a female pseudonym. In the Costume Gothic romances that Joan writes, the heroines' apparel and appearance figure centrally—parodic echoes of her own preoccupations with appearance. Moreover, these texts double as fantasy escapes which, like her oracular poetry, allow Joan to project her emotional dilemmas into her fiction. As Paul tells her, "'Escape literature . . . should be an escape for the writer as well as the reader'" (*LO,* p. 173).

As Joan's life becomes more and more complicated, she eventually realizes what she is trying to flee from: each of her fantasies and different personalities is a strategy for escape from her mother. As an "escape artist," she admits, "the real romance of my life was that between Houdini and his ropes and locked trunk; entering the embrace of bondage, slithering out again. What else had I ever done?" (*LO,* p. 367). The imagery clearly expresses her ambivalent "bondage" to her mother and her need to escape or separate from her.

Lesje Green of *Life before Man* is another of Atwood's escape artists or, more accurately, an "escape scientist." Periodically she retreats to her own wonderland, a lush antediluvian fantasy of the age of dinosaurs, where she observes predatory beasts in safety from her imaginary perch in the trees. Her profession of paleontology is a perfect expression of detached, impersonal self-definition: "This is her knowledge, her field they call it. And it is like a field, you can walk through it and around it and say: These are the boundaries." By contrast, "people aren't her field" (*LBM,* pp. 157, 64). Her own emotions are foreign territory to her.

Like Rennie Wilford of *Bodily Harm,* Offred, the narrator of the futuristic feminist nightmare *The Handmaid's Tale,* struggles against the circumscribing boundaries of imprisonment dictated by the unique, and vulnerable, attributes of the female body. In the Republic of Gilead, she is one of the "two-legged wombs" (*HT,* p. 146) whose sole function is procreation; her body, like that of her co-equal "handmaids," exists literally to be used against her. Subjected to sexual exploitation masquerading as religious fervor and worship of procreation, Offred longs for escape, even contemplating suicide as a way to terminate her understandable distress.

The inner division that afflicts nearly all of Atwood's protagonists can be understood as a manifestation of a female's conflicting possibilities in patriarchy. As a minor character in *The Edible Woman* explains it, an intelligent woman faces a dilemma: while single, she is treated like a "human being," but when she marries, "'[H]er core gets invaded . . . her image of herself. . . . Her feminine role and her core are really in opposition, her feminine role demands passivity from her . . .'" (*EW,* p. 242, final ellipsis in original). In the dystopian *The Handmaid's Tale,* this contradiction is ironically dissolved by splitting female roles along functional lines: Wives, Aunts, Marthas, Handmaids, and "Econowives" perform mutually exclusive functions according to age, fertility, and class, each assigned by male authority. Power and sexuality are absolutely divorced; there *is* no "core" of selfhood.

Yet "core" is suggestively associated not only with selfhood but with food. In Atwood's earlier fiction, the "invaded core" of female selfhood is often expressed through a character's anxieties about literal and symbolic incorporation. Christine Downing, in her study of the mythological dimensions of the feminine, posits that in classical times, "Women were linked with food not only because they cultivated and prepared it but also because their own bodies were a source of food and life"; however, "The nurturing goddess is also the devouring one."[19] In this context the figure of the goddess encodes cultural ambivalence toward female power and the act of incorporation itself: the image of the nurturing/devouring female originates in the earliest infantile experiences of helpless hunger.

Some psychoanalytic interpreters suggest that problems centering on food, eating, and incorporation are symptomatic of anxieties generated in the mother-child relationship that are often renewed during adolescence. These issues, arising during the symbiotic stage of infant development, influence the task of individuation on the part of the child. Furthermore, they are particularly female issues, playing a pivotal role in the perennial mother-daughter conflict.

According to Nancy Chodorow and others, individuation is more difficult for females because of the initial identification with the same-sex parent and the concomitant confusion over ego boundaries. The preoedipal mother–daughter relationship centrally influences the entire course of female maturation, for "separation and individuation remain particularly female developmental issues. . . . [T]here is a tendency in women toward boundary confusion and a lack of sense of separateness from the world."[20] Intense and exclusive attachment, heightened focus on orality and food, struggle between mother and daughter for control over the daughter's body, and the contrary desires to merge and to separate are all boundary issues that are maintained and prolonged in both maternal and filial psyches.[21] In several of Atwood's narratives, a female character experiences disturbed attitudes toward ingestion, maternity, and/or self-definition; these experiences may also express her ambivalence toward her mother or a mother-figure.

As the title of *The Edible Woman* indicates, consumption and female selfhood are central issues in the story. Marian MacAlpin works as an interviewer in a food marketing research organization, Seymour ("seemore") Surveys. She perceives the women with whom she works—in a job with "vaguely defined" limits (*EW,* p. 18)—in terms of her own anxieties about food, boundaries, and the relationship between "inside" and "outside." Observing these matronly women's bodies, she notices their varying contours, contained by "a carapace of clothing and makeup," and imagines "the continual flux between the outside and the inside, taking things in, giving them out, chewing, words, potato chips, burps, grease, hair, babies, milk, excrement, cookies, vomit, coffee, tomato–juice, blood, tea, sweat, liquor, tears, and garbage. . . ." (*EW,* pp. 171–72, ellipsis in original).

Marian's desire for rescue from the all-consuming female world that surrounds her in both her job and her personal life is understandable. Yet her fiancé, Peter, is also associated with predation, both literal and figurative: he collects guns and "shoots" photographs with his several cameras; his best friend is named Trigger. Peter's name is itself suggestive of both male sexuality and the entrapping spouse who imprisons his wife in a pumpkin shell (an idea central to Penelope Mortimer's *The Pumpkin Eater*).

Though Atwood's novel is ostensibly satirical and comic, Marian MacAlpin's anxiety about marriage to a man who will incorporate her precipitates an attack resembling the hardly comic condition of anorexia nervosa, an eating disorder in which the sufferer virtually starves herself to death while inaccurately perceiving herself as fat.[22] One interpretation of this emotional disorder suggests that the repudiation of food is related to the female anorectic's repudiation of sexuality; her fear of obesity reveals acute anxiety concerning impregnation.[23] Avoidance of food as well as sexual intimacy allows the threatened self to maintain "safety" by retaining control over the literal and symbolic boundaries of the body.

In *The Edible Woman*, Marian MacAlpin's incompletely acknowledged feelings of anger and resistance to being consumed by marriage temporarily prevent her from consuming food, as if she loses the boundaries between herself and what is separate from it: food begins as "other" and is mysteriously transformed into "self."[24] As the category of "non-devourable" increases (*EW*, p. 157), Marian is forced to confront her anxieties, not only about Peter, but about sexuality itself; she realizes that her self-destructive abstinence from food is actually a defensive response to her fear of losing herself in marriage. Instructively, Duncan, who evokes a "mothering reaction" in Marian, suggests that "'hunger is more basic than love'" (*EW*, p. 102).

Ultimately achieving at least a partial realization of the sources of her inner confusion, Atwood's protagonist demonstrates the resolution of her crisis of boundary through the creation of yet another distorted female image—one that is, significantly, created to be eaten. Marian bakes a sponge cake (an apt choice[25]) in the shape of a woman, decorates it with the stereotypical accoutrements of her gender, and presents it to Peter. Having confronted the boundary anxieties symbolized by sexual union, matrimony, and incorporation of food, Marian offers the cake woman to Peter, challenging him to eat this projected version of her old consumable self: "'You've been trying to assimilate me. But I've made you a substitute . . .'" (*EW*, p. 279).

After Peter declines her offering and hastily departs, Marian regains her appetite. Exuberantly consuming the cake emblem of her "substitute" or false self, she symbolically demolishes the stereotyped feminine personality who surrenders her "core" and thus participates in her own victimization. When she begins this act of "symbolic cannibalism" (Atwood's own term[26]), she "neatly sever[s] the body from the head" (*EW*, p. 280), an act that suggests a still-unresolved self-division. In contrast to the traditional comic resolution, in this narrative, as Atwood has remarked, "the complications are resolved, but not in a way that reaffirms the social order."[27] However, in departing from the traditional reconciliation and marriage of quarreling or mismatched lovers, the novel affirms a tentatively positive resolution to Marian's crisis—expressed not only through her self-affirming choice of independence at the end but through the narrative form itself.

The first part of the novel is told by Marian in the first-person point of view; the middle section, during which her ambivalence and anorexia threaten to alter both her actual body and the perceived boundaries of her self, is narrated in the third person—for Marian does not during that time possess a unified "I." In the short coda, she demonstrates that she is able to think of herself "in the first person singular again" (*EW*, p. 284). Her recovery of herself as an integrated woman, in control of both herself and her story, is the fitting resolution of her comic/serious schizophrenic odyssey.

In *Lady Oracle,* Joan Delacourt's childhood obesity is the opposite of Marian MacAlpin's temporary eating disorder in its physical manifestations but not in its psychological sources.[28] Consumption becomes an extreme and self-punishing defense against loss of control as well as rage against (in this case) her mother. In recalling her troubled childhood, Joan determines that her overeating began at the point where "the war between myself and my mother was on in earnest; the disputed territory was my body" (*LO*, p. 73). Years later, she retains the image of herself as a fat freak even after losing the excess weight.

The unnamed narrator of *Surfacing* also distorts the eating function as a kind of self-punishing strategy that might help her find her "lost" parents. Sending her companions away, she casts off the "camouflages" of civilization and forbids herself any food that has passed through its transformations, believing that "soon [she] will be able to go without food altogether" (*S*, p. 217).

Fittingly, in the macabre world of *The Handmaid's Tale*, where all forms of nourishment are stunted, eating assumes grotesque associations. Late in the novel Offred witnesses (before breakfast) the punishment by hanging of two handmaids who are convicted of betrayal. Perversely, she confesses, "Death makes me hungry. Maybe it's because I've been emptied; or maybe it's the body's way of seeing to it that I remain alive . . ."(*HT*, p. 293). Moreover, Offred's hunger is intellectual as well as physiological. Starved for mental stimulation, she equates the pieces in her illicit games of Scrabble with the Commander with edibles of stimulating flavors like lime and peppermint. When the Commander indulges her by allowing her the forbidden act of reading, she reads "voraciously . . . trying to get as much into [her] head as possible before the next long starvation. If it were eating it would be the gluttony of the famished . . ." (*HT,* p. 194).

In several of the novels, the eating function is implicitly or explicitly related to the mother-daughter relationship and to the issue of merged ego boundaries between them. In Atwood's fiction, mothers or their stand-ins are narratively absent (*The Edible Woman*), dead or missing (*Surfacing, Life before Man,* and *The Handmaid's Tale*), and/or overwhelming (*Lady Oracle* and *Life before Man*). Moreover, the split within the protagonist is often projected onto or repeated in the image of her mother or a mother figure.

The narrator of *Surfacing,* whose attitude toward her female parent is representative of the daughter's inner division, recalls that when her mother died of brain cancer she had felt only "disappointed in her" (*S,* p. 40), since she had believed in her mother's immortality. Though her original purpose in returning to her parents' cabin is the literal search for her father, the subtext of the narrative is her psychological assimilation of the actual and emotional loss of her mother, whose clothing is impregnated with the "smell of loss; irrecoverable" (*S,* p. 204). The narrative order is significant: in retracing her past, the narrator first recovers her missing father and then—moving backward through her own emotional history—recuperates the anterior attachment to her preoedipal "lost" mother.

According to the psychoanalytic theorist John Bowlby, the loss of a parent, particularly the mother, during early childhood may threaten a child's autonomy so acutely that it may be unable to invest emotionally in later relationships.[29] In Atwood's *Surfacing,* the narrator's relationships are brittle and alienated. Moreover, she projects aspects of her own splitness onto her traveling companions: she figuratively regards her friend, Anna, as "herself" and the two men as her father and brother (*S,* pp. 59–60), leaving as the only role she can occupy in this substitute family that of her mother (*S,* p. 60). That identification becomes central to her eventual recovery.

The narrator's search embarrasses her friends, who "disowned their parents long ago, the way you are supposed to" (*S,* p. 19). Her ambivalence about separation from her own parents—originally dictated by guilt and her failure to be honest with them—leads her to feel both anger and a sense of abandonment. Parents, she claims, "have no right to get old. I envy people whose parents died when they were young, . . . they stay unchanged. I was sure mine would anyway. . . . I thought of them as living in some other time, going about their own concerns closed safe behind a wall as translucent as Jell-O, mammoths frozen in a glacier. All I would have to do was come back when I was ready but I kept putting it off . . ." (*S*, p. 11). Assuming that they would judge her harshly for the choices she made, she gave her parents a fabricated version of events and directed their presumed disappointment upon herself. However, in cutting herself off from them, she has severed herself from her own past as well. Her belated return home becomes a kind of propitiation to the parental "gods" and acknowledgment of mutual loss of trust and connection.

Later, after she has discovered the body of her drowned father, the narrator attempts to re-enter the archaic/primal state before self-division, as if to recover that magical phase when parents are gods to a child. Testing the very boundaries between human and nonhuman, she penetrates more deeply into the primitive levels of consciousness; she merges as completely with nature as she can contrive to do, eating root vegetables, sleeping in a lair. The language of the narrative becomes more fragmented and splintered, mirroring the narrator's nonrational, nonverbal state.[30]

Discarding all material artifacts of her past, she attempts to purify herself sufficiently to earn her parents' spiritual acceptance. Logic itself is a barrier, "a wall, I built it, on the other side is terror" (*S*, p. 205). She begins to discover "rules": her parents' spirits cannot be "anywhere that's marked out, enclosed: even if I opened the doors and fences they could not pass in, to houses and cages, they can move only in the spaces between them, they are against borders. To talk with them I must approach the condition they themselves have entered" (*S*, p. 211).

Eventually she achieves that state of mystical union with nature and is rewarded for her vigilance with momentary visions of each parent: her mother as a nurturing nature-spirit and her father as a wolf, excluded by his own fence "as logic excludes love. He wants . . . the borders abolished, he wants the forest to flow back into the places his mind cleared: reparation" (*S*, p. 218). Her father, in contrast to her earth-spirit mother, had been a kind of boundary-maker: though he was a botanist, "his job was wrong, he was really a surveyor, . . . naming and counting [the trees] so the others could level and excavate" (*S*, p. 218). Ironically, through his fascination with the primitive drawings, the narrator's logical father has led her to her mother's intuitive truth.

Understanding the sacred continuity that exists within nature, she is able to forgive her parents for dying and herself for the sacrifice of her unborn child. As she "ferries" an imagined fetus "secure between death and life" (*S,* p. 197)—the fantasied offspring of her deliberate sexual encounter with Joe—she is no longer impeded by passivity and self-punishing moral boundaries. The "god within" is a more viable fantasy: a synthesis of body and spirit achieved by her integration of the lost past into her conscious selfhood.[31]

The intergenerational ambivalence and attitudes toward loss explored in *Surfacing* assume an ironic, and often reversed, form in *The Handmaid's Tale.* Moreover, although issues of food and incorporation are not as central in Atwood's most recent narratives as they are in the earlier three, it is worth noting that in the Republic of Gilead of *The Handmaid's Tale,* where the female functions are literally stratified among different categories of women, food preparation is performed by the servant "Marthas." The divisions within female identity are thus recast on the level of cultural ideology as well as personal psychology.

At one point Offred associates the kitchen smells of yeast and freshly baked bread with mothers: both her own mother and herself as a mother (*HT,* p. 57). Because she has been forcibly separated from both her mother and her daughter, the nostalgia triggered by the smell of yeast actually points to her own mourning. Separated not only from her loved ones but, symbolically, from both past and future generations, she acknowledges that "this is a treacherous smell" (*HT,* p. 57) whose associations she must repress. Though she has enough "daily bread" in the biblical sense on which she reflects with irony, "[t]he problem is getting it down without choking on it" (*HT,* p. 204).

Unlike the mother figures of the earlier fiction, Offred's mother is not the embodiment of the status quo and its repressive messages about female identity. Rather, she represents the radical ideology that became most threatening to the "Sons of Jacob" who seized power and founded the reactionary fundamentalist Republic of Gilead in which Offred finds herself. Offred's mother, a defiantly single parent and feminist activist, dressed in overalls, participated in prochoice and antipornography demonstrations, and worked for a women's culture.

Though Offred (whose previous name we never learn) admired her mother, she had felt the pressure of her mother's expectations, her hope that Offred would vindicate her values and her life. The daughter, resenting the generational role reversal embodied in her mother's radical values and behavior, had longed for a more orderly, conventional life. Ironically, in the present time of the narrative, Offred and her peers are imprisoned in circumstances whose very existence demonstrates that failure of vision: women of her own generation failed to enact the ideological struggle of their mothers. Offred remarks, "Mother, I think. Wherever you may be. . . . You wanted a women's culture. Well, now there is one. It isn't what you meant, but it exists" (*HT,* p. 137). Through the screen of her repressive life in Gilead, she comes to understand that

> [n]o mother is ever, completely, a child's idea of what a mother should be, and I suppose it works the other way around as well. But despite everything, we didn't do badly by one another, we did as well as most.
> I wish she were here, so I could tell her I finally know this. (*HT,* p. 190)

Two other recurring clusters of images related to boundary concerns in Atwood's fiction are those of drowning—as the literal representation of engulfment—and floating in a void or confronting an abyss—as the figurative equivalent to the experience of blurred or threatened emotional boundary. In *The Edible Woman,* Marian MacAlpin feels engulfed by the women with whom she works, "merged with that other flesh that choked the air in the flowered room with its sweet organic scent; she felt suffocated by this thick sargasso-sea of femininity. . . . [S]he wanted something solid, clear: a man . . . so that she could put her hand out and hold on to him to keep from being sucked down" (*EW,* p. 172). Focusing on a gold bangle worn by one of the women, she imagines the "hard gold circle" surrounding her, providing "a fixed barrier between herself and that liquid amorphous other" (*EW,* p. 172).

This passage explicitly dramatizes anxieties about engulfment and boundary. As Dorothy Dinnerstein has persuasively argued, "[W]hen the active project of selfhood feels too strenuous or too dangerously lonely the temptation is strong in all of us to melt back into that from which we have carved ourselves out": the mother.[32] Though Marian MacAlpin's mother is mentioned only briefly in the narrative, Marian's perceptions of the older women in her office, as well as her dreams of dissolving or becoming transparent, are other forms of this same regressive pull. Various references suggest the figurative "return to the womb." At one point

Marian escapes from Peter and other companions by crawling into a tight space between a bed and wall, where she feels "underground" in a "private burrow" (*EW,* p. 77). Elsewhere in the narrative Marian drifts with the current, floats, and even fantasizes drowning in a bathtub. That fate is reserved for Elizabeth Schoenhof's sister in *Life before Man;* her death dramatizes Elizabeth's own fear of engulfment by the overwhelming negative mother-figure, Auntie Muriel.

The narrator of *Surfacing* asserts that her brother drowned in childhood, before her own birth; only later does she admit the story of his death to be a fabrication. Her falsification is less the result of intentional distortion than the manifestation of repression: like her "marriage" and "baby," the fantasy of her sibling's drowning expresses both denied wishes and unresolved emotional conflicts. As a child she had deplored her brother's penchant for dividing things into absolute moral categories and his capacity to destroy life. In "drowning" him in fantasy, she rejects that part of herself associated with aggression, destruction, and death.

Significantly, the lake in which the narrator's brother and father drown (the first in fantasy, the second in actuality) is her "entrance" into vision (*S,* p. 172). Diving from a canoe poised on the boundary between two worlds—"split between water and air, mediator and life raft" (*S,* p. 166)—she goes under water and metaphorically enters the unconscious.[33] There she confronts, and confesses, the painful memory of the aborted fetus who had "drowned in air" (*S,* p. 168), originally displaced to the invented story of her brother's drowning as a child. Discovery of her drowned father forces the knowledge of both substitutions into consciousness.

Joan Delacourt Foster of *Lady Oracle* stages a fake drowning, ostensibly to escape from her uncontrollably splitting self, but unconsciously to separate from the mother whom, even after her death, Joan experiences as a "vortex" (*LO,* p. 363). Her multiplying personalities are her extreme defense against engulfment by the monstrous mother. On the "other side" (of both the lake she "sinks" in and the ocean she traverses), Joan recognizes her mother's central influence. Furthermore, she projects her "drowning" onto one of her fictional alter egos, the sensuous Felicia of her Gothic romance. Like Joan herself, Felicia emerges from the water alive: the return of the repressed with a vengeance!

The dilemma of psychological engulfment, one consequence of the troubled mother-daughter relationship, is in fact the central subtext of

Lady Oracle. A series of incidents from Joan's childhood—revealed at intermittent points in her retrospective narrative—derive from her seriously disturbed relationship with her parents, particularly her mother. Joan suspects, like Elizabeth Schoenhof of *Life before Man,* that she was an unwanted child whose conception precipitated her parents into a reluctant marriage; even if that circumstance is not factually true, it accurately expresses Joan's perception of her position in her family. Her father—significantly, an anaesthetist—was away in the war for the first five years of Joan's life. Even after his return Joan continued to think of him as "simply an absence" (*LO,* p. 73). By contrast, her mother is an overwhelming presence, while at the same time cold, authoritarian, manipulative, and ambitious for her daughter.

Joan, as a fat child, was a "huge edgeless cloud of inchoate matter which refused to be shaped into anything for which [her mother] could get a prize" (*LO,* p. 71). Yet Joan's obesity is her sole weapon against her mother's tyranny. Hilde Bruch, in her studies of childhood obesity, has concluded that "the outstanding pathogenic factor in the families of . . . obese children is the fact that the child is used by one or other parent as a thing, an object whose function is to fulfill the parents' needs, to compensate for their failures and frustrations in their own lives."[34]

An event from Joan Delacourt Foster's childhood is particularly illustrative in this context. She recalls participating in a dance recital, involuntarily cast as a mothball among little girls attired as butterflies. This "humiliation disguised as a privilege" (*LO,* p. 51) was her mother's betrayal; masquerade and disguise become Joan's repeated defenses against betrayal and violation.

The desperation of Joan's later internal division is accounted for in part by the violence—both physical and psychological—of her childhood and adolescence. She describes being blindfolded and tied to a tree by cruel acquaintances and only some time later rescued by a stranger who may have exposed himself to her on another occasion. Subsequently she wonders, "Was the man who untied me a rescuer or a villain? Or . . . was it possible for a man to be both at once?" (*LO,* p. 67). Virtually every person in Joan's life bears this exaggerated ambivalent quality. The image reappears in *Bodily Harm* as the "faceless stranger" who is both the threatening Other and (later) the catalyst for empathy.

To Joan Delacourt's early boundary confusions, Atwood adds various encounters that involve violations of her protagonist's person/body. Each time, the comic surface belies the sober implications of the experience. One occurs when, as a teenager working in an archery sideshow, Joan is wounded in an ample buttock by a no-doubt intentionally aimed arrow. The infection caused by the wound forces her into a radical weight loss program, which leads directly to one of the narrative's most emotionally laden episodes of violation of boundary, both literal and emotional. Joan's mother, who accurately sees her daughter's loss of weight as evidence of her loss of control over her, stabs Joan in the arm with a kitchen knife, in rage at her daughter's emotional defection. The shock of the attack precipitates Joan's traumatic separation from her mother. Leaving home, she never sees her mother again—except in hallucinations that embody her guilt and her unresolved feelings.

Psychoanalytic theorists of the object-relations school suggest that during the critical phases of a child's psychological separation from the mother in early childhood, the inner image of the ambivalent being who both rewards and punishes may be "split" into a "good mother" and a "bad mother."[35] In *Lady Oracle* Atwood dramatizes that emotional split by making Joan's mother (in the daughter's view, the only perspective we are given) inalterably monstrous and her eccentric Aunt Lou benevolent and supportive.

In a childhood dream generated out of her actual observance of her mother "put[ting] on her face" (*LO*, p. 69), Joan sees her mother reflected in a triple vanity mirror, with three heads (*LO*, p. 70); in unconscious identification, the daughter herself eventually splits into multiple images. Significantly, as a child Joan had pretended that Aunt Lou—her *father's* sister—was her real mother (*LO*, p. 95). Her aunt works for a sanitary napkin company, a hint at the relation between positive female sexual maturation and the image of the "good mother." By contrast, the blood-letting of the knife-stabbing incident fixes the wounding "bad mother" image in the adolescent daughter's mind.

Thus, in the forcible separation that marks the beginning of her "second self" (*LO*, p. 152), Joan attempts to cast off her engulfing "bad mother" and "become" her good mother, Louisa K. Delacourt, her (by-then deceased) aunt. The name "De-la-court" is also a pun on the figures of royal good parents so often encountered in fairy tales and children's fantasies;[36] Aunt Lou is a kind of fairy godmother whose benevolence partially neutralizes the "bad mother's" legacy.

Adrienne Rich, in her discussion of cultural images of motherhood, describes "matrophobia"—the daughter's fear of *becoming* her mother—as "a womanly splitting of the self, in the desire to become purged once and for all of our mothers' bondage, to become individuated and free. The mother stands for the victim in ourselves, the unfree woman, the martyr. Our personalities seem dangerously to blur and overlap with our mothers'; and, in a desperate attempt to know where mother ends and daughter begins, we perform radical surgery."[37]

In Atwood's novel, the internalized "bad mother" stands a stern watch over the daughter's efforts at separation and sexual autonomy. Her apparition appears twice to Joan: once soon after her first sexual betrayal of Paul (a Polish count with whom she loses her virginity) with Arthur Foster—at the moment, she learns soon afterwards, of her mother's actual death; and a second time following her mock drowning. As in *Surfacing,* the "ghost" is the split-off self, in this instance the part of Joan that is still merged with her mother. In fact, returning to Canada for the funeral, Joan feels "as if [she'd] killed her [herself], though this was impossible" (*LO,* p. 199). The guilty wish leads her to gorge herself on food, slipping back into the primitive eating defense against her mother's guilt-inducing power.

Joan's impulsive marriage to Arthur Foster is a consequence of her unresolved negative tie to her overpowering female parent. Psychologically, in fleeing the negative mother the daughter tries "to merge herself with anyone other than her mother, all the while expressing her feelings of dependence on and primary identification with this mother."[38] As Joan eventually sees, "For years I wanted to turn into what Arthur thought I was, or what he thought I should be" (*LO,* p. 235). Dependent on him for approval, she becomes his "Foster" child, as he becomes her Arthur/ author. Believing she has escaped from the negative emotional thrall of her mother, Joan merely transfers her symbiotic needs to Arthur. Only belatedly does she realize that her husband is in important psychological ways a version of her mother.[39] Ironically, Arthur proves to be as internally split as Joan is herself, though, as she phrases it, "I was simultaneous, whereas Arthur was a sequence" (*LO,* p. 236).

Joan's dreams express her anxieties about boundary and engulfment as well as her sense of her mother's alternating emotional wounding and indifference. In one dream, she carries her "three-headed mother" around her neck like "a rotting albatross" (*LO,* p. 238). In another dream, her mother appears on the "other side" of a bridge, which suggestively collapses when Joan reaches the middle; her parent makes no effort to rescue her, not even noticing that "anything unusual was happening" (*LO*, p. 68). Not until Joan is able to cross to the "other side" herself—a symbolic boundary that assumes a variety of meanings, all related to her emotional symbiosis with her mother—does she begin to integrate her fragmented identity.

One of Joan's attempts to reach the "other side" is her hypnotic trance, self-induced with the aid of a candle and, pointedly, a triple mirror identical to her mother's. Under the guidance of automatic writing (a suggestion that she is being driven by something in her own unconscious), she produces sentimental occult poetry, the novelty of which catapults her to instant fame. Her "Lady Oracle" persona is a working out of the figurative journey to the dark psychic underworld where she faces herself in the image of Persephone—the daughter unwillingly separated from her mother—and the crone-mother who presides over the reunion of "lost parts of the self." This is the maze Joan must explore, the "descent into the underworld" that is the puzzle of her own multiple personality.[40] Once, Joan is "trapped" in darkness on the other side. While there she feels as if she is suffocating—the sensation of engulfment that her mother generates in her—until Arthur "rescues" her from her imaginary but true imprisonment.

While Joan's "good mother" is the muse behind her Gothic romances, her unrecognized identification with her "bad mother" fuels her oracular, inverted poetic fantasies. In fact, as Joan ultimately discovers, the two figures are aspects of the same power—other dimensions of her own tripleness. When her mother's apparition appears for a second time, Joan almost succumbs to her thrall, tempted by her pitiable gestures to follow her "down the corridor into the darkness" and "do what she wanted" (*LO*, p. 362). Atwood, inverting the Demeter/Persephone myth, makes the mother the captive of the underworld, where the daughter is drawn to seek her.[41]

Instead of acquiescing to this temptation, however, Joan faces the ambiguous power her mother retains over her: not only the source of her desires for escape and death but also a component of her creative unconscious. Thus does she embody the admitted ambivalence of the mother-daughter bond: "She'd never really let go of me because I had never let her go. . . . How could I renounce her? She needed her freedom also; she had been my reflection too long" (*LO*, p. 363). In recognizing her female parent as her "reflection"—a projected aspect of herself—Joan can reintegrate the emotions split between the "bad" mother and the "good" Aunt Lou and begin to live as a whole person. Seeing her mother as a desperately unhappy, housebound woman (who may even have taken her own life), she begins to loosen the inner ties that have formed her neurotic bondage. Atwood dramatizes the truth that it is not by escaping or denying but by accepting and integrating a negative attachment that one can grow through and beyond its suffocating power.

Like Joan Foster, Elizabeth Schoenhof of *Life before Man* is drawn to a metaphorical "other side" (in this case, of her ceiling) and suffers from boundary anxieties as a result of a seriously disturbed relationship with her maternal parent. Elizabeth's mother was an alcoholic and her father probably a "rounder" (*LBM*, p. 149), though she scarcely knew him since—as is characteristic of the fathers in Atwood's fiction—he disappeared from her life quite early. In fact, Elizabeth's obsessive experience of the void beyond her ceiling dates from her father's desertion (*LBM*, p. 150).

When Elizabeth was a teenager, her mother was fatally injured in a fire ignited by her own careless cigarette while in bed. She survived a week, with half of her body severely burned. Elizabeth had tried unsuccessfully to make contact with her comatose mother through the latter's uninjured "good" side (*LBM*, p. 177). It is much more difficult for Elizabeth to find a "good side" to her stepmother/aunt. According to her Auntie Muriel, her mother had given Elizabeth and her younger sister, Caroline, up for adoption by her own sister. Elizabeth suspects that Auntie Muriel actually kidnapped them, believing self-righteously that, since her sister was a "tramp," she could care better for the children herself.

Whatever the actual explanation, Elizabeth became an orphan, emotional prisoner of an aunt she still hates, even in adulthood; she views Auntie Muriel as a monster who manipulated her into leaving her mother and still practices other cruelties. Elizabeth, a "foster" child in circumstance as Joan Delacourt Foster is in name, also experiences her maternal parent as split into two beings, though the emotional charge is reversed: her aunt is the Wicked Witch of the West in *The Wizard of Oz,* and her scarcely remembered mother is the fairy godmother, Glinda the Good.

As children, Elizabeth and her sister were dressed alike by Auntie Muriel, effectively blurring their individuality. Later, Caroline, the weaker of the two psychologically, went crazy and in effect vacated her body, eventually drowning in a bathtub in two inches of water. In Elizabeth's nightmares of loss, the missing babies in her dreams are not only her two daughters but her lost mother and sister (*LBM,* p. 187). She has always believed that her aunt was somehow responsible for both their deaths.

One of Elizabeth's deepest anxieties is the threat of engulfment by her aunt, who "doesn't know where to stop. Other people have lines they won't step over, but for Auntie Muriel such lines do not exist. Elizabeth's other fear is that these lines do not exist in herself, either" (*LBM,* p. 180). In violating the ego boundaries that separate one from the other, Eliza-beth's aunt has persistently "worked at developing those parts of Eliza-beth that most resembled Auntie Muriel and suppressing or punishing the other parts" (*LBM,* p. 137).

Elizabeth's later self-division can be understood as her defense against Auntie Muriel's invasiveness. As she understands the thrall of her "bad" mother, "Because Auntie Muriel once had all power over her, she will always have some. Elizabeth is an adult in much of her life, but when she's with Auntie Muriel she is still part child. Part prisoner, part orphan, part cripple, part insane; Auntie Muriel the implacable wardress" (*LBM,* p. 123). Yet Elizabeth has never succeeded in separating herself from that malign power. Unlike Joan Delacourt, whose defenses against her emo-tionally voracious mother take the form of overeating and multiple personalities, Elizabeth unconsciously replicates the very manipulative powers she fears in her aunt. Her emotional detachment and predatory control over others are unconscious strategies for neutralizing the threat-ening Auntie Muriel within her.

When Auntie Muriel dies grotesquely of cancer, Elizabeth feels com-pelled to attend her funeral, her feelings split between relief and loss. Unable to bear seeing her aunt "merge" with the earth, she loses con-sciousness: "[T]here's nothing to push against, hold on to. A black vac-uum sucks at her. . . . Elizabeth falls through space" (*LBM,* p. 300). As Atwood has elaborated elsewhere, it is "hatred" against Auntie Muriel that drives Elizabeth. When the powerful negative mother-figure dies, she is "left without anything to push against. She has a great feeling of evaporation. . . . Auntie Muriel has really been part of her. That was a thing that she was locked into."[42]

By contrast, the parents of Lesje Green, the other major female char-acter in *Life before Man,* are rather bland figures, despite their religiously mixed marriage. Lesje's sweet but ineffectual mother, though otherwise quite unlike Elizabeth's Auntie Muriel, sees her daughter as an extension of herself: according to Lesje, her happiness is "her mother's justification" (*LBM*, p. 195). Though Lesje longs for "a mother's blessing" (*LBM*, p. 269), she seeks it less in her mother than in her grandmothers.

In some senses the two central women of *Life before Man* are complementary: Elizabeth, the hard, efficient, dominant woman (on the surface), is so much in control that she coolly observes and virtually orchestrates her husband's liaison with the soft, passive, acquiescent Lesje. They are even physically complementary: Elizabeth is slightly plump, Lesje is tall and slender. Yet despite Elizabeth's apparently greater emotional power over others, both women are troubled by boundary anxieties and feelings of diffuseness. Elizabeth regards the sky above the roof of her house as "the place where there is nothing between her and nothing" (*LBM*, p. 158). Lesje feels that in the absence of a structure like marriage (or even divorce) with its unspoken laws, a relationship like hers with Nate is "amorphous, an endless middle ground" (*LBM*, p. 192). When she finally leaves William—only after he tries to rape her—to live with Nate, she still feels adrift. "Routines hold you in place. Without them she floats, weightless" (*LBM*, p. 209)—like Elizabeth.

Lesje and Elizabeth share a strong sense of "territory," a further manifestation of their involvement with boundary issues. When Lesje first makes love with Nate and learns that they are in Elizabeth's bed, she feels that she has "trespassed" (*LBM*, p. 169). As a child Elizabeth had never understood the meaning of "trespass" in the Lord's Prayer, thinking that it meant "walking on other people's property. A thing she never did; therefore she did not need to be forgiven" (*LBM*, p. 159). Ironically, she invades other people's emotional territories, in repetition of Auntie Muriel's attempt to possess hers.

Even though Lesje apparently takes Elizabeth's husband from her, she derives little satisfaction from her new position, for Nate is essentially "absent," emotionally detained under his wife's thrall. On one occasion, Nate telephones Elizabeth in Lesje's presence to exchange instructions about the children. Several words on his side of the conversation—"home," "love," and "mother"—disturb Lesje. She feels herself exiled, cut off, "gulping for oxygen in the blackness of this outer space" (*LBM*, p. 129).

The three words—*home*, *love*, and *mother*—are crucial emblems in *Life before Man,* evoking the cumulative past emotional losses suffered by each of the major characters. As suggested earlier, psychological separation from the mother is a central stage in each child's formation of ego boundaries. In *Life before Man,* the lonely adults are both attracted to and threatened by the original symbiotic relationship with a powerful Other; each struggles with the tensions of control and submission, aggressive and passive stances within intimate relationships.

Of the three emotionally pivotal images upon which the vulnerability of the major characters is predicated, "mother" is the strongest: motherhood, mothers, stepmothers, and grandmothers are prominent in their thoughts and experiences. Nate had once regarded Elizabeth in the museum as a "Madonna in a shrine, shedding a quiet light" (*LBM,* p. 49). Lesje admires Elizabeth's "competent maternal manner" (*LBM,* p. 21) and views herself, mother of no one, as "officially . . . nothing" (*LBM,* p. 267). By the end of the novel, Lesje suspects, with mixed feelings, that she might be pregnant with Nate's child.

The museum to which nearly all the characters are connected through employment or personal relationships is a fitting location for the emotional drift of its principal human inhabitants. It suggests both a mausoleum of the fossilized (figuratively, repressed) past and a womb-like place of refuge. At the same time it reflects the diffuse boundary anxieties that preoccupy the novel's principal characters. For example, "by a process of discreet seepage, everybody ultimately knew everything" about the private lives of its employees (*LBM,* p. 73). A central cluster of images develops this dimension of "seepage," boundless space, void, and vertigo. Elizabeth Schoenhof's recurring experience of empty space objectifies an inner void. When she is most disturbed about events in her life, she finds herself (involuntarily) in that empty black vacuum—an apt analogue for free-floating anxiety.

If the museum is, figuratively, a giant impersonal womb in which the novel's characters discover solace as well as employment, the dome-shaped auditorium of the nearby Planetarium that Elizabeth visits is "like being inside a breast," where she feels "stifled" (*LBM,* p. 75). Elizabeth's ambivalent attitude toward that suffocating maternal breast is elaborated in several ways. Once, observing an illustration of a tree, she associates it with the sucking voracity of babies, including one of her own daughter's first bites at her breast (*LBM,* p. 60). Later she equates the tree image with the "root" of the word for mother: "*Mummy.* A dried corpse in a gilded case. *Mum,* silent. *Mama,* short for mammary gland. A tree whose hungry mouth is pressed. If you didn't want trees sucking at your sweet flowing breast why did you have children? Already they're preparing for flight, betrayal, they will leave her, she will become their background" (*LBM,* p. 250, emphasis in original).

Other images of sucking are analogues of engulfment or annihilation. In the Planetarium, Elizabeth hears a description of "black holes," the astronomical phenomena that correspond to her own recurring fantasy of engulfment: these hypothetical holes in space "suck energy in instead of giving it out. If you fell into a black hole, you would disappear forever" (*LBM,* p. 77). Elizabeth's Auntie Muriel is a figurative black hole who voraciously absorbs energy instead of giving it out; she is "both the spider and the fly, the sucker-out of life juice and the empty husk" (*LBM,* p. 119).

Nate Schoenhof's view of his mother becomes equally problematic when he learns, to his incredulity, that she had contemplated suicide after her husband's death (Nate's father having died not, as he had thought, of heroism in war but of hepatitis). The discovery of his mother's long-hidden despair, which undermines his perception of himself as the center of her universe, horrifies him. He regards her not with sympathy but as "irresponsible, a bad mother. . . . Potential orphan, he sways at the lip of the abyss which has suddenly gaped in front of him" (*LBM,* p. 287). His reaction reveals his own scarcely controlled boundary anxieties. Like other characters in the novel, he experiences his mother as split into opposing images. Moreover, his new emotional distance from her leaves him threatened by loss from several directions at once: he feels himself "motherless, childless . . . the solitary wanderer, under the cold red stars" (*LBM,* p. 287).

Implicitly, the anxieties concerning "mother" are linked to those concerning "love" and "home." Nate habitually calls both Elizabeth and Lesje "love," and Lesje chafes at the unconscious equation. Though Nate leaves one home for another, Lesje's house, with its bare mattress and minimal furnishings, is scarcely "home" to either of them. In fact, that empty shell expresses Lesje's own sense of lost anchorage: "The house, with no furniture, nothing radiating back to her from the bare walls, absorbs what little energy she has. She feels she's losing weight and that the house is gaining it" (*LBM,* p. 207).

At the same time, Elizabeth attempts (like Penelope Mortimer's

Eleanor Strathearn in *The Home*) to preserve the sense of "home" for her daughters in the wake of her husband's defection. She acknowledges that "her house is not perfect; parts of it are in fact crumbling. . . . But it's a wonder that she has a house at all, that she's managed to accomplish a house. Despite the wreckage" (*LBM*, p. 302). Ironically, her last name— Nate's surname—translates as "beautiful hotel."

In *Life before Man* the absence of the figure who represents the earliest emotional attachment is experienced as a void that simultaneously compels and threatens. Lacking a secure sense of "mother," "love," and "home," each character experiences a kind of emotional vertigo, characterized as a chasm, abyss, cliff, or the "black hole" of outer space itself. Early in the narrative, Lesje, then living with William in a fourteenth-floor apartment, thinks of herself as "a cliff dweller, cliff hanger" (*LBM*, p. 20). Elizabeth had clung emotionally to her lover, Chris: "[I]f he [let] go, she [would] slide down past the edge of the table, the edge of some cliff or quicksand, and be lost forever" (*LBM*, p. 24). Nate experiences the same dread when faced with legal separation from Elizabeth: "[T]he unavoidable vortex has him at last and he's being swept along, out of control, toward some chasm he can dimly perceive" (*LBM*, p. 255).

Even as a teenager Elizabeth had tried to master such anxieties by flirting with self-extinction: in her seduction of a teenaged boy after her mother's death, she had felt excitement and gratification "to be able to do this, go to the edge and almost jump" (*LBM*, p. 178). Thinking of her recent lover's suicide, she recalls the adolescent game of "chicken" and feels "the horrified relief of someone who has stopped just in time to watch an opponent topple in slow motion over the edge" (*LBM*, p. 301). This is Elizabeth's strength: her "survival instinct" (*LBM*, p. 156), her ability to look over the edge of the abyss and resist its negative lure. Defensively, she thinks of space as "a cube around her, she is the center" (*LBM*, p. 162). Yet her intense need to control others inevitably distances her from intimacy.

Each of the disillusioned adults in *Life before Man* confronts the terror of personal extinction, both as a legacy from the past in the form of emotional vulnerability and as a continuing threat in personal relationships. Like Elizabeth, each has "built a dwelling over the abyss, but where else was there to build it?" (*LBM*, p. 302). Each experiences strong anxiety concerning relationships and separations, resulting in fragile emotional attachments. They are all emotionally fossilized. The frequent references to cosmic space and geological time reduce the scale of the human subjects seen against the void.

In several of Atwood's narratives, an inevitable consequence of the female protagonist's experiences of self-division and disturbances in the relationship between herself and her mother is her anxiety about becoming a mother herself. Particularly if she experiences her own mother as overwhelming or as split into two complementary entities, she fears being "sucked back" into the original symbiosis. Maternity is obviously the most dramatic alteration of boundaries, both physical and psychological, for a female. As Julia Kristeva has observed from a psychoanalytic perspective,

> Pregnancy seems to be experienced as the radical ordeal of the splitting of the subject: redoubling up of the body, separation and coexistence of the self and of an other, of nature and consciousness, of physiology and speech. This fundamental challenge to identity is then accompanied by a fantasy of totality—narcissistic completeness—a sort of instituted, socialized, natural psychosis. The arrival of the child, on the other hand, leads the mother into the labyrinths of an experience that, without the child, she would only rarely encounter: love for an other.[43]

For Atwood's female characters who already experience themselves as "split," pregnancy is perceived as a doubly threatening condition. Beginning with *The Edible Woman,* motherhood is viewed as problematic. Both Marian MacAlpin's friend, Clara, and her roommate, Ainsley—with whom she co-exists through "a symbiotic adjustment of habits" (*EW,* p. 14)—dramatize exaggerated attitudes toward maternity. Even before Marian begins to refuse food, she registers her anxiety about procreation in her perceptions of the eternally pregnant Clara, whom she regards variously as the unwilling host of a parasitic, pumpkin-like growth, a pinhead, a "semi-person"; and several people at once (*EW,* p. 117). By contrast, Ainsley is obsessed with the idea of procreation, convinced that "'[e]very woman should have at least one baby. . . . It's even more important than sex. It fulfills your deepest femininity'" (*EW,* p. 40). In one of the novel's delicious ironies, the man whom Ainsley deliberately seduces as part of her strategy to become a mother accuses her of using him only for his body.

The narrator of *Surfacing* suffers guilt from the repressed memories of both her aborted child and the mother from whom she withheld the truth about that crucial event in her life. The sign of healing of her inner split, which comes only after she has achieved a reconciliation with both, is the desire to conceive another child. Her mother's "gift" to her (*S*, p. 175), one of the narrator's own childhood drawings saved in a scrapbook, is both a hieroglyphic message from her own former self and a striking emblem of the original mother–child symbiosis:

> On the left [of the picture] was a woman with a round moon stomach: the baby was sitting up inside her gazing out. Opposite her was a man with horns on his head like cow horns and a barbed tail.
> The picture was mine, I had made it. The baby was myself before I was born, the man was God, I'd drawn him when my brother learned . . . about the Devil and God: if the Devil was allowed a tail and horns, God needed them also. . . . (*S*, p. 185)

This central image conflates the vision of the narrator's origin inside her mother with that of pregnancy itself. In the pictograph, the mother's body literally encapsulates the daughter's. The male figure "opposite" in the drawing represents the opposing male principle: both the father, who is associated with logic and rationality, and the god who, with horns and tail, might fuse the Christian dichotomy between God and Devil, good and evil.

In possession of a new vision of herself "translated" from the pointedly preverbal language of the pictograph, the narrator of *Surfacing* (in contrast to Marian MacAlpin, who fears maternity as a loss of boundary) ultimately seeks impregnation as a means of rejoining the cycle of generativity. She initiates lovemaking with Joe for that precise purpose. The moment of sexual climax releases her from her frigidity and psychic paralysis: "I can feel my lost child surfacing within me, forgiving me, rising from the lake where it has been prisoned for so long" (*S*, p. 191).

Becoming the "miraculous double woman" of the childhood drawing (*S*, p. 207), the narrator experiences herself as a pregnant woman, "transparent, my bones and the child inside me showing through the . . . flesh" (*S*, p. 212). That "transparent" identification with her own mother signals her acceptance of her body and her female sexuality. Through it she validates her capacity not only to give birth—in this case, to her own being—but to accept death. The "lost child" is both the sacrificed (and repressed) fetus and the part of her who, "lost" to her parents, has longed for their forgiveness. Reconciling herself to the irrevocability of both losses, she recovers her own lost self.

Joan Foster of *Lady Oracle* also fears procreation, principally because for much of her story she remains psychologically merged with her "bad mother." Her childhood obesity and her subsequent image of herself as a "Fat Lady" long after she has shed that fat can be understood as grotesque exaggerations of anxieties about maternity.

In *Life before Man,* Elizabeth Schoenhof and Lesje Green provide complementary views of motherhood. One of Atwood's three female protagonists with children (Offred, of *The Handmaid's Tale,* has a daughter from whom she has been forcibly separated), Elizabeth has appreciative but distant relationships with her two daughters; Lesje, unmarried but perhaps pregnant by the end of the narrative, seeks maternity to confirm a fragile sense of herself as a female and to counteract the feeling of "invisibility." The unmarried Rennie Wilford of *Bodily Harm* questions whether her disease, resulting in the loss of part of a breast, will fundamentally alter her future capacity to give birth; she perceives both cancer and the operation as invasions of her selfhood which threaten her female identity.

In *The Handmaid's Tale,* the psychological conflicts associated with pregnancy extend beyond private ambivalence to institutionalized manipulations of female fertility by a perverse and reactionary body politic. Taking as her starting point the profound and irreconcilable contemporary schism between "pro-life" and "pro-choice" ideologies, Atwood imagines a world in which women are defined by their potential fertility (or its absence) and procreation and maternity are simultaneously idealized and dehumanized. In the nightmare future Republic of Gilead, where handmaids serve as vessels for fertilization, maternity is both necessary wish—handmaids are discarded after three unsuccessful attempts at pregnancy—and fear—the baby, unless deformed and declared an "Unbaby," becomes the property of the handmaid's Commander and his Wife. The surrogate mother's function ceases after a brief lactation period following delivery of a healthy child.

Margaret Atwood's first three novels focus on a female character's elusive quest for unified selfhood. In each narrative, concern with ego boundaries—merging and splitting, engulfment and separation—form a cluster of psychological issues that are ultimately clarified for the protagonist as she comes to understand her relationship with her parents (particularly

her mother), a man, or both. In each instance, the structure of the narrative mirrors the central female character's self-division and, later, her
movement toward psychological integration. In each of these narratives,
the first-person narrator shapes part or all of her own story; the very act
of *telling* it demonstrates both the initially unadmitted dimensions of her
self and her eventual advance in self-awareness.

If, as Atwood has said, the underlying pattern of *The Edible Woman* is
a circle, and *Surfacing* traces a spiral,[44] then the narrative structure of *Lady
Oracle* is a maze. Joan Foster's narrative illustrates a deliberate overlapping
of boundaries of the fiction within the fiction: the novel *Lady Oracle* contains the volume of poetry by the same title that the protagonist/narrator
writes, and it is Joan's own pseudonym as well as the key to her complex,
and compound, identity. The interwoven narrative layers demonstrate the
complexity of the female narrative of selfhood: fairy tale, myth, gothic
tale, and psychological puzzle are all contributing, and often contradictory, dimensions of the female scripts of identity. Together they richly
dramatize the overlapping boundaries of female experience.

Life before Man is the only one of Atwood's novels to date with more
than one protagonist. Boundaries and separations affecting each of the
three major characters function as both structure and theme. Accordingly, rather than first-person narration, the triangular focus is dramatized through short, journal-like episodes narrated in both first- and
third-person points of view and in both past and present tenses, in an
astringent, ironic tone (the underside of Atwood's comic vein). The sections, grouped in five major divisions of the narrative and headed by
names and dates like entries in a museum catalog, comprise a two-year
period during which the alignment of affections among the central emotional triangle shifts. Three auxiliary characters (who are not given their
own narrative headings) function as a shadow triangle of the major characters' changing emotional connections.

Since the point of view is split in *Life before Man,* no single perspective
clearly delineates each character. Rather, the reader, like a museum curator painstakingly assembling the shards of a vase, must construct each
image from the characters' own testimonies and the more detached narrative voice. Plays on words and references to two vocabularies (*LBM,*
pp. 95, 148) reinforce the sense of emotional division. Each character is
a repository of artifacts of the buried—repressed—past: not archaeological but psychological. Like museum exhibits, they are fossilized,

"mounted specimens" (*LBM,* p. 268). The narrative catalogues with al-most scientific detachment the events that occur without changing the essentially static characters. Moreover, the void is not only the inner vac-uum experienced by people whose relationships with others are dis-turbed; it is implicitly the condition in which we are all suspended as a consequence of the irreducible difference between "inside" and "outside." One becomes more acutely aware of it in direct proportion to one's sense of separateness and isolation from others.

In both the realistic *Bodily Harm* and the fable-like *Handmaid's Tale,* Atwood develops the themes of selfhood and boundary in more explic-itly feminist terms, focusing on such issues as body image, female sex-uality and fertility, pornography and exploitation, and the nature and perpetuation of male power in patriarchy. Both narratives are also deeply existential works, examining the relation of the individual woman to society: her sense of connectedness to the central social and ideological conflicts of her time; the issues of power and powerlessness; the illusion of exemption from evil; the necessity for being politically and personally engaged; the nature of moral responsibility. In exploring (and exposing) "power politics," both novels demonstrate that female experience cannot be understood apart from the real structures of power. Thus, male aggression and possession, and female passivity and complicity, are seen not only in their private forms but also as expressions of ideology—and vice versa. The body politic is the form writ large of the individual body, in this instance the female body; bodily harm and exploitation in one domain are correspondingly registered in the other.

Both *Bodily Harm* and *The Handmaid's Tale* explore language and the shape of narrative itself in ways that contribute to this unfolding truth in Atwood's fiction. In *Bodily Harm,* three distinct narrative strands consti-tute the experiences of Renata (Rennie) Wilford, a free-lance journalist who tells her story in retrospect. In interweaving Rennie's recent expe-riences with those of her Ontario childhood and of dramatic events on a pair of Caribbean islands that literally change Rennie's life, Atwood il-lustrates that each person contains several "stories" which must somehow be synthesized for coherence of personality. In college Rennie had be-lieved that "there was a real story, not several and not almost real" (*BH,* p. 64). Later in the novel, Paul, an American loner who figures centrally in the events, reiterates, "'In this place you get at least three versions of everything, and if you're lucky one of them is true'" (*BH,* p. 150). Only at the very end of the narrative does Rennie (and the reader) understand how the fragments of her experience are organically connected. In finding that truth, she discovers her inner freedom at a time in her life when, given the circumstances, she might be least expected to do so.

Rennie repudiates her small-town background, or "subground," as she calls it (*BH,* p. 18), regarding it as what she defines herself against. Yet the three negatives she learned as a child among adults—"how to be quiet, what not to say, and how to look at things without touching them" (*BH,* p. 54)—eventually take on entirely different meanings. In fact, the narrative depends on such linguistic modulations. Words like *exempt, neutral, rescue, damaged, normal, luck, invasion,* and *decay* are among the recurring terms whose double or ironic senses are underscored, as Rennie discovers that "what she sees has not altered; only the way she sees it" (*BH,* p. 300).

In *The Handmaid's Tale,* language and perspective are also crucial dimensions of the narrative. A story within a story, Offred's tale demonstrates her effort to "reconstruct" (*HT,* p. 144) her experiences—and to justify the choices she has made under the circumstances as she reveals them. Imagining and inventing different scenarios of what might have happened to her and her family and what might transpire in her life as a handmaid, she is an "unreliable" narrator in the same sense as the narrator of *Surfacing:* her variations and speculations on the "facts" express her uncertain relation to her experiences and the problem of making sense out of a nightmare from which she hopes to awaken. She imagines her husband, Luke, as dead, tortured, or free; the Commander's chauffeur, Nick, may be the middleman for either her freedom or her death. The ironic coda, "Historical Notes on the Handmaid's Tale," transforms the narrative into a retrospective document and implies that the ambiguities are irreducible; no "facts" can be authoritatively confirmed.

Periodically, Offred comments on the process of her own narrative, observing,

> I would like to believe this is a story I'm telling. . . . Those who can believe that such stories are only stories have a better chance.
>
> If it's a story I'm telling, then I have control over the ending. Then there will be an ending, to the story, and real life will come after it. . . .
>
> It isn't a story I'm telling.
>
> It's also a story I'm telling, in my head, as I go along. (*HT,* p. 49)

Offred's act of narration is virtually the only action she is able to initiate and direct. Communication in Gilead, particularly with other handmaids like herself, is cryptic, "amputated speech" (*HT,* p. 211). Reading and writing are proscribed and handmaids are warned (in Atwood's feminist literary pun), "Pen Is Envy" (*HT,* p. 196).

Offred's sense of disconnection from both the past and the future presses her into a state of perpetual ambiguity, boundless and terrible. In continuing to tell her story, she "can will [her]self to go on" (*HT,* p. 280). She wishes for a clearer shape for her story and, implicitly, for her life: "[t]he illusion of depth, created by a frame . . . " (*HT,* p. 153). Apologizing to the unknown audience in whom she must believe for her own survival—the self-generated act of creation that opposes the obligations of procreation—she describes her narrative as if it were herself, "a body caught in crossfire or pulled apart by force . . . this sad and hungry and sordid, this limping and mutilated story" (*HT,* p. 279).

The figurative and literal violations of boundary that in *Lady Oracle* in particular are direct manifestations of the mother–daughter conflict are envisioned in *Bodily Harm* and *The Handmaid's Tale* in broader political, cultural, and gender terms. An event early in *Bodily Harm* foreshadows the insidious links among violence, sex, death, and invasions of boundary that bind the narrative. Rennie Wilford returns one afternoon to her apartment to find a broken door through which an intruder has crashed. Two bullying policemen remind her how lucky she is to have been away when the apartment was forcibly entered; the sinister evidence is a rope lying coiled like a snake on her bed. In her absence, her living space has been invaded, just as her body has been violated by malignant cells. Both the invasion of her dwelling space and the invasive disease of cancer precipitate Rennie's incipient self-estrangement. After the break-in, she begins to see herself "from the outside, as if she was a moving target in someone else's binoculars" (*BH,* p. 40).

Like her mother (who, during her childhood, had made her feel responsible for accidents that happened to her), the policemen investigating the forced entry make Rennie feel as if she had invited it. Throughout the novel, policemen play a sinister role: as agents of authority, they are neutral when they should be involved and involved when they should be neutral. They become symbols for institutionalized manipulation, sanctioned by patriarchal power and by the impersonality of their uniforms.

The detail of the rope remains deliberately unexplained. It accumulates a number of meanings, from the idea of "rape," with which the word resonates, to the image of something coiled like the mythical snake in Eden. Though Rennie's former lover, Jake, is implicated as the intruder who left the rope in her apartment, the identity of that "faceless stranger" broadens to suggest not only several actual men in Rennie's life but also a particular attitude toward experience. In St. Antoine and St. Agathe there are a number of "faceless strangers," including the unknown person who breaks into Rennie's hotel room during her absence, in sinister repetition of the event in Toronto.

The image of rope reappears with equally sinister connotations in *The Handmaid's Tale*. At the "Women's Salvaging" of handmaids who are convicted of betrayal and publicly executed, a long rope "winds like a snake" (*HT,* p. 285) through the reluctant audience of other handmaids and continues onto the stage, where its other end forms the noose that hangs the offenders. The peers of the condemned handmaid are obliged to touch the section of the rope near them "to show . . . unity with the Salvagers and . . . complicity in the death of this woman" (*HT,* p. 288).

In *Bodily Harm*, Rennie Wilford discovers, after the second forcible entry into her living space, that the box she has naively agreed to retrieve from the airport for Lora Lucas (a woman whom she scarcely knows) contains a machine gun. Much later, after she has conveyed the box to its recipient, she realizes that she has been the go-between for the delivery of a weapon that may have facilitated one or more political assassinations. The sequence of events alludes to Pandora, who, like Rennie, was entrusted with an important container whose contents she could not resist knowing. According to the legend, when she opened the container, evil and disease were released into the world; only hope remained within. Rennie writes for a journal named *Pandora* (*BH,* p. 43); by the end of the narrative, she has not only confronted disease and evil but also recovered the saving capacity of hope.

Other images of boxes and containers build on this allusion and also express boundary issues. Jake, Rennie's erstwhile lover, is an advertising package designer. As Rennie eventually realizes, "[S]he was one of the things Jake was packaging" (*BH,* p. 104). Moreover, Jake views her as a "box" in the obscene sense. "You're so closed, Jake said once . . . I want to be the one you open up for. But she could never remember afterwards what he had actually said. Perhaps he'd said, I want to be the one who opens you up" (*BH,* p. 106).

Throughout *Bodily Harm,* men are associated with invasion and violation. Jake had favored sex that included bondage and sadism; he had enjoyed overpowering Rennie with such stage directions as "'Pretend you're being raped'" (*BH,* p. 117). In their bedroom—her bedroom— he had hung two sexually provocative posters of women whose bodies are sadistically bound or distorted. After her operation, Rennie had felt so alienated from her body and from Jake's efforts at lovemaking that she had experienced herself "from outside," watching him with detachment "from her head . . . up there on the pillow at the other end of her body" (*BH,* p. 199)—in unconscious imitation of one of the posters on the wall above them.

The alteration of her body by surgery alters Rennie's sense of the boundaries between inside and outside; she "no longer trusts surfaces" (*BH,* p. 48). She is afraid to look at the healing scar, fearing that she will see "blood, leakage, her stuffing coming out" (*BH,* p. 22). When she sees insects and other repugnant creatures, she morbidly imagines them having exuded from her incision; she dreams she's full of "white maggots eating away at [her] from the inside" (*BH,* p. 83). She worries that the scar will "split open like a faulty zipper, and she will turn inside out. Then she would see what Daniel saw when he looked into her, while she herself lay on the table unconscious as a slit fish . . . he knows what she's like inside" (*BH,* pp. 80–81).[45] The sexual reference implies that all forms of penetration, even love, leave one exposed. Feeling "something missing," Rennie doubts her sexuality.

Together, these images suggest the vulnerability of the female body, its orifices and boundaries subject to penetration and manipulation. They also convey Rennie's sense of having been physically violated, almost like rape: exposed while she was incapable of defending herself, like the forced entries into her living spaces. Even her surgeon, Daniel Luoma (whose name resembles a variety of cancer), has power over her because he "knows something about her she doesn't know" (*BH,* pp. 81–82). In fact, he has literally accomplished what, in another sense, Jake had fantasized: he has "opened her up."

Rennie recalls another doctor, her own grandfather, a country physician of violent temperament whose primitive life-saving methods (as

Rennie describes them) uncannily resemble torturous mutilations of the body: "[H]e drove a cutter and team through blizzards to tear babies out through holes he cut in women's stomachs and then sewed up again, he amputated a man's leg with an ordinary saw" (*BH,* p. 55). Like Rennie's grandfather, Dr. Luoma performs a mutilating operation—one generally practiced by men upon women's bodies—to save Rennie from a process occurring within her own body.

Rennie's exposure to the most overwhelming manifestation of female violation precedes her experiences in the Caribbean—though it is described relatively late in the narrative—when her editor in Toronto assigns her to do a piece on pornography. (The editor believes that articles on the subject in women's magazines miss "the element of playfulness" [*BH,* p. 207].) The descriptions of Rennie's "research" develop the images of rape and brutalization that recur throughout the narrative as symbols of ultimate female violation and express Atwood's powerful condemnation of pornography.

With a companion, Rennie views the "raw material" in a police collection of seized obscene objects; she watches "with detachment" (*BH,* p. 210) film clips of women in positions of intercourse with diverse animals and even sits impassively through several "sex-and-death" pieces that she assures herself must be faked. The graphic and shattering finale, a picture of a live rodent exiting from a woman's vagina, destroys her objectivity entirely. Besides grotesquely echoing Rennie's own morbid fantasies of the fragile boundaries of her body, the image is a stunningly repugnant perversion of birth.

Such shocks form the backdrop for Rennie's reluctant growth from her defensive position of "exemption" to the awareness that she must be involved, must take a position against the exploitation and abuse of women and of the human body. Moreover, in implicitly pairing cancer and pornography as analogous forms of "malignancy"—one in the body, the other in the body politic—Atwood emphasizes a striking cultural congruence. The people of Rennie's conventional Ontario hometown regard cancer as something "obscene" (*BH,* p. 82). Susan Sontag corroborates that word's original meaning as "ill-omened, abominable, repugnant to the senses." She also observes that cancer is too threatening and "scandalous" a subject for literary representation. Where it does appear, this radical metaphor is used "to propose new, critical standards of individual health, and to express a sense of dissatisfaction with society as such."[46]

The latter point precisely describes Atwood's conflation of forms of violation to the boundaries of the body and the self.

When Rennie Wilford is jailed for her presumed involvement in the islands' political upheaval, she experiences the deprivations of the flesh as an intensification of the cell disease within her. She feels "invaded, usurped, germs taking over, betrayal of the body" and imagines that "she's going to burst open" (*BH,* p. 286). Understandably totally disoriented, she feels as if she has been "turned inside out, there's no longer a *here* and a *there*" (*BH,* p. 290, emphasis in original). When she dares to look out the sole barred window of her cell, she watches in horror the sadistic abuse of prisoners by guards who clearly derive pleasure from it. Thus is the pornography of violence linked with the violence of pornography; both are society's "malignant" growths.

As Rennie discovers, "[S]he's afraid of men because men are frightening. She's seen the man with the rope, now she knows what he looks like" (*BH,* p. 290). However, although the urge to power may be more easily identified and located in men—it is in them that power resides in patriarchy—Rennie ultimately discovers that she is not simply their victim. She, too, has participated in events for which she was not prepared to accept responsibility, acts that "she doesn't want to see" (*BH,* p. 293) that may have caused others harm. The deaf-mute man whom Rennie repeatedly observes is an icon of the victimization that accompanies muteness.[47]

In *The Handmaid's Tale,* Atwood recasts in fable form her powerful exposure of the linkages between pornography, female exploitation and mutilation, and patriarchal power. As part of the handmaids' "re-education" in submission, Aunt Lydia (one of the "Aunts," a "female control agency" of women who retain some power in Gilead [*HT,* p. 320]) instructs that to be seen is to be "penetrated" (*HT,* p. 39) and that what they must be is "'impenetrable'" (*HT,* p. 39). With unintentional irony, Aunt Lydia cautions that since God made male flesh weak, it is up to the handmaids "'to set the boundaries'" (*HT,* p. 55). To strengthen their resolve for sexual purity, the handmaids are shown old pornographic films from the seventies and eighties in which women appear in various attitudes of submission, brutalization, and grotesque mutilation.

Offred later reflects that in even the time "before," she was aware of newspaper stories describing "corpses in ditches or the woods, bludgeoned to death or mutilated, interfered with as they used to say, but they were about other women, and the men who did such things were other men" (*HT,* p. 66). People like herself "lived in the blank white spaces at the edges of print" (*HT,* p. 66). More subtly, some desperate women abused their own bodies—"starved themselves thin or pumped their breasts full of silicone, had their noses cut off" (*HT,* p. 231)—to make themselves more attractive to men.

Like Rennie Wilford, Offred struggles for self-preservation in a world of real and symbolic oppression, expressed through boundaries both corporal and political. The landscape she inhabits is a walled enclave, defined by a red brick structure lined with chicken wire; the Wall, which resembles the Berlin Wall,[48] is guarded by sentries and electronic surveillance, and is punctuated by grappling hooks from which the hanged bodies of the executed are instructively displayed. Within the absolute wall are the more immediate walls of the "Re-education Centre" in which the handmaids are housed when they arrive in Gilead. The rebel among them, Moira, reminds them of their complicity in oppression by her own determination to take whatever risks are necessary to escape from it. Yet Moira's daring is itself threatening to the others; she is "like an elevator with open sides. She made us dizzy. Already we were losing the taste for freedom, already we were finding these walls secure. In the upper reaches of the atmosphere you'd come apart, you'd vaporize, there would be no pressure holding you together" (*HT,* p. 143).

Outside the Wall is the "heart" of Gilead, which handmaids can enter for specifically assigned tasks only after passing through a series of checkpoints. Its "edges" are unknown, varying "according to the attacks and counterattacks [of a war still in progress]; but this is the centre, where nothing moves. The Republic of Gilead, said Aunt Lydia, knows no bounds" (*HT,* p. 33). Late in her tale, Offred ironically recalls how she had once understood the absence of boundary in another sense; she had taken the sense of freedom for granted, "as if there were no contingencies, no boundaries; as if we were free to shape and reshape forever the ever-expanding perimeters of our lives" (*HT,* p. 239). Unlike Atwood's other novels, *The Handmaid's Tale* is set not in Canada but in a radically altered location in the United States.[49] In the former time, Offred, responding too late to the signs of impending oppression—when all women were fired from their jobs and stripped of economic and political freedoms—had unsuccessfully tried to flee with her husband and daughter by heading north to the Canadian border with fake visas.

Like her predecessors in Atwood's fiction, Offred experiences her self as split, perceiving self and body in opposition to each other because of the demands imposed upon her. In her former life, she had regarded her body as an "instrument" under her own control—with "limits . . . but nevertheless lithe, single, solid, one with me" (*HT,* p. 84); in Gilead she feels utterly subordinated to the procreative function. "Now the flesh arranges itself differently. I'm a cloud, congealed around a central object, the shape of a pear, which is hard and more real than I am and glows red within its translucent wrapping. Inside it is a space, huge as the sky at night" (*HT,* p. 84). When the doctor who periodically examines Offred for signs of pregnancy offers his own body for the purpose of insemination, she feels frightened without knowing why, since she has "crossed no boundaries . . . given no trust, taken no risk, all is safe. It's the choice that terrifies me" (*HT,* p. 71).

In fact, the boundary issues of self and other that preoccupy Atwood's other protagonists are paradoxically recast in *The Handmaid's Tale.* Offred and the other handmaids are made the property of others, to be used for their own needs and ends. The fertile female is simply a vessel for procreation; anatomy is indeed destiny. The physically confining boundaries of Gilead corroborate the condition of procreative "confinement" to which the handmaids are subject. Under the pressure of terrifying alternatives, Offred (whose name encodes her indentured sexuality: both "offered" and the property "of-Fred") "resign[s] [her] body freely, to the uses of others. They can do what they like with me. I am abject" (*HT,* p. 298)—and object. The "other" is both too close—privileged to violate her body—and too far—there is no intimacy in Gilead. Thus, the Commander's secretive appropriation of Offred for companionship and games of Scrabble betrays the emptiness and utter sterility of a world governed by the dehumanized worship of fertility. As Offred observes, "[N]obody dies from lack of sex. It's lack of love we die from. . . . Can I be blamed for wanting a real body, to put my arms around? Without it I too am disembodied. . . . I am like a room where things once happened and now nothing does . . ." (*HT,* pp. 113–14).

The antithesis of boundary transgression is communion: the reciprocal connection between people that respects the physical and emotional integrity of each individual. In *The Handmaid's Tale,* Offred "hunger[s] to commit the act of touch" (*HT,* p. 21) in a world in which contact can occur only in depersonalized public ceremonies. In *Bodily Harm,* the possibility of that "act of touch" is represented through the symbolism of hands: the emblem(s) for both tangible contact and genuine emotional connection between people. Rennie Wilford had felt, after her operation, as if Dr. Luoma (later Daniel) had "dragged her back into [life] . . . [b]y the hand" (*BH,* p. 32)—a lifesaving act that Rennie ultimately performs for Lora Lucas. Daniel's soul is literally "in his hands" (*BH,* p. 198); Rennie believes that his touch might transform more than her medical fate. On the islands, the ancient woman named Elva is gifted with healing hands—a talent she has inherited from her grandmother, just as Rennie eventually recognizes a similar gift from hers.

In contrast to Jake, who tried to force the "box" of Rennie's sexuality, the mercenary Paul (despite his own alienation) touches Rennie sexually without invading her, accepting the "missing" place (as Robert Schumann does for Muriel Rowbridge in Mortimer's *My Friend Says It's Bulletproof*). Before lovemaking, Rennie feels untouchable, as if "she's died and gone to heaven and come back minus a body" (*BH,* p. 203); afterwards, she feels as if "she's been opened, she's being drawn back down, she enters her body again and there's a moment of pain, incarnation. . . . [S]he can still be touched" (*BH,* p. 204). The language pointedly evokes the idea of resurrection and renewal of the flesh; Paul literally gives Rennie "back her body" (*BH,* p. 248). "Massive involvement" is not the invasive cancer from which Rennie fears she will die but the connections to others that will save her.

In jail, Rennie retreats to memories of touching and loving as antidote to her sense of helplessness and the squalor of her actual environment. Of these recollections, the most central is a haunting recurrent memory of her senile grandmother, wailing that she's lost her hands (a sensation Rennie herself has both dreamed and experienced [BH, pp. 116, 274]). As she wonders what to do with her cell mate Lora's violently gun-whipped and bruised body, Rennie recovers the final piece in that fragmentary recollection: her mother, demonstrating how to assuage the older woman's anguish, had taken hold of her "dangling hands, clasping them in her own" (*BH,* p. 298).

Recovering this crucial memory of human touch and connection, Rennie finally recognizes what has been "missing" in herself. In her discovery that "there's no such thing as a faceless stranger, every face is someone's" (*BH,* p. 299), the sinister symbolism of the anonymous stranger shifts to a positive acknowledgment of mutuality. Lora is Rennie's darker double, the other face of her own being, a woman whose subjection to sexual abuse from childhood makes her the symbolic female scapegoat for patriarchal exploitation. Rennie, reenacting her mother's healing act for her grandmother, administers comfort to Lora's lacerated body, then pulls her through "an invisible hole in the air" (*BH,* p. 299). In bringing the other woman back to consciousness, Rennie gives birth to her own denied consciousness. Having too readily regarded herself as a victim, she saves Lora in order to save herself, to oppose the world that has made the battered woman what she is.

Like the characters in Albert Camus's *The Plague,* who discover that no one is exempt from evil, Rennie Wilford learns that she is not "exempt" from the struggle against violence and dehumanization. Through this recognition about knowledge, personal responsibility, female alliance, and the terrible consequences of their abdication, Rennie is redeemed. Returning to Canada following her release from custody, she determines her new role as a "subversive" (*BH,* p. 301), one who opposes patriarchy's abuse of power through either exploitation or detachment. She is "flying" in more than the literal sense: even with death waiting in the wings, so to speak, she has reason for joy. As she reflects, "She is not exempt. Instead she is lucky, suddenly, finally, she's overflowing with luck, it's this luck holding her up" (*BH,* p. 301). The future is literally in her hands.

In their concern with women's lives in patriarchy, Penelope Mortimer and Margaret Atwood demonstrate their preoccupation with what might be termed the anxieties of relationship and separateness, not only as emotional and social matters, but as existential, cultural, and ideological ones. Like Virginia Woolf (to whom Mortimer occasionally alludes), both authors suggest that to be "free" is both a desire and a threat to their female characters, whose identities are often excessively dependent upon parental confirmation or patriarchal values. The unnamed narrator of Mortimer's *Long Distance* struggles to understand how one can live out the obvious contradiction of "total freedom within limits" (*LD,* p. 12).

The narratives of both authors examine the nature and consequences of attachment and loss in the relationships of heterosexual love and marriage, of daughters and parents, of mothers and children, of self and other. In Mortimer's fiction, marriage is the central emotional relationship and social institution through which adult female identity is both secured and threatened. It is a protective shell which, like its partners—particularly the wife—becomes "emptied out"; over time the boundaries of the relationship rigidify from secure enclosure to prison.

Though narratively realized in quite different ways, Margaret Atwood's female characters also confront and attempt to reconcile themselves with the emotional realities of attachment, separation, and loss. The image of Siamese twins is one of several central metaphors in her ouevre that represent the confusion over boundaries of the self. Other patterns, such as aberrations of body image, eating disorders, various forms of mirror images and mirroring, and imagined or actual violations of the body resonate with this central image of both merging and separation.

However, union is problematic in different ways for Atwood's younger female protagonists. In the earlier novels, her women fear losing themselves in the kinds of marriages in which Mortimer's older women of an earlier generation are imprisoned. Only two of Atwood's protagonists—Joan Foster of *Lady Oracle* and Elizabeth Schoenhof of *Life before Man*—are married (although Offred, of *The Handmaid's Tale*, was once married); for each, infidelity is a symptom of the emotional instability or inadequacy of the relationship. Atwood's other female characters, including Marian MacAlpin, the nameless narrator of *Surfacing,* Lesje Green, and Rennie Wilford, struggle to understand their conflicting needs for protection and autonomy in their erotic liaisons.

Many of Mortimer's and Atwood's women suffer from figurative or literal wounds. Their psychological injuries may be understood as consequences of earlier emotional attachments and unresolved dependencies to powerful mothers or remote fathers—critical past relationships that continue to influence the female characters' fragile or absent sense of their own autonomy and that are often manifested in psychological illnesses like depression, amnesia, agoraphobia, anorexia, obesity, impending madness, and "splitness" or figurative schizophrenia. To their psychic impoverishment, these women characteristically repress the fear and anger originally directed toward (and withheld from) that powerful figure.

In a related sense, nearly all of Atwood's protagonists seek, at least initially, some sort of literal or psychological escape from either their bodies or their "selves," though the forms of escape vary. The extreme form of psychological retreat is exemplified in the wish for or anxiety about death. Most of Mortimer's females worry about mortality; several of them are emotionally "dying of grief" in moribund marriages. Atwood's females' fear of emotional suffocation is frequently represented in the images of engulfment or drowning. Mrs. Armitage and several of Atwood's characters either consider suicide or enact a symbolic suicide as a way of trying to destroy rejected aspects of the self. Both Mortimer's Muriel Rowbridge and Atwood's Rennie Wilford, experiencing the radical fragility of their bodies and diminished sense of themselves as the result of disfiguring breast surgery for cancer, worry about the possibility of dying grotesquely of the disease.

Each of these inner conflicts is, viewed from another angle, a symptom of the struggle for survival—that central theme of Canadian literature, in Atwood's own view. Both authors' fictions explore the issue of *female* survival, a concern that becomes increasingly political and ideological in Atwood's most recent fiction. The recurring escape wishes and fears of actual death or psychological annihilation unfold through the complex dynamics of the female characters' present lives as well as through their—or, at least, the reader's—ultimate recognition of key psychological issues in their past experiences. As Professor Pieixoto—an archivist who addresses the "Twelfth Symposium on Gileadean Studies" held in Nunavit ("None-Of-It") in the year 2195 and whose comments form much of the "Historical Notes" concluding *The Handmaid's Tale*—remarks, the author of the narrative "must be seen within the broad outlines of the moment in history of which she was a part" (*HT,* p. 317).

In several of Mortimer's narratives and in Atwood's earlier ones, this historical context is anchored in the protagonists' relationships with their parents: sometimes their fathers but more often their mothers or mother-substitutes: stepmothers, aunts, and grandmothers. The presence of these female relatives in Atwood's fiction is itself a central motif; the once-removed but powerful female figures amplify positive or negative aspects of relationship split off from the actual mother–daughter bond. Atwood's observation about the three-generational family in Canadian fiction describes, with qualifications, a pattern in her earlier fiction: "rigid Grandparents, grey Parents, and Children who attempt to escape both generations. . . . '[E]scape' pure and simple [is] usually impossible; the solution to the Child's dilemma [is] often seen to involve a coming to terms with the past." [50] Joan Foster and Elizabeth Schoenhof resolve important aspects of their own psychological realities through recognition of the power of aunts who function as stepmothers. Lesje Green and Renata Wilford both see themselves (and in Rennie's case, a new emotional truth) through their grandmothers. In *The Handmaid's Tale,* the "Aunts"—whose names are derived, ironically, from commercial products for women—are the only group of women who have power in Gilead: they are the coercive instructors of "proper" female behavior for handmaids.

Moreover, both Mortimer and Atwood sensitively explore the central mother–daughter relationship and its consequences for the daughter's success or failure in establishing the boundaries of her own autonomy and sexual identity. The loss or death of the mother—occurring either before or during the current time in two of Mortimer's and four of Atwood's narratives—poses an additional imperative for the daughter to come to terms with her ambivalent feelings about her female parent.[51] Her dilemma is the more poignant because, in Adrienne Rich's words, "Few women growing up in patriarchal society can feel mothered enough; the power of our mothers, whatever their love for us and their struggles on our behalf, is too restricted. And it is the mother through whom patriarchy early teaches the small female her proper expectations."[52]

In Mortimer's *The Pumpkin Eater,* it is also the father who "teaches the . . . female her proper expectations." Powerful but unloving, he leaves his daughter with a profound insecurity about her capacity to act in the world. By contrast, in Atwood's narratives, fathers are notably absent. Marian MacAlpin's parents scarcely figure in her narrative. Both parents of Elizabeth Schoenhof and the narrator of *Surfacing* are deceased. In the latter case, the father's mysterious absence precipitates the daughter's search for an understanding of her true filial relationship to both parents. Joan Foster's father is a shadow figure, far less significant than her powerful negative mother; his "resurrectionist" status is ultimately questioned when Joan speculates that he may have been in some way responsible for her mother's death. Elizabeth Schoenhof's father abandoned the family when she was a child; Lesje Green's father is scarcely characterized; even Nate Schoenhof's father died early in his life. Rennie's father, like Elizabeth's, deserted the family early, in the former case to take up with a mistress in another city. In an ironic reversal of the institutionalized paternity in the Gilead of *The Handmaid's Tale,* Offred's own father is a cipher, since her mother chose decisively to be a single parent.

Thus, for one reason or another, Atwood's female characters are shown to have developed in strongly matriarchal environments. The daughter's struggle toward autonomy is made more problematic by the actual or symbolic absence of the male parent, since the mother or her stand-in assumes even greater psychological power over the daughter and also derives her own identity from such power. The very weakness or absence of the father both focuses and emotionally overcharges the relationship between the daughter and her mother or other female adult and makes more problematic the daughter's subsequent relationships with men.

Another manifestation of the anxiety of the females' boundary struggles in both Mortimer's and Atwood's fiction is the issue of maternity. In Mortimer's fiction, the procreative function is characterized simultaneously as a vital source of identity for the mothers and a restriction for the fathers. In Atwood's earlier fiction, maternity, like marriage, is problematic as a possibility rather than an actuality. Joan Foster of *Lady Oracle* fears maternity as long as she is in thrall to her powerful mother. In *The Edible Woman,* Marian MacAlpin's female friends dramatize extreme attitudes toward procreation: Ainsley is obsessed with becoming pregnant while Clara is virtually engulfed by maternity. Marian views both women with scepticism and anxiety. A central problem for the narrator of *Surfacing* is the necessity to come to terms with her denied abortion; the somewhat ambiguous sign of her psychological recovery is her desire to be impregnated by her primitive lover, Joe. In *The Handmaid's Tale,* the terms are reversed: women, not men, are discarded after their role in procreation is concluded. The personal anxieties surrounding procreation, fertility, maternity, and abortion are projected as cultural nightmare and catastrophe.

Thus the issue of the boundaries of female selfhood extends in both directions. For Mortimer's women, molded by the values of the fifties and sixties, the competing demands of motherhood and marriage weaken their capacity to claim themselves as autonomous beings; they remain dependent wives and daughters. Atwood's female characters of the seventies and eighties face, on the one hand, the problematic and often highly emotionally charged bonds between daughter and mother or mother-figure (reinforced by the absence of the father), and, on the other, the daughter's directly related anxiety concerning her own capacities—and the contemporary cultural contradictions—concerning biological motherhood and nurturance.

Not surprisingly, given such conflicts of expectation and actuality, most of Mortimer's narratives end without conclusively resolving the female characters' dilemmas. In this sense, they reflect not only the modernists' eschewing of narrative closure but the psychological limbo of women whose inner growth has been stunted both from within and without. The circular narrative organization of several of her novels (notably the earlier ones) thus structurally reflects the paradoxical sense of enclosure without resolution experienced by the protagonists.

Similarly, in Atwood's fiction, not all of the issues of separation and female identity are resolved, either narratively or psychologically. *Surfacing, Lady Oracle,* and *Life before Man* conclude somewhat irresolutely: the female protagonists—particularly those who articulate their own stories—gain new insight into their personal situations, but that insight does not inevitably alter their relation to the world. In the dystopian fable of *The Handmaid's Tale,* the world itself is radically altered, illustrating the unresolved cultural and ideological forces that corroborate female ambivalence about childbearing in patriarchy; the narrative ends with the resonant interrogative, "Are there any questions?" (*HT,* p. 324). Through irony, ambiguity, and paradox, Atwood's narratives thus structurally represent the boundary issues they explore: conclusion without resolution.

In these narratives of female discovery, development, and crisis, Penelope Mortimer and Margaret Atwood artfully dramatize the paradoxes of boundary—the contrary pulls of union and separation—giving us new insight into central psychological and ideological themes in female experience.

NOTES

1. Atwood, "Canadian-American Relations," in *Second Words: Selected Critical Prose*, ed. Margaret Atwood, (Toronto: Anansi, 1982), p. 392.

2. Marshall McLuhan, "Canada: The Borderline Case," in *The Canadian Imagination: Dimensions of a Literary Culture,* ed. David Staines (Cambridge: Harvard University Press, 1977), p. 244.

3. Russell M. Brown, "Crossing Borders," in *Essays on Canadian Writing,* No. 22 (Summer 1981), p. 155, emphasis in original.

4. Margaret Atwood, conversation with author, November 5, 1981.

5. Atwood, "An End to Audience?" in Atwood, *Second Words,* p. 350.

6. Margaret Atwood, *The Edible Woman* (1969, rpt. New York: Fawcett, 1976), pp. 224, 225. Subsequent references to this edition will be indicated by the abbreviation *"EW"* and page numbers in the text.

7. Margaret Atwood, *Lady Oracle* (1976, rpt. New York: Avon Books, 1978), p. 96. Subsequent references to this edition will be indicated by the abbreviation *"LO"* and page numbers in the text.

8. Margaret Atwood, *Life before Man* (Toronto: McClelland and Stewart, 1979), p. 142. Subsequent references to this edition will be indicated by the abbreviation *"LBM"* and page numbers in the text.

9. Margaret Atwood, *Surfacing* (1972, rpt. New York: Popular Library, 1972), pp. 46, 56. Subsequent references to this edition will be indicated by the abbreviation *"S"* and page numbers in the text.

10. Margaret Atwood, *Bodily Harm* (Toronto: McClelland and Stewart, 1981), p. 67. Subsequent references to this edition will be indicated by the abbreviation "BH" and page numbers in the text. Some portions of the discussion of *Bodily Harm* in this chapter originally appeared in my essay, "Pandora's Box and Female Survival: Margaret Atwood's *Bodily Harm,*" *Journal of Canadian Studies/ revue d'études canadiennes,* Vol. 20, No. 1 (Spring 1985), pp. 120–35. I gratefully acknowledge the journal's permission to use the material in a different form here.

11. Margaret Atwood, *The Handmaid's Tale* (Toronto: McClelland and Stewart, 1985), p. 174. Subsequent references to this edition will be indicated by the abbreviation "HT" and page numbers in the text. Because the novel was published as my book was in press, I have been unable to treat it fully here.

12. Margaret Atwood, *Two-Headed Poems* (New York: Simon and Schuster, 1978), p. 59. The image appears as early as 1963, in the poem "The Siamese Twins" (*Fiddlehead,* No. 59 [Winter 1963], 60).

13. Leslie Fiedler, *Freaks: Myths and Images of the Secret Self* (New York: Simon and Schuster, 1978), p. 203.

14. Atwood, "An End to Audience?" *Second Words,* pp. 348, 353.

15. Nor Hall, *The Moon and the Virgin: Reflections on the Archetypal Feminine* (New York: Harper and Row, 1980), pp. 125, 124. Atwood discusses the symbolism of the triple goddess in Canadian literature in *Survival: A Thematic Guide to Canadian Literature* (Toronto: Anansi, 1972), pp. 199–210. See also Sherrill Grace's references to Atwood's adaptations of the Persephone theme, in *Violent Duality: A Study of Margaret Atwood* (Montreal: Vehicule Press), pp. 121–22; and Sandra Dwja, "The Where of Here: Margaret Atwood and a Canadian Tradition," in *The Art of Margaret Atwood: Essays in Criticism,* ed. Arnold and Cathy Davidson (Toronto: Anansi, 1981), p. 21.

16. Otto Rank has suggested that the fantasy of royal or even supernatural

parents is a common occurrence in children's resolution of the "family romance" during the oedipal phase of psychological development. *The Myth of the Birth of the Hero and Other Essays,* ed. and trans. by Philip Freund (rpt. New York: Alfred A. Knopf and Random House, 1959), p. 93.

17. See Roberta Rubenstein, "Surfacing: Margaret Atwood's Journey to the Interior," *Modern Fiction Studies,* Vol. 22, No. 3 (Autumn, 1976), pp. 387–99) for my analysis of the correspondences between imagery in this novel and in Atwood's poetry. There are numerous other parallels in theme and imagery between the author's fiction and poetry, including such objects and motifs as mirrors, descent, surfacing, drowning, eyes, hands, sexual politics, masquerade, doubling, female victimization, divided identity, etc.

18. Margaret Atwood, Interview with Graeme Gibson, in *Eleven Canadian Novelists,* ed. Graeme Gibson (Toronto: Anansi, 1973), p. 29.

19. Christine Downing, *The Goddess: Mythological Images of the Feminine* (New York: Crossroad, 1981), pp. 11, 12.

20. Nancy Chodorow, *The Reproduction of Mothering: Psychoanalysis and the Sociology of Gender* (Berkeley: University of California Press, 1978), p. 110.

21. Ibid., pp. 109–10.

22. See Hilde Bruch, *The Golden Cage: The Enigma of Anorexia Nervosa* (rpt. New York: Random House, 1979), and Bruch, *Eating Disorders: Obesity, Anorexia Nervosa, and the Person Within* (New York: Basic Books, 1973).

23. Bruch, *Eating Disorders,* p. 219.

24. As Helmut Thoma expresses this relationship in psychoanalytic terms, "[T]he incorporation of nourishment abolishes the spatial barriers between the ego and the object." *Anorexia Nervosa,* trans. Gillian Brydone (New York: International Universities Press, 1967), p. 256.

25. The associations with cake occur in several places during the narrative. In an analysis of the female protagonists of Margaret Drabble's early novels, Ellen Cronan Rose points out that the desire to "have one's cake and eat it too" is an expression of ambivalence about growing up. The observation is equally applicable to Marian MacAlpin's choice of the symbolic cake to represent her recovery of her autonomy and her appetite. *The Novels of Margaret Drabble: Equivocal Figures* (Totowa, N.J.: Barnes and Noble, 1980), p. 7.

26. Atwood, "An Introduction to *The Edible Woman,*" in *Second Words,* p. 369.

27. Margaret Atwood, Interview with Linda Sandler, *Malahat Review,* No. 41 (1977), p. 13. Critics of the novel disagree about whether the novel achieves a positive resolution. For contrasting interpretations, see Catherine McLay, "The Dark Voyage: *The Edible Woman* as Romance," pp. 123–38, and Robert Lecker, "Janus through the Looking Glass: Atwood's First Three Novels," pp. 177–86, both in Davidson, *The Art of Margaret Atwood.*

28. Marlene Boskind-Lodahl suggests that anorexia nervosa, bulimarexia, and adolescent obesity are, despite their differences in physical manifestation, part of the same syndrome. "Cinderella's Stepsisters: A Feminist Perspective on Anorexia Nervosa and Bulimia," *Signs*, Vol. 2, No. 2 (Winter 1976), pp. 342–56.

29. John Bowlby, *Attachment and Loss*, Vol. 2: *Separation, Anxiety, and Anger* (New York: Basic Books, 1973). Margaret Mead has qualified Bowlby's findings by drawing attention to the untypical aspects in the situations of his research subjects. "A Cultural Anthropologist's Approach to Maternal Deprivation," in *Woman: Body and Culture*, ed. Signe Hammer (New York: Harper and Row, 1975), pp. 318–36.

30. In Sherrill Grace's view, Atwood does not follow through this implication by altering the tone in the final section of the novel and thus fails to validate the narrator's change in consciousness with a shift in the language of the narrative itself. See *Violent Duality*, pp. 99–100.

31. Carol Christ analyzes *Surfacing* as a novel dramatizing the successful completion of the female spiritual quest, in *Diving Deep and Surfacing: Women Writers on the Spiritual Quest* (Boston: Beacon Press, 1980), chapter on Margaret Atwood's *Surfacing*. See also Annis Pratt's valuable analysis of the novel in *Archetypal Patterns in Women's Fiction* (Bloomington: Indiana University Press, 1981), pp. 157–61; and Barbara Hill Rigney, *Lilith's Daughters: Women and Religion in Contemporary Fiction* (Madison: University of Wisconsin Press, 1982), pp. 23–30.

32. Dorothy Dinnerstein, *The Mermaid and the Minotaur: Sexual Arrangements and Human Malaise* (rpt. New York: Harper and Row, 1977), p. 111.

33. In *Survival*, Atwood observes that "drowning . . . can be used as a metaphor for a descent into the unconscious" (p. 55).

34. Hilde Bruch, quoted by William Schonfeld in "The Body and the Body-Image in Adolescents," in *Adolescence: Psychosocial Perspectives*, ed. Gerald Caplan and Serge Lebovici (New York: Basic Books, 1969), p. 46.

35. Margaret S. Mahler, Fred Pine, and Anni Bergman, *The Psychological Birth of the Human Infant: Symbiosis and Individuation* (New York: Basic Books, 1975), pp. 88, 117, and esp. 230. In his analysis of the psychological structures of children's fairy tales, Bruno Bettelheim proposes that "[f]ar from being a device used only by fairy tales, such a splitting up of one person into two to keep the good image uncontaminated occurs to many children as a solution to a relationship too difficult to manage or comprehend." *The Uses of Enchantment: The Meaning and Importance of Fairy Tales* (New York: Alfred A. Knopf, 1976), p. 67.

36. See note 16.

37. Adrienne Rich, *Of Woman Born: Motherhood as Experience and Institution* (rpt. New York: Bantam, 1977), p. 238. Lynn Sukenick first used the term "matrophobia" to connote the daughter's fear of *becoming* her mother in her essay

"Feeling and Reason in Doris Lessing's Fiction," in *Doris Lessing: Critical Essays,* ed. Annis Pratt and L. S. Dembo (Madison: University of Wisconsin Press, 1974), p. 102.

38. Chodorow, *The Reproduction of Mothering,* p. 137.

39. As Jane Flax paraphrases Freud, "[W]hat women really look for in their husbands is their mother." See "Mother-Daughter Relationships: Psychodynamics, Politics, and Philosophy," in *The Future of Difference,* ed. Hester Eisenstein and Alice Jardine (Boston: G. K. Hall, 1980), p. 34.

40. Atwood, in her interview with Linda Sandler, says, "The maze I use [in *Lady Oracle*] is a descent into the underworld" (p. 16).

41. Atwood has expressed her pleasure in deliberately inverting traditional narrative forms. In *Lady Oracle,* she inverts certain features of the Gothic romance form, using "the components [of the genre] and then pull[ing] them inside out, as you would a glove." Interview with Betsy Draine in *Interviews with Contemporary Writers,* ed. L. S. Dembo (Madison: University of Wisconsin Press, 1983), p. 371. See also Sybil Korff Vincent's discussion of Atwood's parody of the Gothic form in "The Mirror and the Cameo: Margaret Atwood's Comic/Gothic Novel *Lady Oracle*," in *The Female Gothic,* ed. Juliann E. Fleenor (Montreal: Eden Press, 1983). Arnold and Cathy Davidson discuss the overlap between the Gothic fiction that Joan writes and the romantic and Gothic fantasies that she lives; Joan "deals in the same malady from which she suffers." "Margaret Atwood's *Lady Oracle:* The Artist as Escapist and Seer," *Studies in Canadian Literature,* Vol. 3, No. 2 (Summer 1978), p. 166. Barbara Godard analyzes the novel from the perspective of "subversions": of language as well as of traditional narrative forms such as fairy tales and myths. Several of her observations on Atwood's imagery in *Lady Oracle* parallel my own analysis. See "My (m)Other, My Self: Strategies for Subversion in Atwood and Hébert," *Essays on Canadian Writing,* Vol. 26 (Summer 1983), pp. 13–44.

42. Atwood, Interview with Betsy Draine in Dembo, *Interviews with Contemporary Writers,* p. 369.

43. Julia Kristeva, "Woman's Time," trans. Alice Jardine and Marny Blake, *Signs,* Vol. 7, No. 1 (Autumn 1981), p. 31.

44. Atwood, Interview with Linda Sandler, *Malahat Review,* p. 14.

45. Note the similarity to Mrs. Armitage in Penelope Mortimer's *The Pumpkin Eater,* who observes, after her abortion and sterilization operations, "To be cut open and sewn up makes one realize how much is contained inside skin and muscle: we're only stuffed with life, and can easily burst open." *The Pumpkin Eater* (New York: McGraw Hill, 1962), p. 151.

46. Susan Sontag, *Illness as Metaphor* (New York: Farrar, Straus and Giroux, 1977), pp. 9, 72–73. See my discussion, in part 1 of this study, of Penelope

Mortimer's *My Friend Says It's Bulletproof* (New York: Random House, 1967), a novel in which the female protagonist, Muriel Rowbridge, is also a victim of cancer and mastectomy.

47. As Atwood has written on the subject of victimization, "One of the possibly harmful psychological advantages of being a 'victim' is that you can substitute moral righteousness for responsibility; that is, you can view yourself as innocent and your oppressor as totally evil, and because you define yourself as powerless, you can avoid doing anything about your situation. 'Winning' is not always 'good', obviously, but neither is losing." "Mathews and Misrepresentation," in *Second Words*, p. 134. The theme of female victimization and sadomasochism resonates through Atwood's poetry as well, particularly in *Power Politics* (Toronto: Anansi, 1972). Judith McCombs points out in her analysis of several volumes of Atwood's poetry that even the cover illustration for *Power Politics*—conceived by Atwood in corroboration with an artist—demonstrates this preoccupation: "[T]he warrior and his captive woman are sadomasochism in Gothic dress." "Atwood's Haunted Sequences: *The Circle Game, The Journals of Susanna Moodie,* and *Power Politics,*" in Davidson, *The Art of Margaret Atwood,* p. 47.

48. According to the jacket copy and the author's acknowledgment on the obverse of the title page, Atwood began writing the novel while she was in West Berlin.

49. In answer to an interviewer's question, "Is Gilead imminent?" Atwood recently remarked, "'The United States is where it's going to happen first. . . . Canada is very socially conservative. It's more radical in other ways—socialized medicine, health care, and those things. But . . . people are much more skeptical about sudden change. It was never a revolutionary society. The United States was. . . . The United States . . . is humanity's testing ground. It's like a teeming bacterial culture of everything you can imagine. It's where very different ideas fight it out.'" Cathy N. Davidson, "A Feminist '1984': Margaret Atwood Talks about Her Exciting New Novel," *Ms.* Magazine, February 1986, p. 25, second and final ellipses are in original; others are mine.

50. Atwood, *Survival,* p. 181.

51. Judith Kegan Gardiner has written insightfully on mother-daughter relationships in fiction by women, observing that the death of the female protagonist's mother "becomes a death of childhood repression. Yet, more centrally, the mothers [in narratives by Jean Rhys, Margaret Drabble, Agnes Smedley, and Marge Piercy] are what the daughters fear and must kill in themselves in order to achieve a positive female identity." For a female writer, "creating her own identity, mothering herself, is still so difficult that the woman novelist kills her heroine's devalued mother so that the heroine can achieve power over her own

identity." "The Heroine as Her Author's Daughter," in *Women and Men: The Consequences of Power,* ed. Dana V. Hiller and Robin Ann Sheets (Cincinnati: University of Cincinnati Office of Women's Studies, 1976), p. 144.

52. Rich, *Of Woman Born,* p. 246.

PART 2

Boundaries of Cultural Identity

Pariahs and Community

Toni Morrison

Toni Morrison's fiction, like that of Penelope Mortimer and Margaret Atwood, demonstrates a central interest in the issues of boundary, attachment, and separation, though these concerns are dramatized in considerably different ways. Morrison's characters experience themselves as wounded or imprisoned, not only by virtue of their gender, but additionally by racial and economic divisions within American culture. The boundaries that circumscribe black people of both genders are not only the prejudices and restrictions that bar their entry into the mainstream but the psychological ones they internalize as they develop in a social structure that historically has excluded them.

If woman is the Other within patriarchal culture,[1] then women of ethnic minority groups, as defined by the values of white patriarchy, face a sense of double diminishment. As Pauline Breedlove of *The Bluest Eye* (1970) phrases it, "'Everybody in the world was in a position to give [black women] orders.'"[2] Or, as Margaret Wright expresses it, "Black women have been doubly oppressed. On the job, we're low women on the totem pole. White women have their problems. They're interviewed for secretarial instead of the executive thing. But we're interviewed for mopping floors and stuff like that. Sometimes we have to take what's left over in Miss Ann's refrigerator. This is all exploitation. And when we get home from work, the old man is wondering why his greens aren't cooked on time."[3]

Yet despite this doubled oppression, black women writers have celebrated and written eloquently of their sustaining values. Toni Morrison

125

draws from a rich store of black oral tradition as well as from her own imaginative angle of vision to illuminate the potentialities for both annihilation and transcendence within black experience. In representing such extremes of possibility, she articulates, while not always resolving, some of the cultural contradictions of black women's—and men's—problematic position in white patriarchal American culture.

Morrison's fiction dramatizes both psychological and cultural dimensions of boundary through a number of recurring images and motifs. Concern with the psychological processes of identity formation is expressed through parent–child and peer relationships, often exaggerated in the form of emotionally blurred or distorted ego and body boundaries, as in symbiotic and even incestuous attachments. Another central cluster of images expresses figurative and literal maiming or mutilation. In turn, each of these images has a communal dimension, implying the divisions and splits within individuals that mirror their cultural situation. Thus, constriction of the growth of the self is implicitly linked to restrictive or oppressive cultural circumstances.

Traditionally, black communities have functioned as structures that sustain and preserve the individual, particularly in adversity. Morrison's narratives address the nature and forms of this connection between self and other, individual and group, that may ambiguously both shape people's values and impede their capacity to express them within the community's norms. Morrison also explores the false images and stereotypes that may contribute to this process. Fittingly, another central motif that appears throughout the author's canon is the diverse implications of appearances and perception. The way people regard themselves, and the way they are regarded, permeates every relationship and suggests the intangible boundaries that arise between individuals as well as groups.

Speaking of the visual emphasis in her fiction, Morrison has implicitly drawn a connection between perception and invisible but powerful intercultural divisions: "The interest in vision, in seeing, is a fact of black life. As slaves and ex-slaves, black people were manageable and findable, as no other slave society would be, because they were black. So there is an enormous impact from the simple division of color—more than sex, age, or anything else. The complaint is not being seen for what one is."[4]

In *The Bluest Eye*, this "complaint" functions on many levels. The Breedlove family's sense of utter hopelessness and helplessness is externalized in their appearance: both literal and spiritual poverty manifest themselves as ugliness in a world in which beauty is equated with success: poverty is ugly. Morrison deliberately invokes cultural stereotypes as a way of calling attention to errors of perception. "Cholly" and "Polly" Breedlove are virtually—as their rhyming nicknames suggest—carica-tures: destitute, living in squalor, derelict, "ugly," amoral.[5] In *Tar Baby* (1981), the mysterious Son emerges as if a demon from the white uncon-scious: the anonymous black rapist who creeps menacingly out of the darkness, the proverbial "nigger in the woodpile."[6]

Other stereotypes originating in white culture produce equally false and damaging images. In *The Bluest Eye,* the portrait of family life de-scribed in the "Dick and Jane" frame is a childish oversimplification, not only of language but of reality:

> Here is the house. It is green and white. It has a red door. It is very pretty. Here is the family. Mother, Father, Dick, and Jane live in the green-and-white house. They are very happy. See Jane. She has a red dress. She wants to play. Who will play with Jane? See the cat. It goes meow-meow. Come and play. Come play with Jane. The kitten will not play. See Mother. Mother is very nice. Mother, will you play with Jane? Mother laughs. Laugh, Mother, laugh. See Father. He is big and strong. Father, will you play with Jane? Father is smiling. Smile, Father, smile. See the dog. Bowwow goes the dog. Do you want to play with Jane? See the dog run. Run, dog, run. Look, look. Here comes a friend. The friend will play with Jane. They will play a good game. Play, Jane, play. (*BE,* p. 7)

As in several of Penelope Mortimer's novels, the traditional associa-tions with the idea of home become, in *The Bluest Eye,* ironic comments on both the inaccuracy and the insufficiency of the stereotype. The image of the happy (white) family at home is inverted in the radical homeless-ness of Pecola Breedlove and her destitute family. Even the images of the cat and dog reappear in inverted forms, as Pecola is exploited by male members of her own community in the torment or death of other people's pets: for "Junior," his mother's adored (blue-eyed) cat; for Soap-head Church, his landlady's aged dog.

Moreover, the passage is scarcely an accurate reflection of the segment of American society that it purportedly characterizes.[7] Still less is it pos-sible for a young black girl to recognize herself in it, for the imagination supplies the implicitly white middle-class cast of characters in the roles identified in the sketch. Through what is understood by omission, the invisible boundaries between cultures are eventually defined.

In a world in which many of the qualities deemed desirable are generated by white male fantasies, the Claudia MacTeers and Pecola Breedloves are doubly excluded; both their gender and the color of their skin mark them as outsiders. Beneath the tangible reminders of differentness or exclusion are the intangible but even more powerful expectations and assumptions of the dominant culture. What makes growing up black, female, and poor particularly problematic is that the white definitions of "reality" often do not correspond with either black or female experience. Claudia MacTeer sees that "[b]eing a minority in both caste and class, we moved about . . . on the hem of life, struggling to consolidate our weaknesses and hang on, or to creep singly up into the major folds of the garment" (*BE,* p. 18). Or, as Sula Peace of Morrison's second novel, *Sula* (1973), discovers, the fact that she and her friend Nel Wright are "neither white nor male" means that "all freedom and triumph was forbidden to them."[8]

As an indicator of the subtle seepage of white values into black culture, variations in skin color are evaluated with reference to whiteness. Mary Helen Washington has observed that "the intimidation of color" and the subject of female beauty are recurrent features of the oppressive experience of black women in white culture and are frequently reproduced in narratives by black women writers.[9] In *The Bluest Eye,* Maureen Peal is envied less for her family's greater affluence than for her light skin, whereas to the same peers Pecola's absolute blackness confirms the other delimiting characteristics of her position at the bottom of the social scale; black boys project their "contempt for their own blackness" (*BE,* p. 55) onto her. Those who, on the basis of such arbitrary but powerful distinctions, occupy a "higher" position on this spectrum of pigmentation are nonetheless insecure, because "[t]he line between colored and nigger was not always clear; subtle and telltale signs threatened to erode it, and the watch had to be constant" (*BE,* p. 71).

Measured against white standards of skin color and physical beauty, the black female's options, as depicted in Morrison's first novel, are accommodation, misery, or degradation, if not all three. Unless they are, like Claudia MacTeer, endowed with enough inner strength to believe in themselves in the face of negation, they mature into a condition of inauthenticity, denying or distrusting their own experience. Living out someone else's version of reality, they cannot create themselves.

Such are the "good colored girls" who repress their anger, practice submission, attend college at land-grant institutions, and "learn how to do the white man's work with refinement" (*BE*, p. 68). Conforming to white culture's expectations of them, they become dismembered like Claudia's decapitated white dolls, asexual and stripped of selfhood. Females like Pecola Breedlove, who fall outside the boundaries of even such marginal and self-denying acceptability, are thus radically threatening to "proper" black girls.

Morrison explores the subtle equation between perception and economic status, as if poverty and ugliness were two sides of the same false coin. Families like the ironically named Breedloves survive at the very fringe of society, where the "hem" begins to unravel. Their economic destitution and psychic abjection undermine the very bonds that attach family members to one another and form the basis for community. Barely existing as a social unit, they function even less as an emotional unit, for they lack even the "power of the weak" that characterizes oppressed groups.[10] Pauline Breedlove, disillusioned by her family life, retreats into a dream world purveyed by cinematic imagemakers of white cultural fantasies. Thus she is enslaved, not in the literal sense, but symbolically, by what are to Morrison "probably the most destructive ideas in the history of human thought": romantic love and physical beauty (*BE*, p. 97).

Seduced by appearances, Pauline damns her only daughter at birth. During labor she overhears white doctors commenting on the ease of childbirth for black women: "'They deliver right away and with no pain. Just like horses'" (*BE*, p. 99). Pauline projects onto her undeserving newborn daughter her outrage at such facile and prejudicial judgments. Baby Pecola arrives with a "head full of pretty hair, but Lord she was ugly" (*BE*, p. 100). The emotional crippling shared by Cholly and Pauline is indeed bred into the next generation.

D. W. Winnicott has proposed that the core of what eventually forms as the individual's self-concept begins with the mirroring that occurs between mother and baby. Typically, what the baby sees when it looks into the mother's face is "himself or herself. In other words the mother is looking at the baby and *what she looks like is related to what she sees there.*"[11] In this sense, then, Pecola's first perception is her mother's reflection of her ugliness. From the seed of that initial negation grows her subsequent "fear of growing up, fear of other people, fear of life" (*BE*, p. 102).

In a poignant sense the message Pecola reads first in her mother's eyes and eventually in everyone else's is quite accurate: the people of her community view her as the negation of what they are. Her defenseless condition threatens them with the "static and dread" (*BE,* p. 42) that they repress within themselves. She is the dark shadow, the Other, that undermines both white and black fantasies of female goodness, beauty, and upward mobility. Her position at the bottom of the bottom symbolizes the regrettable need to pronounce someone inferior in order to defend a fragile sense of self-worth.

When the child Pecola hears her parents fighting on the other side of the partition in their makeshift "home," she virtually wishes herself into invisibility: "'Please, God. . . . Please make me disappear.' She squeezed her eyes shut. Little parts of her body faded away" until "[o]nly her tight, tight eyes were left. They were always left" (*BE,* p. 39). Her attempt at psychological suicide ironically recalls the Cheshire Cat of Carroll's *Alice in Wonderland,* whose smile remains after the rest of its form has vanished; for Pecola it is the eyes that remain no matter how hard she wills their disappearance.

Pecola's desire to be *perceived* as a human being in order to exist at all is concentrated in her sad fantasy of obtaining blue eyes. Through them, she might see and be seen as a real person and thus acquire the self-determination denied her by her circumstances as well as by her race and gender. Never able to achieve existence in her own eyes—her own "I"—she exists only in the image reflected by others—by other eyes/I's. Existentially, she is an object, never a subject.[12]

Others of Morrison's characters are also, though more subtly, enslaved by appearances or by false images of selfhood. In *Tar Baby,* both Jadine Childs and Margaret Street are hostage to male idolatry of female beauty. Margaret was, twenty-five years earlier, the "Principal Beauty of Maine," a distinction that led Valerian Street to notice and eventually marry her. Some of the emotional warping of her personality comes from the self-image she was encouraged as a child to cultivate and to which she became enslaved. Initially, Valerian's appreciative attentions had given Margaret the feeling of "consequence under the beauty, back down beneath it where her Margaret-hood lay . . . faceless, silent, and trying like hell to please" (*TB,* p. 83). Years later, she is still caught in the same submissive stasis, though its insufficiency has slowly warped her affections altogether.

Jadine Childs is another dubious benefactor of male worship of female beauty. A "stunning" model who trades on her looks, she lives in the conviction that she has succeeded on her own talent and a bit of luck, when in fact her European education and the opportunities to which it has given her access were subsidized by Valerian.

The trope of vision is adapted to different ends in *Sula.* Nel Wright and Sula Peace initially find "in each other's eyes the intimacy they were look-ing for" (*S*, p. 45). Each virtually creates the other as she sees who she is through the other girl's eyes. Nel later recalls that as girls they were "two throats and one eye" (*S*, p. 126), an image echoed in the detail of "one-eyed chickens" (*S*, p. 47), which in turn suggests the ill-fated Chicken Little. Sula thinks of women without men as "sour-tipped needles featuring one constant empty eye" (*S*, p. 105).

The recurring image of the single or shared eye reinforces the sense of shared boundaries and incidentally recalls the "communal eye" of the mythological Graie sisters, described by Nina Auerbach: "[T]hey have a single eye between them, which is passed unfailingly from sister to sister. They spend their lives endowing each other with vision."[13] After Sula and Nel separate, each suffers from limited vision. When Sula returns to the Bottom after a ten-year absence, Nel likens her reappearance to "get-ting the use of an eye back, having a cataract removed. . . . [Sula] made her see old things with new eyes" (*S*, p. 82).

Later, Sula becomes figuratively "one-eyed" and dis-membered, lack-ing a basic sense of connection to others and to the community. While people *see* themselves more clearly through her, she cannot *see* herself. She is radically free in the sense that Cholly Breedlove is: she has nothing to lose. Moreover, Sula herself is deceived by appearances. When she learns that the one man she can care for is not "Ajax" but "A. Jacks," her illusions are destroyed: if he is not what she has thought him to be, then she cannot trust her own perceptions.

Psychological and cultural eventualities may in a sense overdetermine an individual's limiting and limited circumstances. Pecola Breedlove's radi-cal alienation begins with her mother's rejection of her at birth, to which are added the accumulated insults of poverty and ignorance. The mother is the figure who is, for each infant in most cultures, both the primary object of emotional attachment that enables the self to develop and the transmitter of cultural attitudes and values.[14] In *The Bluest Eye,* Pecola is literally a stranger to her mother, addressing her as "Mrs. Breedlove."

When she goes to the house where her mother is a domestic and nanny for a white female child, Pauline denies even knowing who Pecola is. The cruelty of the scene repeats Pauline's initial rejection of Pecola at birth and accentuates the circular negation of selfhood: the mother becomes a fearful child before the greater power of her young white "mistress"; her own daughter experiences that fear as her mother's preference for her white "daughter," who is privileged to call Mrs. Breedlove by the familiar name, Polly, in marked contrast to Pecola's formal address.

Sula Peace inherits another kind of legacy from her mother: Hannah is literally an easy "piece," thriving on sexual satisfaction because it is the most potent affirmation of her being. From Hannah's casual enjoyment of men, Sula learns that "sex was pleasant and frequent, but otherwise unremarkable" (S, pp. 37–38). Other people in the community simply accept that "It was manlove that Eva bequeathed to her daughters. . . . The Peace women simply loved maleness, for its own sake" (S, p. 35).

When Hannah suffers a horrible death by fire, Sula is mesmerized by the sight of her mother "dancing" in the flames and watches rather than running to her aid. Her recollection of that moment is a haunting revelation of her emotional paralysis. As she phrases it years later, "I didn't mean anything. I never meant anything. I stood there watching her burn and was thrilled" (S, p. 127). Her inappropriate emotional response at the time suggests her distance from the ordinary feelings that bind family members in affection and loyalty. Her words also suggest another meaning: having misunderstood Hannah's overheard comment about loving but "not liking" her daughter, Sula has since believed that she never *meant* anything to her own mother.

Through such misunderstandings Sula becomes a kind of emotional orphan. Like Pecola Breedlove in *The Bluest Eye,* who lives out the meaning of her mother's rejection, Sula enacts her own interpretation of her mother's words, becoming a center of negative energy, withheld emotion, and absence of guilt. In psychological terms, she has no ego: "no center, no speck around which to grow" (S, p. 103). At the core of her personality, where the patterns of self-confirmation and ethical sense should develop, is a void that has existed "ever since her one major feeling of responsibility had been exorcised on the bank of a river with a closed place in the middle. The first experience taught her there was no other that you could count on; the second that there was no self to count on either" (S, pp. 102–3). While men are tempted by Sula's enigmatic charm, women become more attentive to their spouses and children in defense against her charismatic power. She catalyzes the anxieties of those whose paths she crosses because (in others' eyes) she lives out the amoral potentialities that most people repress.

As a result of quite different circumstances, Jadine Childs of *Tar Baby* is a cultural orphan (as well as a literal orphan: her father died when she was two, her mother ten years later) who lacks a clear model for either her female sexuality or her cultural history. As an adult woman she is confronted with the consequences of such inner confusion. When she visits her lover Son's hometown, she stays in his Aunt Rosa's house, where she feels claustrophobically enclosed in a dark, windowless, almost airless box of a room. Looking out to "the blackest nothing she had ever seen" (*TB*, p. 251)—and, figuratively, into her own naked soul—she feels overwhelmed and defenseless. "Maybe if she stood there long enough light would come from somewhere, and she could see shadows, the outline of something, a bush, a tree, a line between earth and sky, a heavier darkness to show where this very house stopped and space began" (*TB*, pp. 251–52). As the language suggests, Jade experiences herself in an unbounded space that threatens the carefully defined limits of her complacent daytime self: "No man had made her feel that naked, that unclothed . . . none of them had made her feel exposed. . . . Obscene" (*TB*, p. 253).

When later Jadine and Son make love, she is inhibited by a group of female demons whom only she can see: her own dead mother; her Aunt Ondine; Son's dead wife, whose sexual charisma is legendary; and a woman in yellow (the image of Jadine's alter ego). All the women except the last expose their breasts to her; the woman in yellow shows her the three big eggs she carries. Jade feels that she must turn her back on these succubi, who remind her of female servitude, whether economic or sexual. Yet her rejection of "breasts" and "eggs" has resulted in her narcissistic self-absorption. Fearing to live out the conventional destiny of her gender (as the night women suggest), Jadine fails to see that her current life is as much a prostitution of her womanhood as the role of Son's wife might be. As the shorter form of her name hints, she is already compromised, from Valerian's financial subsidy of her education to her career as a model who rents out her beauty.

Moreover, Ondine criticizes her niece's self-centeredness, observing that if a girl "'never learns how to be a daughter, she can't never know how to be a woman. . . . You don't need your own natural mother to be a daughter. All you need is to feel a certain . . . careful way about people older than you are. . . . A daughter is a woman that cares about where she come from and takes care of them that took care of her'" (*TB,* p. 281).

Jadine's "failure" as a daughter stems in part from anger she still feels toward her dead mother: "'You left me you died you didn't care enough about me to stay alive'" (*TB,* p. 261). Though one wishes that the thread of Jadine's "motherlessness" were further developed in the narrative, one can speculate that the loss of her mother on the brink of her adolescence is one source of anxiety about her female identity and sexuality.[15] Ondine's self-sacrifice on Jadine's behalf has also distorted their relationship; Ondine has regarded Jadine as "a 'child' whom she could enjoy, indulge, protect and, since this 'child' was a niece[,] it was without the stress of a mother-daughter relationship" (*TB,* p. 96).

Thus, all of the mother figures in Jadine's life—her own mother, Ondine, Margaret, and the collective night women—are in some way threatening to her. Parentless, she lacks a model of either positive mothering or "daughtering"; cultureless, she lacks a clear sense of how to achieve authenticity in either black or white worlds.

In Morrison's narratives, the ambiguous thrall of the parents, or the equally powerful effect of their absence, is an emotional reality that many of her characters, both male and female, confront. In the absence of close bonds with one or both parents, a child seeks some other person who will satisfy the need for a deep, abiding emotional attachment. A central representation of the problems of boundary and attachment that originate in the parent-child bond is that of symbiosis: the mutually dependent emotional connection that ultimately may either facilitate or impede growth of the self.

In *Sula,* three minor characters—homeless boys who come to live in the Peace household—are each called the same name, Dewey, by Eva. For the rest of their lives, they are an inseparable triad. Even their own mothers are unable to distinguish among them for, like figurative Siamese triplets whose physical boundaries are partially shared, each is joined "with the other two to become a trinity with a plural name . . . inseparable, loving nothing and no one but themselves" (*S,* p. 33, ellipsis in original). Fused by Eva's naming of them, "They spoke with one voice, thought with one mind" (*S*, p. 34).

Like the "three deweys" (the capital letter is eventually dropped), Sula Peace and Nel Wright, the only children of "distant mothers and incomprehensible [or absent] fathers" (*S*, p. 44), approach a kind of psychological symbiosis. In Morrison's narrative of a unique female friendship,[16] Sula and Nel initially discover their own essences and begin to grow through their reciprocal connection; each girl seems to have, both materially and metaphysically, what the other lacks. While Sula needs Nel as "the closest thing to both another and a self" (*S*, p. 103), Nel needs Sula to act out the denied dark forces in her own being. Sula, very much her mother's daughter, is sexually free, mercurial, amoral, and as bored by convention as Nel is wedded to it.

Nel is also her mother's daughter; when she marries Jude Greene at eighteen, she acts as an extension of her mother's desires. Her marriage is "the culmination of all [Helene] had been, thought or done in this world" (*S*, p. 68). Moreover, in matrimony she becomes a mirror for her husband, who sees himself "taking shape in her eyes" (*S*, p. 71) and who regards her as an extension of himself: "The two of them together would make one Jude" (*S*, p. 71). Nel's transfer of her symbiotic attachment from Sula to Jude severs the bond between the two girls that had supported both of them. From that point on, they are both partial people, each lacking emotionally what the other originally supplied. Nel participates in the orthodox rites of female maturation: marriage, maternity, childbirth, and—in the pattern typical of the relationships between men and women in the Bottom—abandonment by her husband, in this instance to the thrall of her best friend, Sula.

Sula never finds the other half of her equation again, although for a time she thinks that "Ajax" might occupy that role. Just before her death, she imagines curling into the "heavy softness" of water that might "envelop her, carry her, and wash her tired flesh always" (*S*, p. 128). The "sleep of water" for which she longs is an image of merging into the embracing womb, the mother from whom she has felt radically separated. The image is also linked with preceding events, including Chicken Little's drowning at Sula's hands and the death of Plum, who wanted to crawl back into his mother's womb.

In the same novel, the symbolic return to the womb is expressed on the communal level in the tragic ending to the parade on the Bottom's

135

last National Suicide Day. The people of the community, led to the river's edge by Shadrack, release their rage and anger at the unfinished tunnel—in the construction of which they were barred from employment—by destroying the bricks and timbers at the excavation site. Entering the tunnel, a number of them find themselves instead in a suffocating "chamber of water" (*S*, p. 139) created by the multiplied effect of their assault on the unstable structure in the warm mud. Like Chicken Little, they are swallowed by the river. Thus, Shadrack's vision of collective suicide is literally and tragically enacted.

The event illustrates one of Morrison's recurrent themes, that of energy and passion released self-destructively when there is no positive outlet for its expression. In *Song of Solomon* (1977), Ruth Dead, starved for a closeness and affection that she cannot find in the tyrannical and sexually unavailable Macon, nurses her youngest and only male child well past infancy. The mark of their unusually prolonged symbiotic attachment and merged psychological boundaries is preserved in his name, Milkman. During his childhood, Ruth's son "had never been . . . a separate real person. He had always been a passion." [17] Similarly, Milkman has never regarded his mother as "a person, a separate individual, with a life apart from allowing or interfering with his own" (*SOS*, p. 75). As further evidence of the boundary-blurring among the members of the Dead family, Milkman can scarcely distinguish his much older "baby doll" sisters from his mother (*SOS*, p. 68).

Moreover, Milkman's distorted view of women, derived from his autocratic father's attitude as well as from his clinging mother's and jealous sisters' behavior, warps his later attachments to women and his expectations of the world in general. In early adolescence, he is attracted to his second cousin, Pilate Dead's granddaughter, who is several years his senior. Pilate introduces Milkman to Hagar as her "brother" (*SOS*, p. 43); Hagar's eventual parasitic attachment to him thus figuratively replaces the symbiotic bond originating in Milkman's early attachment to his possessive mother.

Both emotionally dependent women, starved for a sense of their own being, need Milkman to validate their existence; yet for both, love is a prison because it is unreciprocated. Hagar claims that Milkman is her "'home in this world'"; Ruth Dead counters, "'And I am his.'" Pilate chides them both, "'He ain't a house, he's a man'" (*SOS*, p. 138). When Milkman leaves Hagar after more than a dozen years and she realizes that she can neither win him back nor successfully kill him, she dies of grief. Her actual death merely confirms the psychological void within her.

By contrast, Hagar's grandmother and Milkman's aunt, Pilate Dead, is dependently attached to no one. Born to her mother posthumously, she lacks a navel, the mark of each child's original symbiosis with its mother. Though the missing navel initially sets Pilate apart as a freak of nature, its absence represents her unique freedom from the emotional dependencies that characterize the other Dead women. It also makes people believe that Pilate has supernatural, perhaps even demonic, powers. In fact, her arcane knowledge of midwifery, her natural healing powers, her ability to distill wine from plants, her anomalous physical sign, her reputed capacity to "step out of her skin" (*SOS,* p. 94), and her ability to fly "without ever leaving the ground" (*SOS,* p. 340) suggest that she is a kind of benign witch.[18] Yet, although Pilate is Milkman's spiritual midwife, her own daughter and granddaughter are less clearly the beneficiaries of her nurturance; Hagar is fatally crippled by her need for a man to affirm her selfhood.

The metaphorical counterpart to symbiosis and merged boundaries is division, the imagery of which resonates on a number of levels in Morrison's fiction. As in the narratives of Margaret Atwood, "splitness" is a symptom of emotional or spiritual injury. Thus, Pecola Breedlove's division into two "selves" at the end of *The Bluest Eye* represents her inability to see herself as a whole person or, in fact, as a person at all. Soaphead Church's deception (a product of his own self-deception) destroys her last connection to being. Her desire for the most basic confirmation of self in the eyes of others drives her mad, as she splits into the girl with blue eyes and the one "friend" who can corroborate the miracle.

In several instances, division and splitness are dramatized as opposing values or capacities either within a single character or through characters who complement each other. In *Sula,* Sula Peace and Nel Wright are each half of a figurative whole self. Morrison has acknowledged that there is "a little bit of both in each of those two women, and . . . if they had been one person, I suppose they would have been a rather marvelous person. But each lacked something that the other one had."[19]

The girls' respective domiciles are analogues of both boundary and complementarity. While Nel and her mother reside in a compulsively orderly house with "real lace curtains at the window" (*S,* p. 15), Sula lives in a cluttered, "woolly" house of many rooms and stairways: "[T]here were three sets [of stairs] to the second floor—more rooms, doors and stoops. There were rooms that had three doors, others that opened out on the porch only and were inaccessible from any other part of the house; others that you could get to only by going through somebody's bedroom" (S, pp. 25–26). Sula loves the tidiness and material extravagance of Nel's house; Nel covets the disheveled atmosphere of Sula's, where there is more room for the unexpected. While Nel represents the orderly rationality of consciousness and repression, Sula embodies the darker, more mysterious and incongruous dimension of dreams and the unconscious.

When the two girls are separated by Nel's marriage to Jude, Sula ultimately becomes split off from her own feelings. Her moral torpor sets her apart, not only from other people's codes, but also from meaningful connection to them, except through her body. Spiritual lassitude takes the form of promiscuity, for like her mother, Sula's only means of self-verification is her sexuality. During lovemaking, she "needed to find the cutting edge. . . . [T]here was utmost irony and outrage in lying under someone, in a position of surrender, feeling her own abiding strength and limitless power. But the cluster did break, fall apart, and in her panic to hold it together she leaped from the edge into soundlessness and went down howling, howling in a stinging awareness of the endings of things: an eye of sorrow in the midst of all that hurricane rage of joy" (S, p. 106).

Her condition goes beyond loneliness, which assumes "the absence of other people," for "the solitude she found in that desperate terrain had never admitted the possibility of other people" (S, p. 106). Instead, pursuing temporary physical escapes from her inner void, she flirts carelessly and without premeditation with Nel's man, Jude. Unconsciously, her act is a kind of punishment of Nel for betraying the bond that joined the two of them as girls. The single encounter between Sula and Jude eventually destroys Nel's marriage because it introduces dissatisfaction and forbidden desire where satisfaction and complacency had previously reigned.

Heir to the sexual promiscuity of her mother and the indifference to social convention of her grandmother, Sula Peace is radically isolated, even though the community of the Bottom uneasily tolerates her presence. She is drawn to return to the Bottom after ten years because her community is the crucible of her identity. The "freedom" of radical separateness has become an even more oppressive prison; the void ultimately collapses inwardly upon itself. Split off from her feelings, Sula witnesses her death—as she has witnessed much of her life—as a curious but uncommitted observer. It surprises and amuses her that "'it didn't even hurt'" (*S*, p. 128). In the serene detachment of her dying, Sula finds the only real peace of her life.

Through Sula's death, however, her "other self" achieves a kernel of knowledge. Almost twenty-five years later, Eva Peace makes Nel recognize her deeper resemblance to Sula. The doughty matriarch has always believed that the two girls were "'just alike. . . . Never was no difference between you'" (*S*, p. 145). Nel initially rejects this identification, for, ever since she chose marriage to Jude and conventional life, she has regarded herself as different from the wayward, amoral Sula. Eva's words force her to acknowledge that her passivity and silence when Chicken Little drowned were in fact complicity in the event—no different from Sula's detachment as her mother burned.

The interwoven stories of Sula and Nel, of the Peace and Sabat matriarchies with their mixture of wild blood and tamed spirits, suggest that the limiting boundaries of race, class, and gender preclude all but a few narrow avenues to selfhood. In this narrative, the nascent self is represented as split: either suffocated into a repressive virtuousness (like Nel Wright) or drawn to pursue unconventional values (in the community's terms) and sensations that mimic real feeling but lead instead to literal immolation (Plum, Hannah) or emotional isolation (Sula). Nel's wail at the end of the narrative, a howl that has stuck in her throat since she lost both husband and friend years before, wordlessly expresses the sadness of the community of the Bottom and the inequities of the world itself. It is, appropriately, boundless, with "no bottom and . . . no top, just circles and circles of sorrow" (*S*, p. 149).

In Morrison's fiction, the larger divisions within a community are frequently represented through relationships between generations and contrasts between families. In *The Bluest Eye*, the economically and emotionally bankrupt Breedloves are figuratively set against the intact MacTeer family; Mrs. MacTeer's grudging love for her daughters exposes the absence of such affection in Pauline Breedlove's attitude toward Pecola. The Peace and Sabat matriarchies in *Sula* are developed through deliberate contrast; their different values shape Sula's and Nel's very different expectations for themselves.

The complementary families in *Song of Solomon* are both Deads: the self-negating family of Macon Dead and the life-affirming family of his own sister. Pilate Dead, born posthumously to her mother and orphaned in early childhood (her father was shot by whites greedy for his Virginia property), feels "cut off" from other people by her circumstances. Yet, unlike Pecola Breedlove or Sula Peace, her very separateness has led her to acquire a strong sense of her own self; she is set apart in a different sense. "[H]er alien's compassion for troubled people ripened her and— the consequence of the knowledge she had made up or acquired—kept her just barely within the boundaries of the elaborately socialized world of black people" (*SOS,* pp. 149–50).

In contrast to the passive Ruth Dead, Milkman's biological mother, Pilate is Milkman's spiritual mother, who is responsible for his very existence: when "only a miracle" could have produced pregnancy in Ruth (*SOS,* p. 211), Pilate had given her sister-in-law a concoction that had made her briefly both fertile and sexually irresistible to her cold husband, thus presiding over Milkman's very conception. She prevented Macon from killing the baby before it was born and aided Ruth during the delivery. As his spiritual midwife, Pilate enlarges the boundaries of Milkman's suffocating world by introducing him to the sky, "so that from then on when he looked at it, it . . . was intimate, familiar, like a room that he lived in, a place where he belonged" (*SOS,* p. 211). Eventually Milkman discovers the true family history through this woman who, though she lives in the present, is vitally in touch with the past. Milkman, by contrast, has virtually no understanding of the past but is obsessed with it, as indicated by his characteristic concentration on "things behind him. Almost as though there were no future to be had" (*SOS,* p. 35). Pilate's tutelage ultimately results in his liberation through knowledge of his real past, which frees him from his narcissism.

Milkman is aided in the discovery of both his manhood and his family history by another midwife, suggestively named Circe. Years before, this wise old crone, who seems to exist outside time and whose appearance suggests a witch out of Milkman's childhood nightmares, had presided at Pilate's birth from her dead mother. Like Pilate, Circe is also a natural healer who gives Milkman knowledge that is crucial to his discovery of his cultural heritage. Her instructions lead Milkman to the entrance into his ancestry: that most suggestive of female symbols, a cave—the very one in which his father and aunt had once huddled as children and the source of the fabled treasure. Milkman is on a treasure hunt, but the boon he finds is not the one for which he searches.

In *Tar Baby,* divisions operate simultaneously between families and generations. Jadine Childs is anomalously "split" between two pairs of figurative parents, one white and the other black. A quasi-member of both the Street and Childs families, she moves comfortably between black and white worlds and between America and Europe; she is more respectful of and socially at ease with the Streets, her financial benefactors, than with the aunt and uncle who reared and loved her. Through Jadine's brief but intense relationship with Son—a man from an economic and social strata that Jadine initially regards as beneath her—Morrison explores the implications of such psychological and cultural boundary-straddling.

Despite Jadine's apparent savoir faire, one image pointedly suggests her inner division and the vulnerability of her apparently supreme self-confidence. One day at a grocery store in Paris, Jadine had seen a tall "tar-black" woman with scarified cheeks, wearing a long canary-yellow dress. (In Morrison's novels, the most seductive, sexually free women, like Nel Wright's whore-grandmother, Rochelle, and Sula Peace's mother, Hannah, wear yellow dresses.) Jadine, struck as if in a vision, had watched this "woman's woman—that mother/sister/she" (*TB,* p. 46) as she left the market with three eggs balanced in her hand and had followed her with her eyes "all the way to the edge of the world" (*TB,* p. 46). From that location the woman had, inscrutably, spat upon the pavement.

In her incongruity, the woman is a manifestation of Jadine's alter ego: beneath Jade's regal elegance lie a fear of her ancestral African roots and contempt for her social inferiors, as well as anxiety about her female role and her sexuality. The woman in yellow had made Jade feel "lonely and inauthentic" (*TB,* p. 48). Morrison has explained the figure of the woman in yellow as "the original self—the self that we betray when we lie, the one that is always there. . . . [O]ne measures one's other self against it." [20] Ironically, it is the crude, small-town Son who reaches through Jadine's affectations and, for a time, brings out the authentic self restrained beneath her cool hauteur. Yet one of Jade's first reactions to Son—in response to a sexual insult—is to spit at him, in unconscious imitation of the mysterious tar-black woman in yellow.

The splits within and constrictions of the personality as the indirect but terrible result of racism and cultural oppression are dramatized throughout Morrison's fiction. Frequently, her male characters are depicted as infantilized by their position on the fringes of white culture, which dictates their exclusion from all but the most menial forms of employment and self-respect. In *The Bluest Eye,* the first of Cholly Breedlove's "emasculations" (*BE,* p. 37) occurs when, during his initiatory sexual experience, he and the girl are discovered by white men who force the pair to continue at gunpoint for the latters' amusement. From that humiliation, his attitude toward female sexuality is tainted with a mixture of furtiveness, shame, and anger. In the same novel, Soaphead Church is a pedophile; little girls are the only sexual objects who do not threaten his fragile and sterile masculinity.

Additionally infantilized by their often marginal position in a strongly female world, most of the male characters in the novels remain "Sons" or boys, with indicative names like Tar Baby (in *Sula*), a man who can't give up the bottle—in this case, alcohol; and Boy Boy, Eva Peace's husband, who abandons her and their three small children for another woman. Even the little boy whom Sula inadvertently drowns has the diminuitive name of Chicken Little.

The men who actually couple with women are either ineffectual shadows, womanizers, or deserters: from the MacTeers' roomer in *The Bluest Eye*—Mr. Henry, who fraternizes with prostitutes and tries to fondle Frieda MacTeer—to the men of *Sula*—Helene Wright's husband, who vanishes, and Hannah's, who dies three years after siring Sula. The one man whom Sula loves, Ajax, seems to diverge from this pattern; however, as soon as Ajax feels the tug toward permanence, he flees, afraid of relinquishing his maternally cushioned boyhood. Son, the central male character of *Tar Baby*, is an emotionally strong man. Yet his anomalous position is underscored by his status as a man on the lam—his wife's infidelity drove him to accidental homicide—who, finally, has no place to flee except into a legendary past.

The young Milkman Dead of *Song of Solomon* is, for much of his childhood and youth, infantilized by his mother and indulged to the point of satiety by women who adore him and prostrate themselves on his behalf. Accustomed to receiving without giving, he is, like many of the males in Morrison's fiction, allowed to stretch his "carefree boyhood out for thirty-one years" (*SOS*, p. 98). At the same time he is belittled by his cold father and patronized or deeply resented by his elder female siblings, who loathe his privileged maleness. His father, who eventually grudgingly gives Milkman a role in his exploitative business dealings, regards his son as an extension of his own needs, just as the Dead women do.

Morrison implies that if the enveloping white world does not emasculate or infantilize black men, it turns them into Macon Deads, imitators of the most deadening values of white patriarchal society: greed, acquisitiveness, and dominion. Milkman Dead, surrounded by a self-absorbed father and self-effacing or rejecting females, grows up in an exaggerated patriarchal microcosm. However, *Song of Solomon* ultimately provides a distinct contrast to the situation of male characters in the earlier novels, for Morrison makes the infantilized male not only the protagonist but the eventual bearer of knowledge for his community.

Several of Morrison's characters are not only emotionally maimed, as these infantilized male figures suggest, but also literally stunted. The recurrent imagery of deformity and mutilation visually represents the injurious effects of oppression and marginalization, whether resulting from gender, ethnic minority identity, economic circumstance, or their cumulative consequences. Such images or episodes also signal the distortion, violation, or confusion of boundaries of the self or body, as perceived by either the individuals or those who interact with them. Pecola Breedlove's madness in *The Bluest Eye* is the most pronounced manifestation of the difficulty of achieving autonomy in conditions that mitigate absolutely against it. In *Sula*, Shadrack, who walks through Medallion with his genitals exposed, acts out the corresponding psychological emasculation and impotence of his male peers.

The young Claudia MacTeer of *The Bluest Eye* registers the knowledge of exclusion through contempt for the alien objects of her childhood: Shirley Temple milk mugs and white baby dolls for Christmas. Through these emblems, she slowly becomes aware of herself as an outsider. Sensitive to the insult in the presumption that what every girl child desired was "a blue-eyed, yellow-haired, pink-skinned doll" (*BE*, p. 20), she mutilates her dolls and feels—with horror—the same impulse toward little white girls (*BE*, p. 22).

In fact, the figurative mutilation functions in the other direction. As Claudia inevitably accommodates herself to "reality," she learns to do as little black girls (and, more broadly, as most members of oppressed groups who recognize the terms of their survival) traditionally have done: to suppress indignation and affect "fraudulent love" (*BE*, p. 22). Her recognition that such gestures are adjustments "without improvement" (*BE*, p. 22) spares her from total acquiescence to oppression.

In the same novel, each member of the Breedlove family, though alienated from the others, is symbolically linked to the others by various signs of literal or spiritual injury. Pecola's father, Cholly, born a bastard, was left to die by a crazy mother; a more compassionate great-aunt rescued him from abandonment and raised him until, when he was fourteen, she died. He later locates the man he believes is his biological father and is stunned when his putative relative disavows any tie. Bereft of all emotional connection, Cholly wanders about the country as a "free" man, free only in the sense that he is at the bottom, where there is nothing left to lose. In his world, even God is a "nice old white man" with blue eyes (*BE*, p. 106).

Radically disconnected from family or community, Cholly is another of Morrison's cultural orphans. He drifts through life until he meets Pauline, a woman with a physical deformity that parallels his emotional one. Because of her crippled foot, Pauline fears that no man will ever be able to love her; she blames her "general feeling of separateness and unworthiness" on her deformity (*BE*, p. 88). Appearance becomes the false measure of inner worth. Not surprisingly, the two soul-crushed people find solace and even grateful regard in one another.

Their daughter Pecola's inner crippling, begun at her birth with Pauline's declaration of her ugliness, is reinforced as she approaches puberty. When her first menstrual period begins, she believes she is dying; she learns from the MacTeer girls that "ministratin'" (*BE*, p. 25) means that she can generate life. While Claudia and Frieda regard their guest's acquisition of womanhood with envy and awe, the blood Pecola sheds is more accurately a foreshadowing of her spiritual wounding. Her poignant response to the explanation of how babies are created is to wonder, "'[H]ow do you get somebody to love you?'" (*BE*, p. 29). During that same year she is sexually violated and impregnated by her own father, whose unpremeditated but shocking act is depicted as a misdirected expression of his love for her.

Pecola's wounding is advanced by another morally deformed member of the community. Soaphead Church, a man of mixed blood, is a fraudulent "spiritual advisor" to troubled souls. Though he prides himself on his sexual restraint, in his own way he is more destructive than the weak but essentially amoral Cholly Breedlove. Manipulating Pecola's faith in miracles and pressing her to commit a debased act on his behalf by poisoning his landlady's aged dog, he violates her spiritual innocence as surely as her father abuses her physical innocence. By the age that most girls reach sexual maturity, Pecola is already a lost soul, imprisoned in a madness from which she can never flee.

In *Song of Solomon,* most members of the central family are, as their surname hints, spiritually maimed if not dead. Macon Dead, whose entire name is a pun, is a merciless, materialistic slum landlord who reigns over his family as he does his tenants, as an unfeeling autocrat. The members of his family limp through life, each in some crucial way incomplete. The youngest Dead and only son, Milkman, has an actual limp caused by one slightly shorter leg. However, the narrator informs us, "The deformity was mostly in his mind" (*SOS*, p. 62). Macon's two daughters are pathetic, emotionally stunted women. Like fairy-tale sisters awaiting the prince who might free them from the prison of their father's house, they occupy themselves by making fake rose petals out of velvet. Late in her life, the daughter named Corinthians finally is rescued by a man whose affection allows her to replace her false vanity with authentic self-esteem.

In fact, nearly all the females in *Song of Solomon*, except for the indomitable Pilate Dead, are clinging, self-effacing women who are easily humiliated or exploited by men. Ruth Foster Dead, daughter of the town's most successful black doctor and wife of one of its most successful businessmen, lived as a child in "a great big house that pressed [her] into a small package" (*SOS*, p. 124). As an adult woman still occupying that same house, Ruth resembles the domestically confined women of Penelope Mortimer's narratives, finding the patriarchal mansion "more prison than palace" (*SOS*, p. 9), as do her daughters.

Maiming and injury become self-inflicted in *Sula,* as the hint of self-mutilation and dismemberment resonates through the Peace family. Eva Peace, the enigmatic matriarch, is an ambiguous agent of both good and evil who destroys or outlives all three of her children as well as her sole grandchild, Sula. Possessed of only one leg—but a "magnificent" one (*S*,

p. 27)—she is a grotesque but charismatic woman, around whom circle various tales concerning the loss, or perhaps the sale, of the missing limb. Sula's impulsive slashing off of a finger tip with a kitchen knife, to show her confidence when challenged by young white boys, is another manifestation of self-mutilation (*S,* p. 46), as is her mother Hannah's bizarre death by fire.

In *Tar Baby,* the lonely and emotionally stunted Margaret Street had, years before, sadistically abused her infant son, Michael. As Ondine Childs describes it, she had "'cut him up. You cut your baby up. Made him bleed for you. For fun you did it. Made him scream, you, you freak. . . .' Ondine addressed the others, still shouting. 'She stuck pins in his behind. Burned him with cigarettes. Yes, she did, I saw her; I saw his little behind. She burned him!'" (*TB,* p. 208). Ondine has kept this monstrous knowledge to herself for fear that she and Sydney would be "let go" if the truth were exposed.

When people are dehumanized by poverty, prejudice, or restricted opportunity for growth of the self, the capacity for relationship may be radically perverted. In Morrison's fiction, a central and recurring representation of emotional injury as well as violation of the boundaries of selfhood is the distortion of the bonds of affection between people. When such emotional disruption occurs between members of the same family—in several instances involving the abuse of a child by the parent (or another adult) of the opposite sex—the attachment is particularly destructive. Generally the abuse is symptomatic of disturbed family relationships as well as of a parent's excessive dependence upon a child for emotional release from intolerable circumstances.

In each of Morrison's novels to date, that perversion of the affections is dramatized through the family crime of incest. In most of the instances of incestuous attachment or possession, it is the parent's own restricted possibility for growth that precipitates the sexual or physical violation of a child of the opposite sex. The parent oversteps the very psychological boundaries that the child has formed in the process of separation from her or him.

Morrison has claimed that "love or its absence" is one of her central themes: under the name of love, "[P]eople do all sorts of things. . . . The violence is a distortion of what, perhaps, we want to do."[21] In this sense, *The Bluest Eye* is a narrative of both violence and violation—not only of the female body but of potentiality and growth of the self as well as the affections and attachments between human beings. Incest and rape become metaphors for both black and white nightmares of inverted love and suffocation of selfhood.

In that novel, father–daughter incest occurs through Cholly Breedlove's unpremeditated sexual violation of his daughter, Pecola. Even in the MacTeers' emotionally intact household, Claudia and Frieda see their father naked one night and feel "the shame brought on by the absence of shame" (*BE*, p. 59). Mr. Henry, their debonair boarder, fondles Frieda; Soaphead Church's pedophilic fondness for little girls is another expression of the inversion or misplacement of desire, affection, and sexuality itself.

In *Sula*, Eva's only son, Plum, is literally consumed by the power of sexuality that lacks an appropriate outlet. When he returns from the war, mentally broken like Shadrack, to live a mindless, lethargic existence in his mother's house, Eva takes things into her own hands. Finding him one night in his room in his customary drugged, babylike state, she cradles him gently, then douses him with kerosene and sets him afire.

Plum's infantile state externalizes the condition of many of the men of the Bottom who can never be more than "boys" in their world circumscribed by white culture. Eva later explains to her daughter Hannah that Plum had wanted to "crawl back into [her] womb." As she continues,

> I ain't got the room no more even if he could do it. . . . I had room enough in my heart, but not in my womb. . . . I couldn't birth him twice. I'd be laying here at night and he'd be downstairs in that room, but when I closed my eyes I'd see him . . . and he'd be creepin' to the bed trying to spread my legs trying to get back up in my womb. . . . I kept on dreaming it. . . . One night it wouldn't be no dream. It'd be true and I would have done it, would have let him if I'd've had the room. . . . I had to keep him out so I just thought of a way he could die like a man not all scrunched up inside my womb, but like a man. (*S*, p. 62)

Eva is so eloquent in her own defense that the reader is almost persuaded that the incest wish is Plum's. However, taken in context with her other actions, it is clearly Eva's own unacceptable desire—her fear that one night she "would have let him"—that corroborates Plum's infantilized state and fuels his destruction. The shocking infanticide is neither the first nor the last of her almost Godlike manipulations of others' lives.[22]

The incest theme in *Song of Solomon* is expressed through the lonely Ruth Dead, whose attachments to both her father and her son reflect an exaggerated intensity. Though her father had felt her ecstasy at his kisses as excessive, he had delivered both her daughters at their births, to her husband's repugnance. According to Macon Dead, Ruth had lain naked next to the body of her father after he expired. Ruth later gives Milkman a less sensational interpretation of this event. Yet even after her father's death, she expresses feelings toward him more characteristic of a romantic lover; still defining herself as her "daddy's daughter" (*SOS,* p. 67), she worships at his grave several times a year. Ruth's son, Milkman, only belatedly overcomes the exaggerated maternal attachment encoded in his name.

In *Tar Baby,* the incest wish is implied in the relationship between Margaret Street and her son. Margaret lives, like Ruth Dead, in a patriarchal mansion, feeling "drowned . . . in the spaciousness of that house" (*TB,* p. 58). Also like Ruth, Margaret is caught in a loveless marriage and seeks in her son the intimacy she is unable to find with her husband. She unconsciously desires as a lover the son she had abused during his infancy, while priding herself on what she believes is an unpossessive maternal attitude: "[Of] all the people she knew in the world, [Michael] seemed to her the best. . . . She liked his company, to talk to him, to be around him. Not because he is my son, she told herself . . . but because he is interesting and he thinks I am interesting too. I am special to him. Not as a mother, but as a person. Just as he is to me" (*TB,* p. 60). The incestuous quality of her affection is further implied by her desire to live near, or even with, her son rather than her husband.

Margaret's self-justifying response to the disclosure of her earlier abuses of her child reveals her terrible loneliness and emotional insufficiency. As a baby, Michael had imposed his devouring infant needs upon a mother incapable of meeting her own needs for affection. The infant's "implicit and explicit demand for her best and constant self" could never be appeased. "She could not describe her loathing of its prodigious appetite for security. . . . [W]hen she felt hostage to that massive insolence, that stupid trust, she could not help piercing it" (*TB,* p. 236). The ambiguous pronoun "it" indicates the extent to which the baby Michael had been an object, not a person, to Margaret: seen as a part of herself, he was the object upon whom she had projected her self-hatred and self-estrangement.

Though Valerian Street (whose very name indicates his narcotized existence) cannot admit that his own emotional sterility has contributed to Margaret's loneliness and the perversion of her affections, at least he acknowledges that there was "something in the crime of innocence so revolting it paralyzed him. . . . What an awful thing she had done. And how much more awful not to have known it. . . . He was guilty, therefore, of innocence" (*TB*, pp. 242–43). Implicitly, it is this same false innocence that masks Valerian's patronizing attitude toward his dependent black retainers with the pointed surname, Childs.

The representation of boundary is amplified on the collective level in Morrison's characterization of the terms within and against which a black community defines itself. In each of her narratives, a community functions as a moral arbiter, the source of both individual and group norms. Her characters are defined in part through their acceptance of or challenge to certain collective presumptions. Conversely, as a kind of collective conscience, the community either includes or excludes its members on the basis of their accordance with its implicit—though frequently contradictory—values. Thus, separation and division are not only psychological processes but often also social ones, as the figure of the pariah is set apart from the community.

In *The Bluest Eye,* the community is the backdrop to the lives of Claudia and Frieda MacTeer and the Breedlove family, asserting itself primarily in its moral castigation of the Breedloves' misfortunes. Thus, at the end of the retrospective chronicle of Pecola Breedlove's—and the narrator's own—loss of innocence, Claudia MacTeer describes Pecola picking her way "among all the waste and beauty of the world—which is what she herself was. All of our waste which we dumped on her and which she absorbed. And all of our beauty, which was hers first and which she gave to us. . . . Even her waking dreams we used—to silence our own nightmares. And she let us, and thereby deserved our contempt. We honed our egos on her, padded our characters with her frailty, and yawned in the fantasy of our strength" (*BE*, p. 159). Thus is collective anger at the restriction of possibility within a community projected onto its weakest member.

Claudia's words also suggest the way in which the community regards Pecola and her family as tainted—the moral equivalent of "ugly." During the course of the narrative, both Pecola and her father literally soil them-

149

selves: the young Cholly's bowels release when his putative father denies his connection; Pecola stains her dress with the blood of her first menstruation. In traditional societies, such body discharges are associated with pollution and are thus both dangerous and magical.[23] Julia Kristeva's observations on their symbolic aspects may be pertinently applied to images in Morrison's text:

> Excrement and its equivalents (decay, infection, disease, corpse, etc.) stand for the danger to identity that comes from without: the ego threatened by the non-ego, society threatened by its outside, life by death. Menstrual blood, on the contrary, stands for the danger issuing from within the identity (social or sexual); it threatens the relationship between the sexes within a social aggregate and, through internalization, the identity of each sex in the face of sexual difference.[24]

In Morrison's novel, both Cholly and Pecola transgress the social and sexual boundary between allowed and forbidden behavior; however, it is Pecola, the victim, who is punished. Her almost ritual function as the community's scapegoat is prefigured early in the narrative, when her male peers dance "a macabre ballet around the victim [Pecola], whom, for their own sake, they were prepared to sacrifice to the flaming pit" (*BE,* p. 55). Like the sacrificial figures of myth and legend, Pecola is nullifed as a condition of the community's purgation of anxiety and guilt generated by the threat of female sexuality, the violation of blood relationship, and the failure of sympathy. People hate and fear her as a symbol of what they might become themselves and therefore cannot dare to pity.

Claudia and her sister, in tribute to their inarticulate awareness that Pecola is the scapegoat for her community's deepest fears and anxieties about both blackness and sexuality, offer up their own magical sacrifice to nature: "'And when [the marigold seeds] come up, we'll know everything is all right'" (*BE,* p. 149). But of course the seeds, like Pecola and her baby, fail to thrive. Claudia compares Pecola with the moribund seeds: a stunted, deprived potentiality of nature, suffocated before she could blossom. Indeed, nature itself seems poised against those at the very bottom of the social order, buried so deeply that they cannot thrive. As the adult Claudia muses, "This soil is bad for certain kinds of flowers. Certain seeds it will not nurture, certain fruit it will not bear, and when the land kills of its own volition, we acquiesce and say the victim has no right to live. We are wrong, of course . . ." (*BE,* p. 160).

Pecola Breedlove is cut off from community in several senses. Even before she is sexually violated, her father consigns his family to a life "outside"; in a typical drunken rage, he almost burns their shelter down, thus forfeiting all responsibility for its occupants. Pecola's homelessness in the world becomes not only a spiritual but a literal state. Claudia MacTeer, whose family takes Pecola in for a few days, recognizes the horror of the other girl's situation: "Outdoors was the end of something, an irrevocable, physical fact, defining and complementing our metaphysical condition" (*BE,* p. 18). Kathryn Allen Rabuzzi, in her analysis of the symbolism of "home," suggests that "so far beyond the pale of acceptability is homelessness to most people that those who lack homes are perceived as severely threatening to those who have them." [25] Though Morrison's Pecola fatefully returns to her own family (such as it is), who live in an abandoned store, she remains essentially "outdoors"—outside the boundaries of community—for the remainder of her tragic life.

In this latter sense, the Deads of *Song of Solomon* are, although not physically homeless, psychically dislocated from "home"; it is not entirely clear how the family got from Virginia to Michigan. Instructively, Morrison describes their geographical location in terms that mirror their inner boundary confusions and psychological enclosure. They share the experience of people living in the Great Lakes region who are "confused by their place on the country's edge—an edge that is border but not coast. They seem to be able to live a long time believing, as coastal people do, that they are at the frontier where final exit and fatal escape are the only journeys left" (*SOS,* p. 163).

Only Pilate Dead, who has a strong interest in geography, possesses a positive sense of her self in relation to place. As she reminisces, "'Everyplace I went I got me a rock'" (*SOS,* p. 142). This orientation to the earth and its geography is an important stimulus for Milkman's quest for a place in the world. Pilate is his "pilot"; his journey ultimately leads him back to the South and to his historical community—the land from which Pilate's rocks originate.

In *Sula,* the community of the Bottom, in a northern Ohio town called Medallion, is not only a place but a presence—a kind of collective conscience that arbitrates the social and moral norms of its members. Functioning as a life-sustaining structure for its members, it tolerates certain kinds of eccentricity, believing that magic, dreams, and inexplicable forces operate in unpredictable ways. Yet it is also punitive to those who step absolutely outside the boundaries of the communally acceptable. As Morrison has remarked, "It seems to me there were more excesses in women and men [in the past], and people accepted them as they don't now. In the black community where I grew up, there were eccentricity and freedom, less conformity in individual habits—but close conformity in terms of the survival of the village, of the tribe."[26]

Thus, in *Sula* such eccentrics as the crazy Shadrack, a victim of both physical and mental wounds from his service in the First World War, is tolerated by the community in his performance of his bizarre annual rite, "National Suicide Day." While the ritual functions for him as a way to "order and focus" his own inner chaos (*S*, p. 12), it incidentally offers a visible reminder for the community of its own aggressive and self-destructive urges. "Once the people understood the boundaries and nature of [Shadrack's] madness, they could fit him, so to speak, into the scheme of things" (*S*, p. 13).

It is the community of Medallion as much as Sula who is the central "character" of *Sula*. As Morrison has elaborated elsewhere, "[W]hen I wrote *Sula* I was interested in making the town, the community, the neighborhood, as strong a character as I could."[27] The perspective on events is that of the Bottom; when Sula disappears for ten years, no details of her life are confirmed. When she returns, the inhabitants of the community are convinced that she is a source of evil, for she sleeps not only with the women's husbands but, it is rumored, with white men. She is perceived as far more dangerous than someone like Shadrack because she actively threatens the defenses against moral and social transgression that lie hidden in the souls of most people.

No one realizes that Sula's apparent invulnerability masks an acute loneliness and emotional aridity. Dissociated from the values of "neighborhood" or community, she becomes dissociated from herself. Like Pecola Breedlove, Sula provides a negative energy against which members of the community test their own values, a screen upon which they project their needs and fears. As Nel ironically describes Sula's magic (before her friend's betrayal), "Sula never competed; she simply helped others define themselves" (*S*, p. 82). Also like Pecola, Sula is the community's pariah, one who lives out (and dies for) the restriction of possibility of an entire group. As the narrator phrases it, "Had [Sula] anything to engage her tremendous curiosity and her gift for metaphor, she might have exchanged the restlessness and preoccupation with whim for an activity that provided her with all she yearned for. And like any artist with no art form, she became dangerous" (*S*, p. 105).

Both *The Bluest Eye* and *Sula* are narratives of female education and concomitant loss of innocence. The metamorphoses in the lives of the several young girls of the two novels reverberate through the entire communities of which they are a part. In each novel, one female becomes an outcast against whom the group reasserts its values: each is viewed as "evil" because she transgresses, whether willingly or not, the social and sexual mores of her community. *Song of Solomon* and *Tar Baby* extend Morrison's exploration of the vital relationship between the individual and the group. However, in these latter narratives the conflict is dramatized through characters who bear their communities' moral and cultural contradictions more overtly within themselves.

A central manifestation of these contradictions is encoded in names. During the slave era when black families were inhumanly separated, retaining one's true name became a crucial means of keeping track, not simply of identity, but also of place of origin and family bloodline. In this context, Morrison has remarked, "If you come from Africa, your name is gone. It is particularly problematic because it is not just *your* name but your family, your tribe. When you die, how can you connect with your ancestors if you have lost your name? That's a huge psychological scar."[28]

In *Song of Solomon*, Pilate Dead wears her name, in her father's handwriting, as tangible proof of "where she came from": a literal possession connected to her flesh by an earring made out of a box. Milkman's eventual discovery of his grandparents' real names and their ancestry is central to his own self-discovery and achievement of manhood. In fact, his is the most problematic name in the novel. "Dead" suggests the spiritual torpor Milkman must overcome in order to live as an independent man; it also connects him through his father's line to patriarchy itself, with its valuation not of affiliation but of "owning, building, acquiring" (*SOS*, p. 304). Additionally, it is a reminder of the white world's control over black people, for the first Macon Dead's (Milkman's grandfather's) name is the result of a white man's error. The nickname "Milkman" encodes a relationship with his mother of both sustenance and suffocation. Neither is his "true" name; one signifies surfeit and indulgence, the other non-being. Milkman's task is the reconciliation of his two names and the discovery of his true identity behind them.

Names are important, not only as ironic comments on the characters who bear them, but as emblems of the black community's resistance to the white culture's negation of its world. In *Song of Solomon,* locations like Not Doctor Street and No Mercy Hospital (where, until Ruth Dead's son was born, black people were denied admittance) are forms of counternegation of the white world that delimits the black one. It is a measure of women's marginal place within that world that their names are picked by their parents at random from the Bible, whereas many of the men have names that signify functions, trades, places, or objects—all indicators of a public identity.

Milkman's escape from Deadness begins with a literal flight, as he traverses the invisible boundary between North and South in an airplane. In tidewater Virginia, his family's ancestral land, Milkman gradually assembles the diverse pieces of the puzzle of his ancestry, using the names, both true and false, of people in his family as a key. As he restores the corrupted version of a rhythmic childhood chant about the mythical flight of Solomon, he also restores his link to his cultural community by recovering its history.

The collective memory Milkman eventually reconstructs concerns his great-grandfather Solomon/Shalimar, the fabled patriarch of the family, who "flew" back to Africa, leaving his devastated wife and twenty-one children behind. Such stories are part of black American folklore, preserving the dream of rising above the brutal conditions of slavery by escape to Africa, of transcending the literal boundaries of servitude.[29] Flight suggests liberation, whether literal or spiritual; thus, death is one kind of escape or flight and the Dead family name preserves this meaning, though in a corrupted sense.

Morrison's latter two novels both conclude with the equivocal image of flight. Through that image, both narratives explore the conflict between the need for personal autonomy and the temptation of escape from moral responsibility to others, though they implicitly reach different resolutions. In *Song of Solomon,* Milkman's ancestor escaped from slavery by flying away. Yet for those left behind, his flight created further suffering. In a sense, his miraculous escape was irresponsible in the same way that

Milkman's treatment of Hagar was; in the pursuit of his own desires, each left a legacy of misery. In recognizing this correspondence, Milkman realizes how his self-preoccupation and lack of empathy have caused others harm. As he learns through Pilate, acts have consequences for which one must take responsibility; her death is the price he must pay in return for that very knowledge. In fact, two women die in order for Milkman to overcome "Deadness": to come alive as a free—and responsible—agent in his own destiny and to affirm the reciprocal values of the community.

Milkman has inherited his father's and his mother's versions of the Deads' lives; each version contradicts the other, and Pilate's contradicts both. Only as he synthesizes these stories of his family and his past can he construct his own version of the "real." The "Song of Solomon" that he reconstructs commemorates his ancestor's refusal to be owned. However, the true measure of Milkman's own liberation is his recognition that such passion for freedom must be tempered with concern for its effect on others.

He thus unites the complementary strands of moral orientation that, as Carol Gilligan has illuminatingly proposed, have characteristically been gender-defined: the male emphasis on rights and the female emphasis on responsibility to others.[30] Though feminist readers have expressed disappointment with Morrison for making her hero male rather than female,[31] it is equally noteworthy that the author portrays a hero who achieves manhood by assimilating a traditionally female moral perspective into his previously limited vision. Milkman Dead ultimately combines in himself the truths of both patriarchal and matriarchal sides of his heritage: the history of "names" leads him to discover his own identity; the sacrifices on his behalf by Pilate and others generate his new sense of himself as part of a community to which he belongs by virtue of reciprocal responsibility.

Owning his soul, Milkman frees himself to test the possibility that "[i]f you surrendered to the air, you could *ride* it" (*SOS*, p. 341, emphasis in original). In accomplishing "flight," he surrenders his destructive need to be either infantilized or worshipped by women; he heals the rift in himself and, by extension, his community, by fusing the separate truths of male and female moral knowledge. Morrison's story thus articulates a history of separations and re-connections: black culture's radical and involuntary separation from its roots and the hero's personal odyssey of re-engagement. "Boundary," in the senses of both geographical and psychological orientation in the world, is recovered when the hero affirms the genealogy and meaning of his true name.

Song of Solomon is Morrison's most positive depiction of the values of community as a crucial balance between individual liberation and reciprocal obligation, as well as her most artistically accomplished narrative. In *Tar Baby*, the theme of cultural displacement assumes another, somewhat less aesthetically satisfying, expression. Jadine Childs and Son Green regard themselves as cultural orphans, outsiders, neither defined nor limited by the boundaries of black American life. Both try to locate themselves within an ethnic tradition that is multiple and varied; each is forced to confront the meaning of the past and the possibilities of the future; each considers the values of a complex heritage that simultaneously coexists with and opposes the dominant power structure.

Son is characterized as an anomaly, a raw, "natural" man, unpolished but also unscarred by limits, conventions, and compromises. Because of a crime he committed as a result of circumstances that many would regard as almost justifiable provocation, he is a fugitive; he is pointedly "without human rites: unbaptised, uncircumcised, minus puberty rites or the formal rites of manhood. Unmarried and undivorced. He had attended no funeral, married in no church, raised no child. Propertyless, homeless, sought for but not after" (*TB,* pp. 165–66). In his elemental form (symbolically, he emerges from out of the sea or the darkness, or appears as a shadowy reflection in a mirror), he becomes Jadine's tutor, presiding over her temporary immersion in the black culture from which she is estranged.

Like the "good colored girls" of *The Bluest Eye,* who mask their funkiness in order to edge up into the white world's greater opportunities, Jadine initially wants nothing to do with a man who reminds her of what she is grateful to have left behind. Son's elemental rawness alarms her, threatens her sense of civilized restraint. She sees him through the eyes of both sets of her "parents," fearing his aggressive eroticism much as Margaret Street does and loathing his unkempt, animal-like appearance as Ondine and Sydney do. Yet his crudity not only repels but attracts her.

Son is as disgusted with Jade's smug sophistication as she is with his uncut-diamond image. He even calls her a "white girl" because she has sold herself to white values and attitudes toward beauty, sexuality, and money. However, the sheer attraction of opposites temporarily overrides these intellectual resistances. On a picnic they take together, Jade, wearing her "Easter white cotton [dress]—all temptation and dare" (*TB*, p. 168), falls into a pit of tar pitch. In this almost too obviously symbolic scene, Jade's "whiteness" is literally immersed in blackness. Predictably, not long afterwards Jade falls in love with Son.

Like medieval courtly lovers, the two become exclusively absorbed in each other. Jade is nurtured by Son's devotion and care, and comes to feel herself "unorphaned" (*TB*, p. 229) but also emotionally vulnerable. Their courtship is that of the city mouse and the country mouse. The true gap between them is suggested by the geographical distance each must travel to live in the other's world: Jade introduces Son to New York and Son takes Jade to Eloe, Florida, the small, conservative community that he fondly calls home.

To Jade, Son's community is suffocatingly provincial and his friends are uneducated inferiors, "a pack of Neanderthals who think sex is dirty or strange" (*TB*, p. 257). Yet Jadine associates sexuality with animality and is equally concerned to keep her own eroticism "rein[ed] in" (*TB*, p. 124). Son's peers regard Jade as his prize woman, as if "she was a Cadillac he had won, or stolen, or even bought for all they knew" (*TB*, p. 254). Though this view offends Jade, it is no different an image than the one she consciously cultivates in her life as a model.

In resisting Eloe, Jade believes that what she is rejecting is the women who haunt her dreams, a "coven" of women who have "nothing to show but breasts" (*TB*, p. 262). The real nature of her conflict is both personal and cultural: the struggle within herself for who and what she is, and a contest of wills between her and Son to claim "authentic" black values; each lover implicitly questions whether the other is "really a member of the tribe."[32] Each attempts to pull the other "away from the maw of hell. . . . One had a past, the other a future[,] and each one bore the culture to save the race in his hands. Mama-spoiled black man, will you mature with me? Culture-bearing black woman, whose culture are you bearing?" (*TB*, p. 269).

The lovers' ecstatic but doomed connection symbolizes a kind of radical division between the educated and the uneducated; between power and powerlessness; and between urbanity, material well-being, rationality, and privilege on the one hand and emotional intensity, provincial values, and spiritual well-being on the other. Both protagonist and antagonist struggle to identify themselves within and against these competing claims. In the rather too programmatic clash of wills and beliefs,[33] Morrison examines the gap between outsiders and insiders, education and cultural rootedness, and competing definitions of authenticity within black experience.

Though the relationship between Jade and Son suggests a dialectical tension between opposites, a synthesis is never achieved. In fact, such diametrically opposing values are rarely reconciled except in the symbolic terms of myth and legend, and it is through those that Morrison equivocatingly concludes her narrative. In the folk tale of Tar Baby, Bre'r Rabbit is enmeshed in the deceptive lure but uses his wits to extricate himself and regain his freedom.[34] In Morrison's novel, Son cites the story to illustrate his contention that women like Jadine are tar babies—ensnarers of black men. Convinced of the necessity for preserving the traditional culture, he regards the tar baby as the white world's corrupting lure for upwardly mobile black people. Once they are caught by the lure of affluence, they become psychologically and materially enslaved. For Jade, spoiled by the worldly pleasures that beauty, education, privilege, and money can buy, the tar baby is the "coven" of women who would ensnare her in domestic, sexual, and procreative functions—much as, earlier in the narrative, she is mired in the swampy tar pit.

To a certain extent, the conflict symbolized in the image of the tar baby transcends its ethnic sources. The tar baby is that which would ensnare and overwhelm one, threaten one's ego boundaries and one's efforts at separation from the forces, whether external or internal, that might engulf the self. It is that shadowy aspect of the Other that must be confronted as a prelude to authenticity and autonomy.

The symbolism of the tar baby is not clarified by the novel's end. Morrison has remarked elsewhere that "the tar baby came to mean the black woman who can hold things together."[35] Yet the novel does not entirely fulfill this sense and thus fails to resolve the set of tensions the author has dramatized. One questions whether Jade's encounter with Son so changes her that she relinquishes her narcissistic self-worship to become a hardworking "queen ant" struggling for the survival of her people. Instead, her flight from Son and both sets of her "parents" seems an ironic inversion of Milkman Dead's flight into authenticity and a return to her self-indulgent life.

In giving the narrative's final scene to Son, Morrison brackets Jadine's flight and comments on it with his. In one of two narrative "parentheses" that enclose the numbered chapters,[36] Son returns to Dominique, hoping to regain Jadine, even at the expense of Eloe and what it signifies. But his willing sacrifice never takes place; Jadine has already departed, and another kind of sacrifice is intended for him. He enters the darkness from which he emerged at the beginning, to be symbolically absorbed into the legend of the mythical horsemen descended from African slaves: elemental, inhuman powers of the universe. Like the Son of God, whose image is suggested in his generic name and in his appearance at the pointedly named L'Arbe de la Croix, he eventually becomes the scapegoat for the internal contradictions of a cultural group.

The figure of the pariah is clearly central to Morrison's vision, as the emblem of different levels and forms of exclusion. In her fiction, the community is understood as both a specific social structure—the vehicle through which behavior is expressed and reinforced—and a set of values (frequently contradictory) operating within that structure. As the author has remarked in this context, "The black community is a pariah community. Black people are pariahs. The civilization of black people that lives apart from but in juxtaposition to other civilizations is a pariah relationship. . . . But a community contains pariahs within it that are very useful for the conscience of that community."[37] From a variety of perspectives, Morrison's fiction expresses the complex dynamics of experience through which individuals are formed, or deformed, by the often conflicting values of their respective communities. The emotional reality of Morrison's characters may thus be understood as both a response to and a reflection of the benign or destructive boundaries of community.

NOTES

1. Simone de Beauvoir, *The Second Sex*, trans. H. M. Parshley (New York: Alfred A. Knopf, 1971), pp. 139, 141, and passim.

2. Toni Morrison, *The Bluest Eye* (1970, rpt. New York: Washington Square Press, 1972), p. 109. All subsequent references in the text, indicated by the abbreviation "*BE*," are to this edition, indicated by parenthetical footnotes.

3. Margaret White, "I want the right to be black and me," in *Black Women in*

White America: A Documentary History, ed. Gerda Lerner (New York: Pantheon, 1972), p. 607.

4. "'The Language Must Not Sweat': A Conversation with Toni Morrison," Conducted by Thomas LeClair," *The New Republic,* March 21, 1981, p. 29.

5. Cholly Breedlove's sexual violation of his daughter, Pecola, echoes Jim Trueblood's similar act in Ralph Ellison's *Invisible Man.*

6. *Tar Baby* (New York: Alfred A. Knopf, 1981), p. 83. Subsequent references, indicated by the abbreviation "TB" and parenthetical page numbers, refer to this edition.

7. Morrison has explained that the Dick and Jane story is "a frame acknowledging the outer civilization. The primer with white children was the way life was presented to the black people. As the novel proceeded I wanted that primer version broken up and confused, which explains the typographical running together of the words." "'The Language Must Not Sweat,'" p. 29. For an analysis of the relationship between these primer sections and the characters, see Phyllis R. Klotman, "Dick-and-Jane and the Shirley Temple Sensibility in *The Bluest Eye,*" *Black American Literature Forum,* Vol. 13, No. 4 (Winter 1979), pp. 123–25.

8. Toni Morrison, *Sula* (1973, rpt. New York: Bantam, 1975), p. 44. Subsequent references in the text, indicated by the abbreviation "*S*" and parenthetical page numbers, are to this edition.

9. "The subject of the black woman's physical beauty occurs with such frequency in the writing of black women that it indicates they have been deeply affected by the discrimination against the shade of their skin and the texture of their hair. In almost every novel or autobiography written by a black woman, there is at least one incident in which the dark-skinned girl wishes to be either white or light-skinned with 'good' hair." See Mary Helen Washington, "Teaching *Black-Eyed Susans:* An Approach to the Study of Black Women Writers," in *All the Women Are White, All the Blacks Are Men, But Some of Us Are Brave: Black Women's Studies,* ed. Gloria T. Hull, Patricia Bell Scott, and Barbara Smith (Old Westbury, N.Y.: The Feminist Press, 1982), p. 210.

10. See Elizabeth Janeway, *Powers of the Weak* (New York: Morrow, 1981), esp. pp. 3–48.

11. D. W. Winnicott, *Playing and Reality* (New York: Basic Books, 1971), p. 112, emphasis in original.

12. C. O. Ogunyemi observes that the novel's title is also a pun: "'the bluest I,' the gloomy ego, the black man [sic] feeling very blue from the psychological bombardment he is exposed to from early life to late." "Order and Disorder in Toni Morrison's *The Bluest Eye,*" *Critique,* Vol. 19, No. 1 (1977), p. 114. Cynthia Davis discusses Morrison's fiction from an existentialist perspective, noting that "[w]omanhood, like blackness, is Other in this society, and the dilemma of woman in a patriarchal society is parallel to that of blacks in a racist one: they are

made to feel most real when *seen.*" "Self, Society, and Myth in Toni Morrison's Fiction," *Contemporary Literature,* Vol. 23, No. 3 (Summer 1982), p. 329, emphasis in original.

13. Nina Auerbach, *Communities of Women: An Idea in Fiction* (Cambridge: Harvard University Press, 1978), p. 3.

14. Nancy Chodorow, *The Reproduction of Mothering: Psychoanalysis and the Sociology of Gender* (Berkeley: University of California Press, 1978). See Introduction to this study, pp. 5–7.

15. John Bowlby's psychoanalytic studies emphasize the critical role that attachment between the child and its parents plays in the development of personality. The child's separation from the parents, particularly the mother, and particularly the traumatic separation of death, may have profound effects upon the individual's subsequent capacity to form and maintain positive emotional attachments. See John Bowlby, *Attachment and Loss,* Vol. 2: *Separation, Anxiety, and Loss* (New York: Basic Books, 1973).

16. Morrison emphasizes that friendship between women is a rare subject in fiction; it is "special, different, and has never been depicted as the major focus of a novel before *Sula.* Nobody ever talked about friendship between women unless it was homosexual, and there is no homosexuality in *Sula.*" In *Black Women Writers at Work,* ed. Claudia Tate (New York: Continuum, 1983), p. 118. As Elizabeth Abel observes in her illuminating reading of *Sula* in this context, "Friendship in *Sula* is both the vehicle and product of self-knowledge, the uniquely valuable and rigorous relationship. By combining the adolescent need for identification with the adult need for independence, Morrison presents an ideal of female friendship dependent not on love, obligation, or compassion, but on an almost impossible conjunction of sameness and autonomy, attainable only with another version of oneself." See "(E)Merging Identities: The Dynamics of Female Friendship in Contemporary Fiction by Women," *Signs,* Vol. 6, No. 3 (Spring 1981), pp. 413–35, esp. p. 429.

17. Toni Morrison, *Song of Solomon* (1977, rpt. New York: New American Library, 1978), p. 131. Subsequent references, indicated by the abbreviation "*SOS*" and parenthetical page numbers in the text, are to this edition.

18. In medieval lore, there were many associations between the umbilical cord and midwives. Furthermore, witches were often healers and were frequently associated with "flying," a central motif in Morrison's novel. One source on witchcraft describes a "flying ointment" which, smeared on the naked body, enabled magical flight. See Thomas Rogers Forbes, *The Midwife and the Witch* (New Haven: Yale University Press, 1966), p. 118.

19. Morrison, in "Intimate Things in Place: A Conversation with Toni Morrison," conducted by Robert Stepto, in *The Third Woman: Minority Women Writers of the United States,* ed. Dexter Fisher (Boston: Houghton Mifflin, 1980), p. 170.

20. "An Interview with Toni Morrison" conducted by Nellie McKay, *Contemporary Literature*, Vol. 23, No. 4 (Winter 1983), p. 422.

21. "'The Seams Can't Show': An Interview with Toni Morrison" by Jane Bakerman, *Black American Literature Forum*, Vol. 12, No. 2, p. 60.

22. In an important essay examining the use of language by women writers, Margaret Homans suggests that Eva "claims God's power of life and death" in her destruction of Plum; however, "the monological power of God can be appropriated by a black woman only at the exorbitant cost of self-mutilation." "'Her Very Own Howl': The Ambiguities of Representation in Recent Women's Fiction," *Signs*, Vol. 9, No. 2 (Winter 1983), p. 191.

23. See Mary Douglas, *Purity and Danger: An Analysis of Concepts of Pollution and Taboo* (New York: Routledge and Kegan Paul, 1966).

24. Julia Kristeva, *Powers of Horror: An Essay on Abjection*, trans. Leon S. Roudiez (New York: Columbia University Press, 1982), p. 71.

25. Kathryn Allen Rabuzzi, *The Sacred and the Feminine: Toward a Theology of Housework* (New York: Seabury, 1982), p. 73.

26. Morrison, in "'The Language Must Not Sweat,'" p. 28.

27. Morrison, in "Intimate Things in Place," p. 168.

28. Morrison, in "'The Language Must Not Sweat,'" p. 28. The author's earlier name was Chloe Anthony Wofford. See Tate, *Black Women Writers at Work*, p. 117.

29. For example, "People Who Could Fly," in *Black Folktales*, retold by Julius Lester (New York: Richard W. Baron, 1969), pp. 147–51, and "Flying Africans," in *A Treasury of Afro-American Folklore*, collected by Harold Courlander (New York: Crown, 1976), pp. 285–86.

30. See Carol Gilligan, *In a Different Voice: Psychological Theory and Women's Development* (Cambridge: Harvard University Press, 1982), esp. pp. 24–63.

31. Cynthia Davis criticizes Morrison for failing to alter the stereotypical gender roles of myth, in which males are heroes and females are supporting figures in a male story. All of Milkman's models are male; even Pilate, though she "embodies Morrison's values . . . is not the complete hero that Milkman is, for she lacks his recognition of meaning." Furthermore, "Until women like Pilate recover their heroic female line, they cannot replace false images with true ones, and they will be left in a world, as Morrison shows, where mothers and daughters reject one another, female friendships are difficult to sustain, the dominating models of female selfhood are baby dolls and pinups, and even heroic women like Pilate cannot pass on their values to their children and grandchildren." "Self, Society, and Myth in Toni Morrison's Fiction," pp. 339, 340–41.

Morrison counters such objections by remarking, "I could write a book in which all the women were brave and wonderful, but it would bore me to death, and I think it would bore everybody else to death. Some women are weak and frail and hopeless, and some women are not. I write about both kinds, so one should not be more disturbing than the other. In the development of characters, there is value in the different effects." Later she adds, "I chose the man to make that journey [in *Song of Solomon*] because I thought he had more to learn than a woman would have." "An Interview with Toni Morrison," McKay, pp. 419, 428.

32. Ibid., p. 422.

33. As Maureen Howard observes, "Son and Jadine come at each other like running commentaries on black men and black women, on education, debt, freedom." "A Novel of Exile and Home," Review of *Tar Baby, The New Republic,* March 21, 1981, p. 30.

34. "Tar Baby," *The Book of Negro Folklore,* ed. Langston Hughes and Arna Bontemps (New York: Dodd, Mead, and Co., 1958), pp. 1–2.

35. Morrison, in "'The Language Must Not Sweat,'" p. 27.

36. Morrison's own phrase in McKay, "An Interview with Toni Morrison," p. 425.

37. Morrison, in Tate, *Black Women Writers at Work,* p. 129.

Bridging Two Cultures

Maxine Hong Kingston

Several of the female characters in the fiction of Penelope Mortimer and Toni Morrison suffer from the effects of cultural nearsightedness; they either experience themselves as invisible or seek the condition of invisibility as a way of hiding from themselves or those who judge them. The trope of perception expresses the authors' focus on their characters' experiences as women and/or as black people of both genders in white patriarchy. In a parallel sense, the women about whom Maxine Hong Kingston writes experience themselves as muted and suffer because they cannot be heard—again, as the doubled effect of both gender and ethnic origin.[1] The symbolic meanings attached to the phenomena of hearing, naming, language, and their correlatives are particularly important to the understanding of Kingston's two form-straddling works.

Moreover, Kingston's narratives dramatize several different aspects of boundary, including the experience of marginalization as a consequence of both gender and cultural circumstance; the establishment of individual ego boundaries as a daughter achieves psychological individuation and separation from her parents[2]—a process with special ramifications in a culture that traditionally scorned female children; the definition of certain female events as boundary conditions that are culturally perceived as negative or dangerous; and, in a literary sense, the mediating quality of Kingston's narratives themselves, which straddle or conflate diverse narrative forms.

A reader may question the inclusion in this study of such apparently nonfictional works along with the novels considered in other sections. In answer, I suggest that the very challenge to conventional narrative boundaries is what gives Kingston's works their special status as both fiction and nonfiction. Though the author calls *The Woman Warrior: Memoirs of a Girlhood among Ghosts* (1976) a memoir,[3] the work incorporates practically every narrative form from fairy tale to autobiography, from epic to moral tale. The basis for such narrative diversity is the Chinese tradition (and the author's own family tradition) of "talk-story," an oral form composed of indeterminate portions of fact, embellishment, invention, and fantasy.

Each of the five separate sections of *The Woman Warrior* is comprised of numerous smaller segments related to the central subject of the author's memories and recreations of childhood experiences, along with distilled family recollections and legends about a China she had not seen until years after the memoir was published.[4] Though each section is self-contained, it also implicitly comments on those before and after it; ultimately the narrative accumulates a network of interpenetrating themes and meanings. In this sense, Kingston's memoir shares many aspects of the form of female autobiography. As Estelle Jelinek has observed,

> [I]rregularity rather than orderliness informs the self-portraits by women. The narratives of their lives are often not chronological and progressive but disconnected, fragmentary, or organized into self-sustained units rather than connecting chapters. The multidimensionality of women's socially conditioned roles seems to have established a pattern of diffusion and diversity when they write their autobiographies as well, and so by established critical standards, their life studies are excluded from the genre and cast into the "non-artistic" categories of memoir, reminiscence, and other disjunctive forms.[5]

From a different perspective, Joanna Russ suggests that women writers who find the traditional plots, strategies, and archetypal themes of the narrative mode inadequate to express their vision either structure their narratives according to the lyric mode—"the organization of discrete elements . . . around an unspoken thematic or emotional center"—or use as their model "the structure of [their] own experience."[6] Maxine Hong Kingston has in fact applied both of these alternative principles of narrative organization in her memoir. The theme that ultimately unifies the apparently "disjunctive" segments or points to an unspoken "emotional center" of her narrative is the relationship between female generations, expressed in both communal and uniquely personal terms.

In the communal sense, Kingston explores the multiple and often conflicting strands of the experience of growing up female in the rigidly patriarchal Chinese culture, whose customs have become further petrified as a result of emigration to the United States. The elders, born in one world and surviving as adults in another, experience a bifurcated reality. Their offspring born in America inherit this split between cultures without ever having seen their ancestral land, except imaginatively, through their elders' eyes. Kingston, attempting to understand this patchwork vision of the world, tells her story not only for herself but also on behalf of first-generation Chinese-Americans like herself who lack a coherent heritage: "Chinese-Americans, when you try to understand what things in you are Chinese, how do you separate what is peculiar to childhood, to poverty, insanities, one family, your mother who marked your growing with stories, from what is Chinese? What is Chinese tradition and what is the movies?" (*WW*, p. 6). Additionally, the author recounts her struggle to find value in her gender in a culture in which females are called "maggots" (*WW*, p. 222) and in which even parents disparage their daughters with comments such as, "'Better to raise geese than girls'" (*WW*, p. 54).

More personally, Kingston explores the tangled threads of her relationship with her own mother, who is both the transmitter of tradition and a possible model for escape from its most imprisoning features. In reconstructing the gradual, painful process of separating herself from her female parent while maintaining her connection to the experiences, fantasies, and perceptions that are her mother's legacy to her, Kingston shapes her narrative around the "unspoken center" of the mother-daughter relationship.

Thus the memoir begins with the tale of "No Name Woman"—"a story to grow up on" (*WW*, p. 5) told by Kingston's mother to her at the onset of menstruation. A cautionary tale associated with female coming-of-age, the story carries a double message: not only the poignant account of transgression and humiliation, but also the implicit warning that what happened to the forgotten aunt in China "'could happen to you'" (*WW*, p. 5).

No Name Woman, Kingston's father's sister, became pregnant long after her husband of a "hurry-up wedding" had left for the Gold Mountain (America). The villagers registered their contempt for her and her family by rampaging through their home in masks and slaughtering their domestic animals. Shamed for herself and her family, the unfortunate woman bore her child alone and out of doors in darkness and then, in spite, drowned the infant and herself in the family well. Her gesture (as Kingston imagines her plight) made concrete the moral pollution for which she was condemned.

Kingston speculates that the villagers ostracized her aunt for acting in violation of the community's mores, "as if she could have a private life, secret and apart from them" (*WW*, p. 14). She had transgressed the boundaries of the community, making "a break . . . in the "'roundness'" (*WW*, p. 14). Furthermore, "This roundness had to be made coin-sized so that she would see its circumference: punish her at the birth of her baby" (*WW*, p. 15). Her suffering, as imagined by her niece, is the loss of that protective boundary, experienced from within: during labor and the birth of the child she experiences a kind of vertigo, feeling "flayed, unprotected against space" (*WW*, p. 16). Like several of Penelope Mortimer's and Margaret Atwood's agoraphobic and boundary-threatened women, No Name Woman plunges into "black space," experiencing herself "alternately [as] body and space" (*WW*, p. 16). The pain she suffers in childbirth arises not only from the baby's physical separation from her body but from her own radical separation from her community; like Toni Morrison's Pecola Breedlove, she is punished for being the innocent victim of sexual violation.

In this closed social structure, the act of self-destruction is a radical violation of social as well as (obviously) bodily boundary. According to Margery Wolf, suicide, which was more common among women than men in prerevolutionary Chinese society (in contrast to the higher proportion of male suicides in Western culture), "is not only an individual act, a gesture of personal despair, but also an act that implicates others. For a young person it is the ultimate rebellion in a society that requires respectful submission to the will of one's seniors, and for a woman it is the most damning public accusation she can make of her mother-in-law, her husband, or her son." [7]

The community of No Name Woman in turn punished her by condemning her spirit to oblivion. Kingston, recognizing that she has inadvertently participated in this conspiracy of silence, imagines and articulates the story of her aunt's rape, suffering, and suicide as a way to vindicate her spirit and those of other unnamed female victims of a repressive social structure. Moreover, she identifies herself with this aunt, her "forerunner" (*WW,* p. 9), whose transgression occurred through victimization, not choice: "Unless I see her life branching into mine, she gives me no ancestral help" (*WW,* p. 10).

To be nameless for eternity is a special form of ostracism in a culture in which descent lines are vitally important and the connections among relatives are the essential fabric of social confirmation. Names are congruent with identity; without a name, the spirit cannot find its way back to its home village (*WW,* p. 89). In America, the immigrant Chinese, like the members of the black community in Toni Morrison's *Song of Solomon,* use names to neutralize threatening circumstances beyond their control. For the black people, this power of naming is used to oppose the labels imposed upon them by their white oppressors; for the Chinese immigrants, it is to "[confuse] the gods by diverting their curses, misleading them with crooked streets and false names" (*WW,* p. 6).

As David Gutman has suggested, "When the self derives its definition and its 'names' from the groupings to which it belongs, the distinctions between the self and other members are blurred over. We identify ourselves with a name—and we thus identify and recognize ourselves in the other who derives his 'name' from our common affiliation."[8] The blurring of individual ego boundaries within a tightly defined group was a central aspect of the Chinese village life of Kingston's mother's generation and before. To be stripped of one's name by such a group, as was No Name Woman, was to be condemned to non-being, disaffiliated for eternity.

That Maxine Kingston's mother tells her the story of her aunt's transgression of social boundaries just as the daughter crosses the physiological boundary into womanhood is an admonitory comment on the vulnerable position of women in Chinese culture. Both the time of the story's occurrence in Maxine's personal history and its placement at the beginning of her narrative emphasize the links between female sexuality and fear, pollution, and taboo in a cultural group in which women occupy the inferior gender position. In Chinese culture, both menstruation and childbirth are regarded as "polluting" conditions. As Emily M. Ahern has elaborated, events that bridge the categories of bodily or social boundaries are considered polluting and prevent the tainted person from communicating with the gods: "Things the Chinese consider unclean threaten the order of or are a result of disorder in the family or in the human body. Disorder here has two specific meanings: anything that pierces the boundaries of these two entities is unclean, whether it is something that enters or something that leaves; anything that tends to undermine the tenets of order, any external threat to orderly entities, is unclean."[9]

In traditional Chinese culture, women are in a permanent transitional state as "outsiders" in relation to the dominant (male) cultural categories; because "the kinship system is focused on male lines of descent . . . women are depicted on the boundaries, breaking in as strangers. It may be events that are polluting rather than women *per se,* but polluting events are events that intrude new people or remove old ones in a male-oriented kinship system."[10] In a different cultural context, Mary Douglas has analyzed the social significance of such boundary concerns, observing that marginal positions within a group are perceived as threatening because of their ambiguity: "Danger lies in transitional states, simply because transition is neither one state nor the next, it is undefinable."[11]

Just as No Name Woman "crossed boundaries not delineated in space" (*WW,* p. 9), other women whom Kingston describes challenge various rigidly defined boundaries of traditional life. Since the villagers "depended on one another to maintain the real" (*WW,* p. 14), any violation of the consensus of wholeness was threatening to the community. Kingston describes several "crazy" women, including another aunt, who comes to America only to retreat into madness when she unsuccessfully seeks reunion with her (remarried) husband, who had emigrated thirty years earlier. As a child, the author had even suspected herself crazy, when she realized that others did not, as she did, "'talk to people that aren't real inside [her] mind'" (*WW,* p. 221). Much later, she understands the way in which the Chinese children of her generation in the United States threatened their parents' sense of the "real": their determination to "get things straight . . . name the unspeakable" (*WW,* p. 6) undermined their parents' different constructions of reality.

The most central boundary issues of Kingston's memoir, then, are the shifting ones demarcating "reality" from fantasy, "fact" from fiction, truth from invention. The blending of these narrative categories not only results in the unique form of *The Woman Warrior* but also dramatically reflects the narrator's confusion of those realms in her actual experience.[12]

As she once complained to her mother, "'You won't tell me a story and then say "This is a true story," or "This is just a story." I can't tell the difference. I don't even know what your real names are. I can't tell what's real and what you make up'" (*WW,* p. 235). Through her own "talk-story," she attempts to clarify the boundaries of a world made both fabulous and perilously unpredictable by that blurring between recollection and invention.

Presumably the close but ambivalent mother–daughter bond is typical of intergenerational female relationships in Chinese culture. As Francis Hsu has written of prerevolutionary Chinese society, "[P]arental discipline in West Town [the location for his field observations] is more severe on girls than boys. Fathers do not have very much to do with their daughters, but mothers, who have complete control of their children before ten, are more severe with their daughters than with their sons." Additionally, "Boys . . . are never barred from any occasions of ritual importance; girls, on the other hand, are excluded from most prayer meetings. Boys have very few taboos to observe; girls suffer from a good many ritual disabilities."[13]

Moreover, in such a traditional community the consequences of a daughter's rebellion against social constraints were punitive enough to suppress rage (as No Name Woman's story illustrates). Because a daughter joined her husband's family through marriage, she was permanently separated from her mother and could look forward only to many years of powerlessness within her husband's family. The husband's mother found in her relationship with her daughter-in-law an outlet for her own long-suppressed desire for control. Thus, the contempt for daughters was reinforced in each aspect of the family structure, for mothers of sons (but not of daughters) eventually gained a modicum of familial power.[14]

Fittingly, two of the most compelling sections of Kingston's memoir are those dramatizing the contrast between the powerless outer self and the heroic inner self of both the author and her mother. There is a deliberate irony to these two central clusters of stories of female courage, power, and significance. On the one hand, the young Maxine and her female peers concluded from their mothers' "talk-stories" that "we failed if we grew up to be but wives or slaves. We could be heroines, swordswomen. . . . Perhaps women were once so dangerous that they had to have their feet bound" (*WW,* p. 23). In their actual lives, on the other hand, girls and women were utterly subordinate and unvalued. The invention of a potent magical self is a kind of defensive fantasy that imaginatively counteracts the experience of insignificance and the generalized contempt for females in Chinese culture.

In this context, Kingston recreates an early fantasy that reveals her imaginative identification, not with her ambivalent mother, but with the mythical warrior woman, Fa Mu Lan. This classic story celebrates the virtues of a brave young woman who took her father's place in battle by "passing" as a male warrior; following her victories, she eventually revealed herself as a woman, to the surprise and acclaim of her people.[15] Kingston invents the childhood and initiation of this woman warrior (the portion of her life that precedes the events described in the original legend), following the pattern of the archetypal hero story.[16] The author's imaginative poetic embellishments in the story of Fa Mu Lan make it the brilliant centerpiece of her memoir.

Identifying herself with the hero, Maxine/Fa Mu Lan responds to a call and leaves her own parents, to be tutored in the role of warrior by supernatural parents.[17] She undergoes initiatory tests of physical endurance, journeys to the dead land, and achieves a mystical vision through abstinence from food. After years of training, she enters a marriage with a "spirit bridegroom" who loves her for who she is in her deepest self and eventually she avenges her people.

A difficult part of the warrior woman's training is "dragon lessons," through which she learns to challenge the invisible forces of evil. "'You have to infer the whole dragon from the parts you can see and touch,'" she is told (*WW*, p. 34). That mission seems of special personal significance, for both Kingston and her mother were born under the sign of the dragon, and the author specifically mentions the dragon powers of her mother more than once.

In the magical realm, the woman warrior's first menses signals not pollution and sexual prohibition—as in the monitory tale of No Name Woman—but her bond of blood with the unborn and the dead. Not long after crossing that crucial female threshold, Maxine/Fa Mu Lan experiences her greatest trial of blood: when she returns to her true family, her parents carve their people's grievances into the flesh of her back with knife and ink. She is so lacerated that if she were flayed by an enemy "the light would shine through [her] skin like lace" (*WW*, p. 41). Kingston (like Mortimer and Morrison) uses this and other images of literally wounding words and mutilation as emblems of female victimization in patriarchy.[18]

Eventually Fa Mu Lan subdues her people's enemy overlord and claims the land as far as "the northern boundary of the world" (*WW*, p. 50). By contrast, as a child Maxine had "feared the size of the world" (*WW*, p. 116). The fantasy identification with the woman warrior allowed her to transcend the boundaries of her claustrophobically narrow world and to achieve an imaginary identity of power and autonomy precluded by her actual circumstances as a child and a female.

Yet even the image of the woman warrior reinforces traditional gender roles, for Fa Mu Lan achieves her distinction by "passing" as a man and emulating the postures of aggression, albeit for a noble cause. Moreover, unlike the woman warrior, the author as a child had no means of avenging her family's suffering and loss during the Chinese Revolution—or even of achieving a sense of her positive worth. (Kingston reports learning only in adulthood that the revolution in China resulted in the abolition of foot binding and in greater equality for women.) "I am useless, one more girl who couldn't be sold," she mourns (*WW*, p. 62). Feeling un-valued within both her own culture and the surrounding American cul-ture—the latter with its own prejudices against people of Asian descent—the young Maxine sought validation in the less bounded world of fantasy.

Ironically, it was Kingston's mother who opened that imaginative realm to her; thus, "talk-story," which originated in the primary attachment of daughter and mother, eventually comes to comment on it.[19] The emo-tional intensity of the mother-daughter relationship is further under-scored by Kingston's central placement in the narrative of the section about her mother, Brave Orchid, significantly entitled "Shaman." Through this story within a story, Kingston reconstructs the process through which she came to understand and forgive her mother. Concur-rently, she pays homage to the storytelling tradition that she inherited through the matriarchal side of her family.

To her daughter, Brave Orchid is a paradox: both the courageous woman who dared to be a "new woman" in the old country—a practic-ing midwife—and the ritual-bound, almost paranoid mother of Kings-ton's American childhood. The cluster of tales and memories concerning Brave Orchid unfold in several movements, spanning the time before

Maxine Kingston's own birth, through her adult reconciliation with her mother.

Despite the low status of women in prerevolutionary China, midwifery was one of the few acceptable professions, particularly suitable for a properly married woman whose husband had gone to seek his fortune and might be gone for years—or might never send for her to join him. Still, few women "got to live out the daydream of women—to have a room, even a section of a room, that only gets messed up when she messes it up herself" (*WW,* p. 72). (The desire for a "room of one's own," given such enduring expression by Virginia Woolf, transcends its original cultural context.) Kingston's mother, a generation older than her student peers, came to be regarded as a kind of dragon power, fearless and brave in the face of unknown dangers. Brave Orchid's most spectacular manifestation of courage is her confrontation with "ghosts" in a reputedly haunted room of her medical school. During that frightening night alone in the room, she outlasts the malign spirits by talking back to them fearlessly and by chanting her lessons as if she were alone in a well-lit room.

When Brave Orchid returns victorious from her overnight "trial" of courage in that nether region, she recounts her experience, embellishing and exaggerating the details, in the manner of all successful storytellers, to affect her young, impressionable audience. She gives both her young student peers and later her daughter Maxine an extraordinary lesson in the efficacy of courage, magic, and belief, as well as in the power of storytelling itself.

Kingston in turn recounts her mother's experiences as if she had been in the ghost room in Brave Orchid's place. Thus, the "medical-student" section of "Shaman" is the narrative equivalent of Chinese boxes, consisting of three levels of or variations on a single theme: Brave Orchid's adventurous pursuit of a medical education in defiance of the traditional female roles; the harrowing experience, as recapitulated to her peers, of her night in the ghost room; and, finally, the seamless sequence that Kingston reconstructs, with her own additional embellishments, from her mother's "talk-story."

After graduation from medical school, Brave Orchid buys a young female slave to train as her nurse and proceeds to practice medicine and midwifery in her village. Some of her nightmarish cases included a baby boy born with the "defect" of blue eyes. (Recalling Pecola Breedlove's desperate wish for such eyes, one realizes the cultural relativity of the symbolism associated with physical characteristics.) Kingston wonders whether her mother ever condoned female infanticide and regrets that Brave Orchid seems to have thought more highly of her slave than her daughters. Kingston's own sister wanted to grow up to be a slave (*WW*, p. 96), because slaves received more respect than daughters; one Chinese word for the female "I" is equivalent in meaning to "slave" (*WW*, p. 56). While condemning such attitudes, the author attempts to preserve the legacy of imaginative invention generated by her mother's experiences and recollections.

However, the daughter can never verify the details of her mother's experiences, beyond the proofs of medical diplomas and photographs of Brave Orchid with her graduating class. In America, the mother Kingston has known from infancy is a ritual-bound traditionalist, unable to transfer her professional training from one culture, language, and social context to another. Thus she is, for her daughter, ambivalently both a woman of exceptional power within the female world of her culture and a powerless female in the larger bicultural situation. Either she had actually had the extraordinary life in China that she describes for her daughter, or she had invented it. In either case, the daughter knows that she has grown up "in the presence of great power" (*WW*, p. 24). Brave Orchid's stories stimulate Kingston's vision of a China she will never see, for the Revolution altered their country of ancestral origin irrevocably.

From these once-removed memories, the author invents a place more magical and mystical than her disappointingly prosaic American reality. As a child, Kingston "could not figure out what was [her] village" (*WW*, p. 54). Fairy tales gave way to culture shock, as the daughter attempted to invigorate her ordinary experience with fantasies like her mother's. However, the "White Ghosts" and "Machine Ghosts" of Maxine's American childhood are pale imitations of the mysterious and poetic grotesques of Brave Orchid's tales. While Brave Orchid never lost her connection to that mythicized China of her youth, her children have no choice but to accommodate themselves to a different world.

To reconcile her relationship with both her mother and her Chinese tradition, Kingston straddles the boundaries, melding the conflicting dimensions of her heritage into a single vision. This necessity is fundamental to the universal process of psychological maturation: the need to reconcile the discrepancy between the supernatural parent as seen through the young child's eyes and the humanly limited figure one must accept in adulthood. Kingston, herself a brilliant storyteller, recreates this process with poetic beauty and poignancy.

As an adult, the author achieved, and preserves in her narrative, a rare moment of true intimacy and mutuality with her elderly mother. The description of their recognition and mutual forgiveness occurs at almost the exact midpoint of *The Woman Warrior*. Returning for a visit with Brave Orchid after having left home for good, Maxine comforts her mother's sadness that there is "no more China to go home to" (*WW,* p. 125) by explaining, "'We belong to the planet now, Mama. . . . [I]f we're no longer attached to one piece of land, we belong to the planet[.] Wherever we happen to be standing, why, that spot belongs to us as much as any other spot'" (*WW,* p. 125). Some time during their meeting, Brave Orchid sighs, "'[H]ow can I bear to have you leave me again?'" to which her grown daughter silently asks herself, "How can I bear to leave her again?" (*WW,* p. 118). Their exchange registers the pain of separation between mother and daughter immortalized in the archetypal story of Demeter and Persephone.

Such separations are necessitated by the daughter's profound but inevitably ambivalent attachment to her female parent. As Dorothy Dinnerstein has argued, even while the mother provides

> vital support for the early growth of the self, [she] is inevitably felt as a menace to that self. She is the outstanding feature of the arresting, sometimes overwhelming, realm within which the self's boundaries must be defined.
>
> . . . There is of course no such thing as a wholly benevolent mother. . . . But even if there were, she would be experienced by the child, in its struggle to become [an autonomous being], both as an interfering influence and as a lure back into non-being.[20]

In a culture in which women traditionally were assigned the devalued social position while holding responsibility for child-rearing, a daughter's identification with her female parent would inevitably ratify their inferior gender status. Nancy Chodorow's analysis of different avenues of ego development for females and males[21] might be reconsidered in a cultural context in which female subordination was maintained through such extreme practices as female infanticide and footbinding. The daughter's achievement of autonomy would presume a difficult separation from the figure associated not only with nurturing but, in social terms, with oppression and, in psychological terms, with repression.

In Kingston's memoir, Brave Orchid implicitly acknowledges the ambivalence of the mother-daughter relationship by expressing a rare endearment to her daughter. At that moment, Maxine feels the release of her mother's possessive grip; she is free to tell this narrative, her own story.

The first three of the five major divisions of *The Woman Warrior* might be viewed respectively as a morality tale, a fairy-tale epic, and a series of "ghost stories" and adventures completed by the reconciliation between mother and daughter. The fourth section, "At the Western Palace," is a tragedy, and the final one, "A Song for a Barbarian Reed Pipe," is a combination of confession and legend. While the first three sections focus on personal histories within the traditional Chinese culture, filtered through Kingston's once-removed perspective, the last two emphasize the broader dislocations attendant upon straddling two cultures. Each section also reinforces the life-saving powers of imagination and language. Cumulatively, the five major sections form a composite story of magical enclosure within parental and cultural constructs of reality, followed by separation and acquisition of selfhood in an equally ambiguous bicultural world view.

The true tragedy of the collision between two dissimilar cultures is dramatized in Kingston's account of her aunt's arrival to the United States in her old age. Her mother, Brave Orchid, still hostage to her old culture's views of matrimony and privilege, urges her more timid sister, Moon Orchid, to pursue and claim her Chinese husband, who had immigrated to America thirty years before. Though he considered himself a "good husband" because he had faithfully sent her money (*WW,* p. 177), he had never sent for her to join him in America. Instead, he had married an American-Chinese woman and achieved success in Western terms as a brain surgeon. From facts only gleaned third-hand (from Maxine's brother's account to their sister) of the meeting between Moon Orchid and her former spouse, Kingston reconstructs the poignant sequence of events that culminate in her aunt's tragic disillusionment. Moon Orchid is virtually bullied by her more aggressive, indignant sister into a confrontation that she cannot win. To the elderly alien aunt's considerable feelings of helplessness in a strange country is added the sudden loss of the illusion that has sustained her for most of her adult life.

Like Kingston's other tragic aunt, No Name Woman, Moon Orchid is stripped of her one claim to identity—marriage—and is left with no defined place in the social structure of her immigrant community. As Mary Douglas has written of such peripheral people, "It seems that if a person has no place in the social system and is therefore a marginal being, all precautions against danger must come from others. He cannot help his abnormal situation."[22] Moon Orchid's acute sense of displacement is also exacerbated by her nephews' and nieces' irritation at her peculiar Chinese ways. Caught in the cracks, as it were, between Chinese and Western traditions, Moon Orchid lapses into fear, paranoia, and, finally, madness. The "Western Palace" of which she had dreamed is an illusion; the only "home" left for her is the state mental asylum. There, she feels the pathetic security of a woman who has only "one story" to tell over and over (*WW*, p. 184). From this tragic conclusion to their aunt's odyssey, Maxine and her sisters find a paradoxical affirmation; they vow "fiercely that they would never let men be unfaithful to them" (*WW*, p. 186).

Kingston admits that her brother's version of Moon Orchid's ill-fated rendezvous "may be better than [hers] because of its bareness, not twisted into designs" (*WW*, p. 189). Here, as elsewhere, she acknowledges that her reconstructions of family history are embellished by her own invention of the details. In defending her penchant for "designs" of language and story, Kingston traces her development as a storyteller from an unlikely beginning as an imaginative but acutely tongue-tied young girl who "flunked kindergarten" (*WW*, p. 192) and who discovered the power of language by abusing it.

In great detail, as if confessing to us, her readers, Kingston recounts her bullying of a younger Chinese girl who never spoke in school or outside of it; the child represents in extreme form a handicap Kingston herself suffered as a child attending schools taught in the "foreign" language of English. In the girls' lavatory after school one day, she tormented the terrified younger child interminably, trying to force her to speak. Powerless in the world of adults, White Ghosts, and Americans, the young Maxine had found a rare opportunity to wield power over someone else. Sadly, as she acknowledges in retrospect, she used that power destructively. However, through the experience she also discovered poetic justice: she spent the next eighteen months "sick in bed with a mysterious illness" (*WW,* p. 211).

Kingston's mother had told her as a child that she had cut her frenum so that Maxine would not remain tongue-tied. One anthropologist has proposed that the condition of being culturally tongue-tied or "muted" is a general consequence of being female in a patriarchal social structure. As Edwin Ardener states,

> One of the problems that women [as ethnological subjects] presented was that they were rendered "inarticulate" by the male structure; that the dominant structure was articulated in terms of a male world position. Those who were not in the male world-position were, as it were, "muted." . . . [A group] is muted simply because it does not form part of the dominant communicative system of the society—expressed as it must be through the dominant ideology, and that "mode of production," if you wish, which is articulated with it. [23]

Although Ardener's observation applies to a "technically defined condition of structures—not some condition of linguistic silence," [24] his concept of muting is particularly suggestive when both senses are demonstrable, as in Kingston's story of the mute child and, in fact, *The Woman Warrior* as a whole. Young females in a repressively patriarchal system had "nothing to say" that was given serious consideration. This muting—both structural and linguistic, both consequence and reinforcement of inferior gender position—is made explicit in Kingston's account of her own "tongue-tied" childhood and her torment of her even more profoundly muted peer.

Much of Kingston's memoir is a repudiation of the paralyzing muted state. As she comments elsewhere in a sketch for an unfinished story, "I can't follow this story any longer. First I have to finish the stories I couldn't write during childhood because of the years it took to acquire vocabulary." [25] "Vocabulary" refers to her acquisition not only of English but of a language that would enable her to articulate the formerly unverbalized dimensions of her experience. Storytelling itself is a way of giving poetic expression to the once inarticulate. The tales of No Name Woman, whose very name and history were "muted" to complete silence, and Moon Orchid, who was driven to repeat her "one story," are forceful variations on this central theme. So too are the images of the Woman Warrior, with the "scarwords" of her people's grief carved into her back, and the female captive of the barbarians, whose mournful songs precipitated her freedom.

Even the author's childhood attempt to "confess" her sins reveals the ambivalence in the effort of moving from silence to articulation and from symbiosis to independence from her mother. During a phase of accumulated guilt, the young Maxine resolved to confess one "bad deed" or "true thing" about herself per day to her mother in order to purge her sense of unworthiness. She thought that if her mother knew these shameful details, "[S]he—and the world—would become more like me, and I would never be alone again" (*WW*, p. 230). Yet the more she confessed, the larger the list of bad deeds grew. Even more remarkable to the young Maxine, however, was her mother's total indifference to the momentous truths being disclosed to her.

Reconsidering such discrepancies between children's and parents' perceptions, Kingston reflects that much of her childhood was—as is true in some way for all children—a mystery; the youngest members of the family were uninformed participants, observers, and even offenders of obscure rituals, ceremonies, and taboos. She wonders how, when so little of the old tradition was articulated for the young, the Chinese people "kept up a continuous culture for five thousand years. Maybe they didn't; maybe everyone makes it up as they go along. If we had to depend on being told, we'd have no religion, no babies, no menstruation (sex, of course, unspeakable), no death" (*WW*, p. 216).

Kingston could never verify the family stories since the very sense of what is "true" is culturally defined. Instead, straddling two cultures, she wonders if perhaps "what I once had was not Chinese-sight at all but child-sight that would have disappeared eventually without such struggle. . . . I continue to sort out what's just my childhood, just my imagination, just my family, just the village, just movies, just living" (*WW*, p. 239). The only way Kingston could test these overlapping strands of experience was to leave the home and language of her parents. In order to appreciate her tradition and her mother's gifts, she was compelled to separate herself from "the village" of her family and childhood, and enter the complex bicultural realities of the outside world through the world of her imagination.

However, the capacity she inherited from her culture and from her mother, to "make it up as one goes along," provided Kingston with her vocation. Rejecting her mother's entrapment in a culture that devalues females, yet identifying with Brave Orchid's talent—and in tribute to her—Kingston became a storyteller, committed to giving expression to the muted females of her culture. In *The Woman Warrior,* Kingston reconciles the contradictory messages of her personal and cultural heritage by appropriating her mother's powers, not only as a storyteller, but, symbolically, as a midwife. In fabricating "twisted designs" out of the garbled mixture of observation, recollection, and imagination, Kingston gives birth to the meaning of these particular and generic female experiences by assisting their difficult transition from one state to another.

Fittingly, the final segment of the *Memoirs,* "A Song for a Barbarian Reed Pipe," is a corroboration begun by the mother and completed by the daughter "when I told her I also talk-story" (*WW,* p. 240) that validates that achievement. In this parable of the significance of art to the Chinese people, Kingston identifies herself with another woman warrior: the second-century poet Ts'ai Yen, who, kidnapped by barbarians, eventually "brought her songs back from the savage lands" (*WW,* p. 243). Like her, and like her own mother, Kingston has smuggled her stories out of the "ghost land" of her early years, the "savage land" of childhood. Replacing the warrior's sword with the word—as the latter word is literally contained within the former—Kingston determines to vindicate the history written "at [her] back" (*WW,* p. 63) by the nameless, powerless, muted females (and males) of her culture.[26] At the same time, by achieving a unique perspective on the relationships among the experiences of childhood, gender, and Chinese heritage, she pays tribute to the rich but ambivalent tradition bequeathed her by the matriarchal side of her family.

The final words of Kingston's narrative (referring to Ts'ai Yen's song) are "It translated well" (*WW,* p. 243). The same can be said of her own narrative: with a remarkable and powerful voice she has transmuted silence into poetry, creating not only a discourse but a narrative form that accommodates the contradictory strands of imaginative and imagined history.

In *China Men* (1980), Maxine Hong Kingston explores some of the same issues (and others) considered in the first volume by focusing on the male side of Chinese tradition—again, through cultural and family history as well as legend, folktale, recollection, and imaginative reconstruction.[27] However, in the author's consideration of her patriarchal tradition, the boundary between historical event and imaginative invention is more sharply drawn, just as it is in the actual experience of its male members.

In the first memoir, fact and fabrication often blur into one another; Kingston's own gender identification underscores her confusion about the distinctions between them. In *China Men,* she observes as her father's daughter or as a niece or female relative of men. In contrast to the embellished autobiography in *The Woman Warrior, China Men* is cultural biography. Of the eighteen segments of the latter narrative, only a third are imaginative legends or parables from Chinese tradition; the rest are historical reconstructions or anecdotal accounts of the male members of Kingston's extended family. Perhaps because the author's close identification with the principal figures of the narrative is absent, the "talk-story" that animates the earlier narrative gives way to a more detached historical record interlarded with legends.

Nonetheless, *China Men* is an important complementary volume, rounding out Kingston's exploration of her heritage by illustrating the other strand of her gender-defined cultural history. To understand her male ancestors and relatives, she attempts to comprehend patriarchy as it operated in Chinese culture, both in its original context and in its collision with American customs and mores. Unlike her mother, Kingston's father was a reluctant source for either fact or story; implicitly, he indicated "with the few words, and the silences: No stories. No Past. No China" (*CM,* p. 14). Thus Kingston was obliged to examine her father's implicit attitudes toward the women in his family and his culture as evidence for the male perspective. Her acute discomfort at the many Chinese curses that refer to the female body prompts her to formulate an urgent request that she could never actually demand of her father: for him to say that "those curses are only common Chinese sayings. That you did not mean to make me sicken at being female" (*CM,* p. 14). Even if he did not, of course, the curses, whether personal or impersonal, expose the culture's deeply ingrained contempt for females.

Yet Kingston also describes pleasant childhood memories of "father places" like the cellar and attic; as a child accompanying her father on his chores, she was privy to nooks and crannies of mystery. She also felt privileged to visit his business establishments, including the room where he managed the gambling enterprise and the basement of the family's commercial laundry. Kingston had not realized before those special discoveries that her family had owned "such an extravagance of empty space" (*CM,* p. 239). At another point, she talks with an aunt recently arrived from Hong Kong and confesses, "I had thought perhaps people from Hong Kong didn't need room, that Chinese people preferred small spaces" (*CM,* p. 202). These assumptions reflect most upon the author's own feeling of physical and psychological constraint (no "room of her own") in her hybrid Chinese-American female identity. Chinese men, despite their restricted place in American culture, had more "space" than Chinese women.

In this narrative, Kingston underscores the fact that history in nearly all cultures and times has been both made and recorded by men. The actual stories of those ancestors about whom Kingston writes are a representative record of several waves of Chinese immigration to the United States during the nineteenth century, as well as a recapitulation of the obstacles and prejudices that impeded the way. From the so-called "coolie" laborers of the Hawaiian cane fields to those who helped to build the great American railroad, they were overworked and underpaid. They risked the hardships of the ocean passage as well as illness, loneliness, homesickness, opium addiction, economic exploitation, and the appalling discrimination that came with the jobs. Their one recourse was the sense of community and shared misery. Kingston documents the generalized American prejudice against an ethnic group which, because its members were exploited as "cheap labor," threatened economic competition once the need for their skill and manpower had ended.

Thus, while *The Woman Warrior* explores the prohibitions and traditions associated with being a Chinese female, *China Men* illustrates these restrictions in terms of an entire ethnic group attempting to survive in an inhospitable host country. One section of the narrative is a recital of the laws, treaties, and judicial decisions on record between 1868 and 1978 that specifically limited, regulated, or affected the lives of people of Chinese descent. The situation of the Chinese ethnic group as a whole in American culture was analogous to the condition of Chinese women in their traditional culture: both were abused, economically exploited, denigrated, dehumanized. Within Chinese-American culture, females were thus doubly marginalized.

Interspersed with Kingston's reconstructions of actual historical events are folktales and parables that comment on these factual records, frequently to highlight the contrast between male and female experiences regardless of time and place. As a thematic bridge between the earlier

182

memoir and this one, *China Men* begins with the fable "On Discovery," in which a China man named Tang Ao seeks the Gold Mountain, only to find himself in the Land of Women. There, he is subjected to the practices with which Chinese women had been intimately and painfully acquainted for centuries through their subjection to male prerogatives: the threat of having the lips sewn together to enforce silence; ear piercing; the excruciating practice of footbinding, which involved breaking bones in the feet to alter their shape, inhibit their growth, and make walking impossible; elaborate facial makeup; and instruction in serving food. The "discovery" announced by the title of the legend is thus an ironic one; the hapless man experiences the torments that his own gender has perpetrated upon the other.

In another morality tale on the theme of gender, Kingston relates the story of the origin of death in the world. Tu Tzu-Chun is told that he has an opportunity to gain a gift from the gods, but with one crucial condition: he must maintain a vow of eternal silence for the length of his sojourn in illusion. He travels silently through hell and is reborn as a deaf-mute female, which will presumably make his task easier. In this second life as a woman, Tu Tzu-Chun grows up, marries, and bears a child, all without uttering a sound. But "her" silence is broken when her husband, irritated by her muteness, deliberately tortures their child to provoke a sound from her lips. Her scream breaks the formula that would have won "immortality for the human race" (*CM*, p. 121).

Pertinently, it is the powerful love of the mother for her child that breaks the silence. Her inability to remain silent in the presence of suffering is both the woman's strength and her weakness. As in the Greek myth of Pandora, female "weakness" is blamed for the mortal limit of human existence. What gives the tale additional poignancy is its irony: the "she" of the story began as the man, Tu Tzu-Chun. The responsibility for mortality thus implicitly is shared by both sexes.

In this parable, silence is regarded in moral terms as both a virtue and a flaw. The image of the mute(d) female resonates with Kingston's recollections in *The Woman Warrior* of her own tongue-tied youth and her torment of a mute girl. In *China Men*, Kingston also recalls a grandmother who "jabbered like a monkey" (*CM*, p. 86) when she came to America. No one responded to her, since "'Who knows what she was saying anyway?' She fell mute" (*CM*, p. 86).

In another fable about gender relationships and attitudes, a young man lost in a storm seeks shelter at an unfamiliar doorstep. The occupant of the house, a widowed young noblewoman, cares for him lavishly. The overnight visit extends into years, during which time the man is satiated in every desire and appetite by the marvelous courtesan. Finally, the pleasure of total gratification palls; the man, longing for the stimulus of competition in his profession or trade in the actual world, regretfully leaves the courtesan.

The "archaic" component of the fantasy is emphasized by the man's eventual discovery that he has virtually stumbled into the past; the woman with whom he has apparently spent the better part of his life in fact lived and died centuries earlier. He recognizes that hunger and deprivation had brought him to a fantastic place, a dream world energized by a powerful wish-fulfillment fantasy. The all-giving female (originally the mother) becomes a sexually alluring courtesan who responds to the young man's every need. He awakes to reality because he is "unable to remain joined, connected" (*CM,* p. 80) in this self-indulgent but regressive union. He is (and we are) surprised when he wakes to find himself a young man with his life still ahead of him. Returning gratefully to his actual wife and family, he can fully appreciate their human gifts.

Through such fables, Kingston suggests the myriad ways in which, even in fantasy, China Men's experience differed in opportunity, status, and variety from Chinese women's much more restricted possibilities. Many of the details of female inferiority emerge between the lines of male history and tradition. For example, in describing her own father's birth, the author notes the special, joyous celebrations associated with the arrival of a male child. By contrast, when a female child is born, parents and relatives sigh, "'It's only a girl. . . . Just a girl'" (*CM,* p. 18).[28] There are occasional, if infrequent, exceptions to this undervaluation of females. Kingston's own grandfather desperately desired a daughter in his family of five sons and actually attempted to trade the newborn baby boy (Kingston's father) for a baby girl born into a neighbor's all-female family. The exchange was revoked by Maxine's horrified grandmother.

Because the traditional gender attitudes were so marked, Kingston thought as a child that males and females were altogether dissimilar and attempted an experiment in social anthropology to prove it. When she kicked a boy at school and he did not cry, she claimed proof to her girlfriends of her hypothesis that males have an "immunity" to pain: "It was the same with Chinese boys, black boys, white boys, and Mexican and Filipino boys. Girls and women of all races cried and had feelings. We had to toughen up. We had to be as tough as boys, tougher because we only pretended not to feel pain" (*CM,* p. 252).

The "double bind" implied in this experiment is the distinction between male power, associated with "immunity to pain," and female weakness, associated with vulnerability to it. The distinction between the sexes is carried into adult life in another form: men, not women—except for mythical women warriors—fight wars, as if they were "immune" to pain. Though Kingston's father had escaped induction because he was under regulation weight for the army, her youngest brother served in Vietnam in the navy and survived it. The author's reconstruction of his experience reveals how unhappy the Vietnam era was for Americans— of either sex—of Asian descent. Like their immigrant ancestors, they were still victims of racial discrimination; America would, as the Asian-American soldiers phrased it, "send a gook to fight the gook war" (*CM,* p. 283).

The reality of men fighting in contemporary wars emphasizes the distance between the poetic vision of the woman warrior of Kingston's earlier memoir and the later, more reality-bound narrative. In tracing the male dimension of her personal and cultural experience through history and legend, Kingston concedes that she has invented what she cannot know of men's lives and perceptions, just as she has imagined the country of her ancestral origin. In a sense, she is a foreigner to both.

NOTES

1. Asian-American women may also experience themselves as unseen. See Mitsuye Yamada, "Invisibility is an Unnatural Disaster: Reflections of an Asian American Woman," in *This Bridge Called My Back: Writings by Radical Women of Color,* eds. Cherríe Moraga and Gloria Anzaldúa (Watertown, Mass.: Persephone Press, 1981), pp. 35–40.

2. See my Introduction, pp. 5–7.

3. Maxine Hong Kingston, *The Woman Warrior: Memoirs of a Girlhood among Ghosts* (1976, rpt. New York: Random House, Vintage Books, 1977). All subsequent references to this edition are indicated in the text by the abbreviation "*WW*" and parenthetical page numbers.

4. In 1984, Kingston finally visited the country of her ancestors, despite the protestations of her mother. As Harrison E. Salisbury wrote of her experience as one of a group of writers who visited China, Kingston's "mother had been on the telephone to her two and three times a day before she left for China. She was convinced that her daughter would vanish into China and never return. 'You've written some very bad things about the regime,' her mother said. 'Tell them you didn't mean it. Tell them you take it all back.' On the next call she would urge Mrs. Kingston, who was understandably nervous, to give up the trip. Her family had left before the Communist victory and had never been friendly to the regime.

"But her fears proved groundless. When she reached Canton everyone seemed to know her writing. . . . Everyone claimed to be a relative. No one complained about what she had written about the Communists.

"To Maxine Hong Kingston it was coming home to a home where she had never lived but where everything somehow seemed warm and familiar and, she was glad to learn, a place where with the passage of years the intense hostility against Chinese émigrés that her mother had feared had begun to fade into the distance. China, she felt, was beginning to become China again." "On the Literary Road: American Writers in China," *The New York Times Book Review,* January 20, 1985, p. 25.

5. Estelle Jelinek, Introduction to *Women's Autobiography: Essays in Criticism,* ed. Estelle Jelinek (Bloomington: Indiana University Press, 1980), p. 17.

6. Joanna Russ, "What Can a Heroine Do? or Why Women Can't Write," in *Images of Women in Fiction: Feminist Perspectives,* ed. Susan Koppelman Cornillon (Bowling Green, Ohio: Bowling Green University Press, 1972), pp. 12–13.

7. Margery Wolf, "Women and Suicide in China," in *Women in Chinese Society,* ed. Margery Wolf and Roxane Witke (Stanford: Stanford University Press, 1975), p. 112.

8. David Gutman, "Woman and the Conception of Ego-Strength," *Merrill-Palmer Quarterly of Behavior and Development,* Vol. 11, No. 2 (1965), p. 235. I am indebted to the work of Nancy Chodorow for discovery of this essay.

9. Emily M. Ahern, "The Power and Pollution of Chinese Women," in Wolf and Witke, *Women in Chinese Society,* p. 207. See also Julia Kristeva's comments on menstruation as a boundary condition, in chapter 3, p. 150 of this study.

10. Ahern, "The Power and Pollution of Chinese Women," p. 213.

11. Mary Douglas, *Purity and Danger: An Analysis of Concepts of Pollution and Taboo* (New York: Routledge and Kegan Paul, 1966), p. 96.

12. On this subject Kingston remarked in an interview, "The reason people are confused about whether my books are fiction or non-fiction is that *I* keep asking this question. I say, Is this real? Is this true? The readers pick up on my asking, and they ask that because I've planted the question.

"But the truth is I answer that question." "This is the Story I Heard: A Conversation with Maxine Hong Kingston and Earll Kingston," conducted by Phyllis Hoge Thompson, *Biography,* Vol. 6, No. 1 (Winter 1983), p. 4.

13. Francis L. K. Hsu, *Under the Ancestors' Shadow: Kinship, Personality, and Social Mobility in Village China* (rpt. Garden City, N.Y.: Doubleday, 1967), pp. 227, 222.

14. Julia Kristeva describes the segregation of female roles in Chinese culture, observing that artistic creation and procreation were mutually exclusive. The courtesan was privy to the arts but excluded from domestic security. "With Confucianism, two barriers are erected to insure the cohesion of the feudal social order: the first is the door to the bedchamber, the second is writing and knowledge in general. A woman cannot cross them both at once: either she leaves the bedchamber to be acknowledged—but only as genetrix—the mother of the father's sons; or she gains access to the social order (as poet, dancer, singer) but behind the door of the bedchamber, an unacknowledgeable sexual partner." *About Chinese Women,* trans. Anita Barrows (New York: Urizen Books, 1977), p. 76.

15. The story has been rendered in several versions. See, for example, "The Ballad of MuLan," in *The Temple and Other Poems,* trans. Arthur Waley (New York: Alfred A. Knopf, 1923), pp. 128–30.

16. Joseph Campbell describes these stages, with variations, as the call to adventure, crossing of the threshold, tests and encounters with powerful forces or figures of darkness (including a dragon battle), descent into death, receipt of magical aid, sacred marriage, award of boon or elixir of knowledge, and return to the ordinary world. See *The Hero with a Thousand Faces,* 2nd ed. (Princeton: Princeton University Press, 1968).

Annis Pratt, in her valuable reformulation of the archetypal rebirth journey as it applies to female experience and is manifested in narratives by women, describes the five phases of the adventure as the splitting off from family, husbands, lovers; the green-world guide or token; the green-world lover; confrontation with parental figures; and the plunge into the unconscious. In her view, the transformed hero who survives the journey into the unconscious is "unlikely to be able to reintegrate herself fully into 'normal' society." *Archetypal Patterns in Women's Fiction* (Bloomington: Indiana University Press, 1981), pp. 139–43, esp. p. 143.

17. Otto Rank describes the "family romance," wherein during preoedipal and oedipal conflict with parents, children express the fantasy that these are not their actual parents; the fantasied parents are of noble birth or idealized goodness. Rank's discussion of the congruence between oedipal fantasy and myth focuses on male heroes and male children; female experience is dismissed in a footnote,

without reference to the conflict for girls during the same phase of development. See *The Myth of the Birth of the Hero and Other Essays,* ed. and trans. Philip Freund (New York: Alfred A. Knopf and Random House, 1959), esp. p. 93.

18. The image of words carved into the flesh also recalls Franz Kafka's story "In the Penal Colony."

19. The connection between language and the early phase of the mother-daughter relationship has provocative implications. Julia Kristeva speculates that because the Chinese language is tonal when spoken, and because babies understand differences in tone before they understand language, "children surrounded by tonal speech do retain [the tonal variations], and quite early on. Thus, Chinese children begin taking part in the code of social communication that is language at a much younger age (5 or 6 months) than children in other cultures, since they are capable so early of distinguishing the fundamental trait of their language. And, as the dependency on the mother's body is so great at that age, it is thus the psycho-corporeal imprint of the mother that shapes tonal expression and transmits it without obliterating it. . . . Does the Chinese language preserve, then, thanks to its tones, a pre–Oedipal, pre-syntactic, pre-symbolic (symbol and syntax being concomitant) register, even if it is evident that the tonal system is not fully realized except in syntax . . . ?" *About Chinese Women,* pp. 55–56.

20. Dorothy Dinnerstein, *The Mermaid and the Minotaur: Sexual Arrangements and Human Malaise* (rpt. New York: Harper and Row, 1977), p. 111. See also Nancy Chodorow, *The Reproduction of Mothering: Psychoanalysis and the Sociology of Gender* (Berkeley: University of California Press, 1978), esp. pp. 111–29.

21. Ibid. See also my Introduction to this book.

22. Douglas, *Purity and Danger,* p. 97.

23. Edwin Ardener, "The 'Problem' Revisited," in *Perceiving Women,* ed. Shirley Ardener (New York: John Wiley and Sons, 1975), p. 22.

24. Ibid.

25. Kingston, "The Coming Book," in *The Writer and Her Work,* ed. Janet Sternberg (New York: W. W. Norton, 1980), p. 182.

26. In her analysis of Kingston's memoirs as an example of female autobiography, Suzanne Juhasz notes, "It is through words—through finding them, forming them, saying them aloud, *in public*—that Kingston reaches selfhood." "Towards a Theory of Form in Feminist Autobiography: Kate Millet's *Flying* and Maxine Hong Kingston's *The Woman Warrior,*" in Jelinek, *Woman's Autobiography,* p. 236, emphasis in original. See also Margaret Miller's excellent analysis (which I came to after completing this chapter) of the memoir as autobiography: "Threads of Identity in Maxine Hong Kingston's *The Woman Warrior,*" *Biography,* Vol. 6, No. 1 (Winter 1983), pp. 13–33.

27. Maxine Hong Kingston, *China Men* (New York: Alfred A. Knopf, 1980).

All subsequent references in the text are from this edition, indicated by the abbreviation "*CM*" and parenthetical page numbers.

28. In a comparable example, Margery Wolf quotes an old village woman in Taiwan who bore many daughters and gave them away. When asked how she felt about parting with them, the woman answered quite emphatically, "'Why should I want so many daughters? It is useless to raise your own daughters. I'd just have to give them away when they were grown, so when someone asked for them as infants I gave them away. Think of all the rice I saved.'" Margery Wolf, *The House of Lim: A Study of a Chinese Farm Family* (New York: Appleton-Century-Crofts, 1968), p. 40.

Boundaries of the Cosmos

Leslie Silko

In an observation that applies to American as well as Canadian literary traditions, Margaret Atwood has noted that until very recently Indians appeared only as characters in books by white authors.[1] However, in the past fifteen years, Native American writers have remedied this one-sided situation, enriching American literature through both poetry and fiction. Until quite recently, only one novel had been published by a Native American woman: Leslie Silko (who is also a published poet). Her novel, *Ceremony* (1977), is an intricate, moving narrative of an American Indian's struggle to locate himself in his world.[2] The male protagonist, Tayo, struggles against the same cultural structures that infantilize women, and people of both genders belonging to ethnic minorities, by perpetuating their dependency and powerlessness and restricting their access to conditions that promote self-worth.

Ceremony is noteworthy in several respects. In addition to its evident artistry, it is also the story of a man's recovery of meaning and selfhood in a culture in which many of the organizing values are what would traditionally be considered female. This in itself is a reversal of many novelistic premises wherein, regardless of whether the writer and/or the protagonist are male or female, the larger social context is patriarchal. Much recent feminist criticism has focused on the representation of women in literary texts by both female and male authors; the representation of men as protagonists in narratives by women poses decidedly different questions for literary and feminist criticism.

The psychologist David Bakan has defined the opposing modes of relation to experience that are often stereotypically labeled "masculine" and "feminine" in the more neutral terms of "agency" and "communion": "agency for the existence of an organism as an individual, and communion for the participation of the individual in some larger organism of which the individual is a part. Agency manifests itself in self-protection, self-assertion, and self-expansion; communion manifests itself in the sense of being at one with other organisms. Agency manifests itself in the formation of separations; communion in the lack of separations."[3] Bakan's terminology is useful because it acknowledges that people of both genders participate in both modes, each under certain circumstances. In a given culture, the proportion of activity accorded members of each gender in each mode may be strictly set; furthermore, the culture itself may be characterized by emphasis on one more than the other.[4]

Most Indian cultures of the pueblos and plains traditionally based their lives upon a web of values that resembles Bakan's concept of "communion," or the dominant American culture's definition of the feminine. Unaggressive and affiliative rather than achievement oriented, the Pueblos participated in an agricultural economy and structured their lives in harmony with the rhythms of nature. In the Pueblo culture, in particular the Keresan-speaking Laguna Pueblo (Silko's cultural group), family structure is matrilineal and matrilocal; the principal creation and fertility deities are female.

Additionally, Pueblo culture is distinguished by its emphasis on directional and cosmological boundaries. As Alfonso Ortiz has observed, all Pueblo Indian groups "set careful limits to the boundaries of their world and order everything within it. These boundaries are not the same but, more important, the principles of setting boundaries are since all use phenomena in the four cardinal directions, either mountains or bodies of water, usually both, to set them. . . . All peoples try to bring their definitions of group space somehow into line with their cosmologies, but the Pueblos are unusually precise about it."[5]

Boundaries, then, are both metaphorical and metaphysical constructs within the Pueblo world view that frame experience for both the individual and the community. This fact produces a tragic irony, for the sacred boundaries of the Pueblo cosmos are juxtaposed with demarcations of a very secular and political nature: the reservations themselves are surrounded spaces, enclosed by fences on all sides. In Silko's narrative, literal and figurative images of boundaries or their absence are significant sym-

bolic points of reference. Fences, webs, and entanglement recur throughout *Ceremony,* suggesting both the positive and negative forms of
connection and separation in both individual and cultural contexts.

Moreover, Silko, writing about a racially mixed man's difficult struggle
to achieve identity and selfhood within his chosen cultural group, dramatizes Tayo's dilemma as a problem of boundaries, both cultural and psychological. Her protagonist is caught between two social structures with
incompatible ideological organizations. Tayo must reconcile the two
sides of his biological and cultural heritage, the split itself symbolizing
contradictory personal and cultural modes of being.

According to Silko's rendering of Laguna oral tradition, before the
white man entered the world, "the people shared the same consciousness." But eventually, outside of their unified clan, "the fifth world"—of
human beings—became "entangled with European names . . . all of creation suddenly had . . . an Indian name and a white name" (*C,* p. 70).
The story of the white people's arrival thus also describes the first knowledge of separation, the recognition of a rift in the unity and wholeness
of things in both individual and communal experience.

The nature of the protagonist's cultural dislocation and inner illness
and the manner of their cure unfold in *Ceremony* through two distinct
narrative styles. One style forwards the present time of the story and the
events leading to it (Tayo's childhood and youth, and his more recent war
experience); the other relates the timeless traditional tales that comment
on it. Thus, the narrative itself is a figurative web, as traditional songs
are interwoven with events from the life of a particular individual. Silko
is both the mediator of the traditional story in the mind of the creator-
deity, Thought Woman, and herself the creator of a narrative in which
those cultural stories are incorporated.

While the three prefatory poems express images of the interrelated web
of reality and the ceremonies of creation and renewal central to Pueblo
tradition, the early images of the prose narrative that follow suggest total
alienation. At the center of this symbolism is Tayo's own inner division.
The illegitimate son of a Laguna woman and an anonymous white man,
he was abandoned by his mother when he was a child, a casualty of her
own alienated life as a loose woman who associated indiscriminately with
white and Mexican men. Tayo was left in the care of his mother's sister,
an "Auntie" who (like Elizabeth Schoenhof's Auntie Muriel in Margaret

Atwood's *Life before Man*) fulfills one meaning of that term: "anti"—the equivalent of the negating stepmother of fairy tales.

From his birth, Tayo's Auntie had reinforced all of his own feelings of self-contempt and worthlessness, deliberately making him feel rejected. She had wanted Tayo "close enough to feel excluded, to be aware of the distance between them" (*C*, p. 69). She had also pushed her own son, Rocky, to excel in white schools and sports in order to gain a position in the white world. By such efforts, she had hoped to erase the shame caused by her sister's careless life. Yet Tayo had internalized the hatred felt by Indians toward whites as self-hatred of his "white" side.

Silko, herself of mixed parentage, has commented on the ambiguous consequences of such a heritage. As she remarks, "I suppose at the core of my writing is the attempt to identify what it is to be a half-breed or mixed blooded person; what it is to grow up neither white nor fully traditional Indian. It is for this reason that I hesitate to say that I am representative of Indian poets or Indian people, or even Laguna people. I am only one human being, one Laguna woman."[6] In a land in which Indian ethnic groups have historically been so visibly segregated from the rest of American culture, to be accepted by neither one nor the other group is to be a victim of radically confused identity. Like William Faulkner's Joe Christmas, who was also an orphan (of uncertain but probably mixed parentage), Tayo struggles for a sense of who he really is in the absence of either an unambiguous group identification or parents—those figures who normally provide the crucial context for the child's formation of personality.

Yet, in Silko's novel, the fact of ethnically mixed parentage becomes a sign of special powers. People with hazel eyes (one of whom is the protagonist, Tayo) are involved in the transitions that enable the culture to adapt and survive. Tayo himself ultimately joins this select group of wise people.

Through flashbacks, the reader learns that Tayo and his cousin Rocky had enlisted together for the U.S. Army during the Second World War. Rocky was killed by the Japanese (in Tayo's presence), while the latter survived. Eventually hospitalized for what is presumably shell shock, the young man had suffered from distortions of perception. Besides experiencing himself as invisible, he had been able to see only the flat outlines of his environment without their meaningful details. He had "inhabited a gray winter fog on a distant elk mountain where hunters are lost indefinitely and their own bones mark the boundaries" (*C*, p. 14).

Tayo's lingering nightmare of that period is "quicksand with no bottom or top, no edges" (*C*, p. 246). Other dreams of loss of boundary and engulfment by the Philippine jungle express his terrible guilt about his part in the war against Japan: he believes that he killed his uncle, Josiah, the only father he has ever known, in the body of a Japanese soldier. His recognition that the enemy soldier's skin was "not much different from his own" (*C*, p. 7) had precipitated a madness originating in his own racial confusion. Additionally, Tayo believes that his blasphemous prayers for an end to the interminable Philippine rains were the direct cause of six years of drought for his people in Laguna, New Mexico. Only much later do these disturbances evolve into a positive truth, namely that all human beings (who have not been corrupted by evil) are the same under the skin, "one clan again, united by the fate the destroyers planned for . . . all living things" (*C*, p. 258).

In psychological terms, Tayo suffers from the effects of acute loss: the traumatic separation from his mother in childhood (exacerbated by his subsequent family life); and survivor guilt as he outlived both Rocky, his "brother," in the war and Josiah, his uncle/father, who died while Tayo was in action—and for whose death he feels responsible. Silko's story dramatizes not only how the illness induced by separation and loss is healed within Tayo but also how it mirrors and is embedded in cultural loss, guilt, and separation from the earth—the ultimate mother in Pueblo tradition. Yet in another sense Tayo's story transcends its immediate cultural context to address the alienating legacy of patriarchy in Western culture as well.

When Tayo returns to his own pueblo after the war, he is repeatedly reminded of the arbitrary boundaries of his homeland. Along the highway that parallels the reservation fence, there is a string of bars that the local Indians call "'going up the line'" (*C*, p. 24). Most of Tayo's Laguna war buddies virtually drown themselves in liquor, trying to "silence their grief with war stories about their courage, defending the land they had already lost" (*C*, p. 178). Silko has suggested elsewhere that the Second World War brought out "destructive powers and sadism," not only in her people, but in the world at large—a conviction clearly elaborated in this novel.[7]

Tayo seeks out his war buddies because they are the only people who might be able to share his misery. But the other men's pride in their war experiences sickens him even further. They regard their days in uniform as a time when "'they got respect'" (*C*, p. 43). When they became civilians and Indians again, all of the cultural prejudices returned. As Tayo remarks, emphasizing his anomalous status, "'I'm half-breed. . . . I'll speak for both sides. First time you walked down the street in Gallup or Albuquerque, you knew. . . . The war was over, the uniform was gone. All of a sudden that man at the store waits on you last . . . '" (*C*, p. 43).

Between scenes that depict Tayo's malaise, Silko interweaves segments of several stories from Laguna oral tradition. One central tale concerns the community's struggle to earn forgiveness and purification following a punitive drought that causes great disharmony within the pueblo. As the story goes, the Laguna people, in their fascination with magic, neglect the altar of mother corn (whose name literally means "earth"[8]); the angry mother Nau'ts'ity'i retaliates by withholding rain clouds and crops, challenging the Lagunas to live off magic "if they like [it] so much" (*C*, p. 50). When the people realize their error and feel their painful separation from the earth mother, they seek her forgiveness. That task proves to be a complex one, involving a sequence of conditions and propitiations accomplished with the aid of animal representatives. Finally the people earn purification and forgiveness from their angry mother, and the rains and crops return to the land. Nau'ts'ity'i cautions the people, "'Stay out of trouble/ from now on.// It isn't very easy/ to fix up things again./ Remember that/ next time/ some ck'o'yo magician/ comes to town'" (*C*, p. 268).

This traditional story parallels Tayo's quest for purification and forgiveness from the "angry mother" who withholds the rain. His ceremony is "not easy" either and it similarly involves several distinct tasks and stages. Tayo makes a crucial connection between the earth mother and his own mother when he recalls the latter's death during another very dry time. He remembers that traditionally Spider Woman, the creator of the world, knew how to "win the storm clouds back" (*C*, p. 99); the spider "waited in certain locations for people to come to her for help" (*C*, p. 98). That aid comes unbidden before he leaves for the war: a spider emerges from the ground and, soon afterwards, rain comes "spinning out of the thunderclouds like gray spider webs" (*C*, p. 100).

195

On that very day, Tayo has his first sexual experience—with a woman old enough to be his mother. The Mexican woman, a former cantina dancer who calls herself Night Swan, is his Uncle Josiah's own tender prostitute. To Tayo, the woman is synonymous with mystery and life, "like the rain and the wind" (*C,* p. 103), thus suggestively identified with Spider Woman. When she initiates lovemaking with Tayo, "[H]er rhythm [merges] into the sound of the wind shaking the rafters and the sound of the rain in the tree" (*C,* p. 104). Night Swan tells Tayo that people are afraid of change and thus fearful of half-breeds like themselves with their hazel eyes, since their appearance challenges tribal norms. Her wisdom ultimately contributes to Tayo's successful struggle to accept himself and to unify his identity within his culture.

By the time Tayo returns to New Mexico after the war, everything has changed—except for his aunt's scorn. Rocky and Josiah are dead, Josiah's spotted Mexican cattle—also half-breed—are missing, and Tayo feels dead within. Still sick in spirit after visiting the local medicine man, he is sent to an unorthodox healer who lives in the foothills near the ceremonial dancing grounds in Gallup.

The medicine man, Betonie, whose name alludes to medicinal plants,[9] is of mixed (Indian and Mexican) blood; like Tayo, he has hazel eyes. Betonie's hazel-eyed Mexican grandmother was a medicine woman who, as he tells Tayo, had appeared mysteriously in a tree to a party of Laguna deer hunters. With his old grandfather, she had combined medicinal powers to re-enact the same ceremony of purification and opposition to evil in which Betonie later instructs Tayo. Initially, Tayo is puzzled by Betonie, whose obscure comments refer less to Tayo's malaise than to a perennial process, the struggle between good and evil. His "text" is a Laguna legend concerning the origin of evil and destruction in the world.

Before there were white people in the world, Betonie explains, there was a "contest" in "dark things" (*C,* p. 140), with powerful witches from various Indian tribes exhibiting their charms and powers. One witch— of indeterminate sex—did not perform any magical feats but merely told a self-actualizing prophecy, "creating" white people, who "[grew] away from the earth" and its bounty (*C,* p. 142). Because they turned their backs on living things, these people feared the world and began to destroy what they feared, including themselves. The ceremony of evil unleashed by the most malign and powerful witch continues to this day;

once the story gave form to reality, it could not be revoked but only opposed.

Here, as elsewhere in *Ceremony,* Silko suggests the power of storytelling itself. The witch of Betonie's story is the dark antithesis of Thought Woman's projection of ideas "outward into space and what she thought became reality." [10] When Tayo is most in touch with his own tradition, he sees "a world made of stories" (*C,* p. 100) in every living being and object; Betonie's vision becomes "a story he could feel happening" (*C,* p. 194). The world is animated by stories; once a story exists, it continues to affect the world, for either good or ill. The "destroyers" want to alter the ceremony by changing the "end of the story" (*C,* p. 243). Only unceasing human vigilance allows the restorative ceremony of life to persist in opposition to the witch's evil; the traditional rituals must change precisely in order to resist the new threats to them. [11] Silko's narrative thus participates in and extends the storytelling tradition of her culture, for she incorporates timeless stories and mythical tales into a contemporary narrative of transformation and renewal.

The transformation begins when Betonie guides Tayo through a ritual ceremony of purification and describes his vision. As Tayo understands the meaning of these rituals and signs, "there were transitions that had to be made in order to become whole again, in order to be the people our Mother would remember" (*C,* p. 178). The language is particularly resonant: Tayo's struggle for wholeness is bound up with the memory of his actual mother and other lost loved ones, as well as the generative female spirits of his culture. His alienation and his anxieties over the separations forced upon him are inextricably connected to the losses of his culture and to his community's fear of loss of their land.

The ritual initiation prompts Tayo's epiphany of a cosmos with "no boundaries; the world below [the mountaintop] and the sand paintings inside became the same that night. The mountains from all the directions had been gathered there" during his initiatory ritual (*C,* p. 152). The imagery of boundary thus shifts from the negative experience of terrifying loss of selfhood through engulfment or invisibility to the positive experience of identification with the cosmos.

Tayo's mission is interrupted on several occasions by his beer-swilling buddies—the form of temptation he must overcome in order to complete his ceremony of renewal. More positively, one day a strange woman appears beneath an apricot tree. Like both Night Swan and Betonie's grandmother, the young woman with "ocher" eyes (*C*, p. 185) is marked by significant natural signs: she carries a small willow staff and wears a blue silk shawl and moccasins with rainbirds carved on the silver buttons; her blanket bears a design of rain clouds.

Significantly, Betonie's grandmother was also Mexican, had eyes of an unconventional color, and appeared from a tree wearing a blue (lace) shawl (*C*, p. 154). Night Swan, who is also associated with rain, wind, and trees, wore a blue satin kimono (*C*, p. 102) and lived in an apartment with blue flowers painted on the walls. The repeated features of unconventional eye color and dominant colors and symbols of nature underscore the three women's common connection to restorative or creative female earth powers; the woman beneath the apricot tree, whose name is Ts'eh,[12] is a spirit woman and the most important female presence in the novel. Eventually, Ts'eh, like Night Swan, initiates lovemaking with Tayo, who fears "being lost" in her (*C*, p. 188). However, something makes him release himself into Ts'eh's power, and through her he begins to find himself.

Tayo leaves Ts'eh to search for his Uncle Josiah's missing herd of spotted Mexican cattle. Eventually locating the herd behind a white man's reinforced boundary fence, he realizes that they are not lost but stolen; he cuts a hole in the fence wide enough for the cattle to escape through it. In recovering Josiah's legacy, he finds a partial antidote to his own sense of homelessness. In a larger sense, however, Tayo's placelessness can never be ameliorated. His people's historical loss of their land is a deep and terrible injury that challenges their collective identity.

Two white cowboys intercept Tayo on the mountain just after he makes the hole in the boundary fence. Trapped like an animal and imagining that he might die at their hands, he takes sustenance from the earth beneath him.

> The magnetism of the center spread over him smoothly like rainwater down his neck and shoulders. . . . It was pulling him back, close to the earth . . . and even with the noise and pain in his head he knew how it would be: a returning rather than a separation. He was relieved because he feared leaving people he loved. But lying above the center that pulled him down closer felt more familiar to him than any embrace he could remember; and he was sinking into the elemental arms of mountain silence. (*C*, p. 210)

In Pueblo culture, Hamilton Tyler notes, the "center" symbolizes a place of "stability and balance which can only be achieved in the true home where one's heart lies."[13] This passage in Silko's narrative articulates most explicitly the identification of earth with woman and mother, the female sources from whom Tayo has felt himself radically separated. Distanced from both his actual mother and his affiliative culture, Tayo initially fears the earth's encompassing embrace, believing that his own energy "would leak out and take with it all barriers, all boundaries; he would seep into the earth and rest with the center, where the voice of the silence was familiar and the density of the dark earth loved him. He could secure the thresholds with molten pain and remain; or he could let go and flow back. It was up to him" (*C*, p. 211).

The language powerfully evokes an image of symbiosis—that state in which we all began but which, particularly for males and in Western culture, is fraught with the anxiety of loss of autonomy. Although one must be careful in applying observations based upon one culture's domestic arrangements and resulting psychological patterns to those of other cultures, certainly the absolute dependence of an infant on a nurturing figure or figures (who is/are in most cases female) is a constant in human experience.[14] Within the communal Laguna culture, Tayo *must* "flow back," reconnect with that powerful female force, before he can be fully recovered. As he did with Ts'eh, Tayo acquiesces to what frightens him and "merges with the center." Paradoxically, instead of relinquishing his potency in this submission, he affirms it.

Later imagery makes unmistakable the association between the earth and the regenerative female powers of Pueblo tradition. When subsequently Tayo dreams of lovemaking with Ts'eh, he feels that she is literally indistinguishable from the earth: "He couldn't feel where her body ended and the sand began" (*C*, p. 232). Through that sensation, he understands that his ambivalence about intimate connection with a woman is a manifestation of his "terror at loss" (*C*, p. 229): the excruciating anxiety of separation exaggerated by his mother's abandonment of him in childhood, perpetuated by his aunt's contempt, and made still more painful by the losses associated with his war experiences.

Tayo's despair at "something lost forever" (*C*, p. 229) eventually gives way to a realization that, if he views himself not in isolation but as a part of the interconnected cosmos, "[N]othing was lost; all was retained be-

199

tween the sky and the earth, and within himself" (*C,*, p. 229). Silko thus emphasizes here (and elsewhere) her concern with "communion"—both among people and between the individual and nature. As she phrases it, "'What I'm concerned about are relationships,'" for "'That's all there really is. . . . You have to come to terms, to some kind of equilibrium with those people around you, those people who care for you, your environment.'"[15] In *Ceremony*, the "destroyers" are not simply white people but any people who "destroy the feeling people have for each other" (*C,* p. 240).

As if to verify the connection Tayo feels between the expansive state of his own being and the state of the earth, rain arrives, ending the drought that began while he was away at war. It is not that his blasphemous prayers in the Philippine jungle had actually produced the drought in New Mexico. Rather, his intuitive insight during the war—that what happened there was somehow related to what happened elsewhere on earth—has become a more generalized truth. Within the Pueblo perception, the world is indeed a vast, interconnected web, and the apparently limited acts of good or evil affect the common fate of all living beings on the earth.

With Ts'eh's final reappearance, the rains continue and the land becomes green again. The sexual union between the hero and the female earth spirit revitalizes Tayo and symbolizes his position as a fulcrum in the ceremony of collective restoration;[16] the spirit woman tutors Tayo in his renewed relationship with the earth through both lovemaking and herbal lore. Moreover, the recovery of the lost, mixed-breed cattle through the break in the boundary fence is emblematic of the lost, half-breed Tayo's own breakthrough as he accepts himself in connection to others and to the earth.

Through Ts'eh, Tayo realizes how his anger and pain have turned inward, numbing his feelings. It is his "white" half with which Tayo has self-destructively identified—the part associated not only with his unknown white father but with aggression and division. The healers he encounters guide him to the recovery of his Laguna identity, which becomes synonymous with the affiliative female dimension of his heritage. Though the spirit woman Ts'eh eventually leaves Tayo, as has every other person to whom he has felt a deep emotional attachment, this time he retains the confidence that he can survive separation. "[H]is connection with the ground was solid" (*C,* p. 242); he has integrated within himself the traditional female powers of reverence for life and generativity that Ts'eh embodies.

The final and most dangerous phase of the ceremony is Tayo's encounter with his war buddies, who he has erroneously believed are his friends and not men already poisoned by their entanglement in destructive rituals. After a drunken interlude, the men leave Tayo near an abandoned uranium mine shaft. The place, which corresponds with images in Betonie's retelling of the witch's story, marks the point of origin in the path of evil that eventually resulted in the atomic bomb, which in turn led to the detonations over Hiroshima and Nagasaki while Tayo was fighting the Japanese "enemy" in the Philippine jungles. Further, the destruction of man (and earth) by man "knew no boundaries; and he had arrived at the point of convergence where the fate of all living things, and even the earth, had been laid. . . . [T]he lines of cultures and worlds were drawn in flat dark lines on fine light sand, converging in the middle of witchery's final ceremonial sand painting. From that time on, human beings were one clan again, . . . united by a circle of death that devoured people in cities twelve thousand miles away . . ." (*C*, pp. 257–58).

The elements of the very earth itself are thus ambivalent on a grand scale, depending on their use; the terrible power that can destroy the entire world can be neutralized only by the power of human beings in community. It is this struggle between the powers of creation and destruction that is encoded in Betonie's parable—and in Silko's narrative. The uranium site is a symbolic center, where Tayo sees the entangled strands of his experience converge in a central meaning: "[A]ll the stories fit together—the old stories, the war stories, [the destroyers'] stories—to become the story that was still being told. . . . He had only seen and heard the world as it always was: no boundaries, only transitions through all distances and time" (*C*, p. 258).

The completion of Tayo's ceremony occurs during a natural solar transition, when "the darkness of night and the light of day [are] balanced" (*C*, p. 259): the autumnal equinox, an important astronomical event in the Pueblo ceremonial year.[17] The timing underscores what Tayo has learned about the interconnected web of human and natural events. At the uranium site in the gathering dusk, Tayo's "buddies" try to entangle him in their barbaric rituals. Tayo almost fulfills their malign plan. Instead, newly strengthened by Ts'eh's tutelage, he subdues his murderous urges. As propitiation for his temptation to kill, he locates a plant designated by Ts'eh that will create "light"; its seeds will reproduce new plants as "strong and translucent as the stars" (*C*, p. 266). In this emblematic act, Silko's protagonist celebrates the recovery of the female forces in himself: achieving enlightenment, he participates in the earth's regeneration.

As Tayo crosses the river at the symbolic renewal time of sunrise (references to which frame the narrative), the transition is completed with his multiply suggestive reflection: "He thought of her then; she had always loved him; she had never left him; she had always been there" (*C*, p. 267). The ambiguous feminine pronoun simultaneously suggests Ts'eh, Tayo's own mother, Laura, and the Great Mother, the earth. As Silko has commented, "It all comes together in the end, his being loved, the mother, the creator."[18] Tayo, forgiving himself for having survived his dead loved ones, feels at home in the world at last and returns to his pueblo renewed and whole.

Thereafter, Tayo himself assumes the role of the storyteller adumbrated in the narrative's opening poem (*C*, p. 2), recounting for his people his path of ritual purification and self-recovery.[19] His evil-worshiping "buddies" are entangled by their own destructive aggressions. Symbolically, evil can never be destroyed but only overcome in a process that recurs eternally. The dialectic of opposing forces—and the power of the word—resonate at every level of the polarized Pueblo universe.[20]

The seven works considered in this section reflect diverse renderings of the relationship between individual and cultural identity. Though Toni Morrison, Maxine Hong Kingston, and Leslie Silko artistically represent experience in quite distinct manners and narrative forms, their several works reflect a common concern with issues of boundary in both psychological and cultural terms. The dilemmas of selfhood that in the fiction of Penelope Mortimer and Margaret Atwood result from the mediations within personal relationships—daughter and mother, wife and husband, self and other, and within the self—are given additional resonance within the larger context of cultural position.

In *The Woman Warrior* and *China Men*, Kingston delineates the double bind of patriarchal devaluation of females in both Chinese and American cultures and, additionally, the conditions of exclusion shared by both men and women of Chinese ancestry. Morrison, in each novel but most explicitly in *Tar Baby,* dramatizes the conflict of values between dominant and minority groups as well as within black culture. Jadine Childs's figurative dual parentage, like Tayo's literally mixed parentage in *Ceremony,* illustrates the dilemmas of cultural exclusion or contradiction: the difficulty of establishing identity when barriers resulting from skin color, ethnic origin, economic class, or their combination reduce access to opportunity for the minority culture as a whole.

In each writer's narratives, the ethnic community functions as "the boundary maintained from within,"[21] the common cultural knowledge that, even though it contains contradictions, provides the frame of reference for social behavior, moral judgment, and acceptance or exclusion. Thus, in *The Bluest Eye, Tar Baby,* and *The Woman Warrior,* the mother-daughter relationship is complicated by the mother's ambivalent role as transmitter to her daughter of negative or ambiguous cultural attitudes toward her gender and sexuality. While this is implicitly true in several of the narratives by women writers who belong to the mainstream culture, the experiences of exclusion on the basis of appearance, language, or other ethnically distinct traits underscore the impediments to the achievement of female selfhood in patriarchy.

In the narratives in which the protagonist is male, the story traces his recovery of traditional values or cultural memories that have been lost to his entire community. In fact, the female author's projection of a cultural dilemma through a male character highlights the distinctions between exclusion on the basis of gender and ethnic origin; the central male character is the locus for boundary issues that both include and transcend gender. In *Song of Solomon* and *Ceremony,* the male protagonist achieves manhood, identity, or inner wholeness by restoring his connection to cultural values that may themselves be in "transition." That achievement directly depends on a female mentor who guides him toward his integration of the female dimension of his personal or cultural heritage. Concern with "geography" or the land of origin, the names of people or places, and the recognition of reciprocal responsibility elaborate the male character's affirmation of connection to others and the continuity as well as the flexibility of his cultural tradition.

In *Ceremony,* the forces of destruction in history and myth are set against the capacity for renewal present in both, as they operate in the cosmos and the individual. Through such renewal, Silko's protagonist, Tayo, is able to resist the powers of aggression and division that would destroy both him and his cultural community. He heals his inner split—his acute sense of loss of his loved ones, his heritage, and the land—by joining forces with the elemental restorative powers of the earth.

In that resolution, the narrative illustrates in cultural terms, as each child eventually learns in personal terms, that the "good mother" and the "angry mother" are two sides of the same primary entity. Silko's story implies that the aggressive urges more traditionally associated with the male are held in balance by those forces conceived in Laguna mythology (and in Western tradition) as the female powers of the universe. By implication, these capacities for regeneration and communion might well be integrated, not only in a culturally mixed man like Tayo, but in Western culture itself.

Victor Turner, in his analysis of ritual transitions within traditional cultures, uses the term "liminality" to indicate an individual's position "between fixed points," a situation that is "ambiguous, unsettled, and unsettling."[22] In this sense, Silko's Tayo is the most obviously liminal character; the term "transition" describes his movement through and completion of the ceremony of renewal as he himself changes. More broadly, the characters in these narratives frequently occupy an anomalous or liminal position "betwixt and between the categories of ordinary social life."[23] Whether as women, as members of ethnic minority groups, or both, they are simultaneously shaped by and excluded from the dominant structures of power and validation. The figure of the pariah and the theme of cultural orphanage that recurs in Morrison's novels embody the experiences of separation and loss not only as psychological processes but as mediations between the "inside" and the "outside" in collective or cultural terms.

In their depictions of communities with partially overlapping attitudes toward women and people of both genders who are ethnically distinct, these three authors invoke the power of language and story telling to fuse the conflicting strands of experience. Each writer enacts that imaginative synthesis through the relationship between narrator, text, and reader. Morrison invites the reader to participate in the mediation of paradox by leaving "holes and spaces" in the language "so the reader can come into it."[24] Kingston's two memoirs, distinguished by their selective focus on female and male cultural experience, exemplify complementary narrative strategies. *The Woman Warrior* is inevitably the more artistically compelling of the two because it interweaves personal and cultural, particular and general, to meld several different layerings of female experience into an imaginative whole. By contrast, the author's greater actual and critical distance from the male side of her heritage imposes aesthetic limitations on such synthesis; the obvious discrepancies between history and invention make the latter work a less lyrical narrative.

Ultimately, however, both memoirs are unique renderings of the relationship between storytelling and experience, between fiction and reality. Kingston expresses her desire (since satisfied) to visit the land of her ancestral origin in order to compare "China, a country I made up, with what country is really out there."[25] Yet she knows that the place her relatives (of both genders) describe no longer exists. In blurring the narrative boundary between "real" and "imaginary," Maxine Hong Kingston invents not only her ancestors' China but the past, since there is no other way to visit them.

Like Kingston, Silko extends the boundaries of narrative form in order to give expression to her story of cultural bifurcation. *Ceremony* is a continuation of the traditional narrative activity that creates and recreates the world. Itself a web of interconnected stories and images, it fuses two different kinds of narrative traditions. The novel is framed by segments of traditional oral chants or poems; other orally transmitted legends from the author's Laguna culture are translated and incorporated in poetic form, deliberately contrasting with the prose both in style and in their placement on the page. Thus the text itself reflects the synthesis of diverse frames of reference.

Furthermore, in identifying herself with both the female creator, Thought Woman, and the culturally mixed male protagonist Tayo, Silko imaginatively straddles the categories of gender.[26] Her narrative inscribes the way in which the fate of all people, regardless of gender or ethnic origin, is fundamentally interconnected; what human beings do to each other and to the earth, for good or ill, reverberates throughout the cosmos. The changing boundaries of the self, with its capacities for both creation and destruction, are analogous to the dynamic state of the world.

NOTES

1. Margaret Atwood, *Survival: A Thematic Guide to Canadian Literature* (Toronto: Anansi, 1972), p. 91.

2. Leslie Marmon Silko, *Ceremony* (1977, rpt. New York: New American Li-

brary, 1978). All subsequent references, indicated by "*C*" and parenthetical page numbers in the text, are to this edition. Three novels by American Indian women published since Silko's appeared are *Love Medicine* by Louise Erdrich (New York: Holt, Rinehart and Winston, 1984), *The Woman Who Owned the Shadows* by Paula Gunn Allen (San Francisco: Spinsters, Inc., 1984), and *The Jailing of Cecelia Capture* by Janet Campbell Hale (New York: Random House, 1985).

3. David Bakan, *The Duality of Human Existence: Isolation and Communion in Western Man* (Boston: Beacon Press, 1966), p. 15.

4. See also Carol Gilligan's discussion of the difference between male and female moral perspectives, *In a Different Voice: Psychological Theory and Women's Development* (Cambridge: Harvard University Press, 1982).

5. Alfonso Ortiz, "Ritual Drama and the Pueblo World View," in *New Perspective on the Pueblos,* ed. Alfonso Ortiz (Albuquerque: University of New Mexico Press, 1972), p. 142.

6. Silko, *Laguna Woman* (Greenfield Center, N.Y.: Greenfield Review Press, 1974), p. 35.

7. Silko, in "Stories and Their Tellers: A Conversation with Leslie Marmon Silko," in *The Third Woman: Minority Women Writers of the United States,* ed. Dexter Fisher (Boston: Houghton Mifflin, 1980), p. 22. See also Scott Momaday's novel, *House Made of Dawn* (New York: New American Library, 1969), for an important treatment of the effect of World War II on Indians who fought in it. Charles R. Larson, in his study of Native American fiction, places both Silko's and Momaday's novels in the context of narratives written by Indian authors and provides a fine, concise analysis of *Ceremony. American Indian Fiction* (Albuquerque: University of New Mexico Press, 1978).

8. Hamilton Tyler, *Pueblo Gods and Myths* (Norman: University of Oklahoma Press, 1964), p. 118.

9. According to the *Oxford English Dictionary,* "betony" (with a number of variant spellings, including "betonie") is a plant once believed to have not only medicinal but magical properties.

10. See Tyler, *Pueblo Gods and Myths,* p. 89, and *Ceremony,* first prefatory poem, p. 1.

11. Edward Dozier has observed that "[c]eremonial activity is the Pueblo's contribution to maintaining a harmonious balance which is believed to be the natural state of affairs. In Pueblo belief, as long as ceremonies are consistently and properly performed, nature will respond by providing the necessities of life. Thus, man and nature cooperate to maintain universal balance. Man alone, however, may upset the balance; he may do so by refusing to engage in ceremonial activity, by harboring ill feelings, by failure to observe minute details of costuming and performance." *The Pueblo Indians of North America* (New York: Holt, Rinehart and Winston, 1970), p. 200.

12. Kenneth Lincoln notes that Ts'eh's full name—Ts'eh Montaño—is a conflation of several Laguna words: "'Ts'i' is Keresan for water and 'montaña' Spanish for mountain, hence 'Water-Mountain' spirit-woman, perhaps, in the two languages, translated into English, that fuse Silko's own linguistical-genetic heritage." *Native American Renaissance* (Berkeley: University of California Press, 1983), pp. 240–41. Lincoln's reading of *Ceremony* is both illuminating and valuable for his knowledgeable interpretation of a variety of Laguna rituals, words, colors, and figures.

13. Tyler, *Pueblo Gods and Myths,* p. 115.

14. As Dorothy Dinnerstein has phrased it, the mother is typically "the helpless child's main contact with the natural surround, the center of everything the infant wants and feels drawn to, fears losing and feels threatened by. She is the center also of the non-self, an unbounded, still unarticulated region within which the child labors to define itself and to discover the outlines of durable objects, creatures, themes." *The Mermaid and the Minotaur: Sexual Arrangements and Human Malaise* (rpt. New York: Harper and Row, 1977), p. 93.

15. Silko, in Fisher, *The Third Woman,* pp. 21, 22.

16. *Ceremony* is a fertility legend like that of the Fisher King: the restoration of the land by rain is conditional upon the cure of, in this case, the hero's own illness. See Jessie Weston, *From Ritual to Romance* (rpt. Garden City, N.Y.: Doubleday, 1957), esp. pp. 113–36. I noticed this connection before discovering Allan Velie's discussion, "Leslie Silko's *Ceremony:* A Laguna Grail Story," in Velie, *Four American Indian Literary Masters: Momaday, Welch, Silko, Vizenor* (Norman: University of Oklahoma Press, 1982), pp. 107–11, 120–21.

17. Alfonso Ortiz emphasizes the importance of the solstices and equinoxes in Pueblo culture. These points of the solar calendar form a kind of "axis mundi" symbolism upon which other ceremonies are organized. For the Laguna Pueblo, the equinoxes rather than the solstices were primary points of transition. "Ritual Drama and the Pueblo World View," p. 144. Kenneth Lincoln writes, "Laguna [Pueblo] may be regarded as a Pueblo of transitions—geographically, genetically, linguistically, culturally, and historically." *Native American Renaissance,* p. 233.

18. Silko, in Fisher, *The Third Woman,* p. 22.

19. As Kenneth Lincoln phrases it, "Silko's novel is a word ceremony. It tells Tayo's story as a curative act." *Native American Renaissance,* p. 237.

20. Hamilton Tyler notes that Pueblo thought is distinguished by a persistent dualism and a concern for oppositions: "'everything both ways.'" *Pueblo Gods and Myths,* p. 142.

21. Anya Peterson Royce, *Ethnic Identity: Strategies of Diversity* (Bloomington: Indiana University Press, 1982), p. 29. See the Introduction to this study, page 7.

22. Victor Turner, *Dramas, Fields, and Metaphors: Symbolic Action in Human Society* (Ithaca: Cornell University Press, 1974), p. 274.

23. Ibid., p. 273. As Turner elaborates, "Structure, or all that which holds people apart, defines their differences, and constrains their actions, is one pole in a charged field, for which the opposite pole is communitas, or anti-structure . . . representing the desire for a total, unmediated relationship between person and person, a relationship which nevertheless does not submerge one in the other but safeguards their uniqueness in the very act of realizing their commonness. Communitas does not merge identities; it liberates them from conformity to general norms, though this is necessarily a transient condition if society is to continue to operate in an orderly fashion" (p. 274).

24. Toni Morrison, in an interview conducted by Claudia Tate in *Black Women Writers at Work,* ed. Claudia Tate (New York: Continuum, 1983), p. 125. Elsewhere Morrison has compared her use of the narrative form to black musical forms: "I think about what black writers do as having a quality of hunger and disturbance that never ends. Classical music satisfies and closes. Black music does not do that. Jazz always keeps you on the edge. There is no final chord. . . . There is always something else that you want from the music. I want my books to be like that—because I want that feeling of something held in reserve and the sense that there is more—that you can't have it all right now." "An Interview with Toni Morrison" conducted by Nellie McKay, *Contemporary Literature,* Vol. 23, No. 4 (Winter 1983), p. 429.

25. Maxine Hong Kingston, *China Men* (New York: Alfred A. Knopf, 1980), p. 87.

26. Silko has commented, "Writing the novel was a ceremony for me to stay sane. . . . My character [Tayo] is very sick, and I was very sick when I was writing the novel. . . . And as Tayo got better, I felt better." Fisher, *The Third Woman,* p. 20.

PART 3

Reformulating Boundaries

Transformations of the Ordinary

Marilynne Robinson

Like the women of Penelope Mortimer's fiction, the central female figures of Marilynne Robinson's single novel to date, *Housekeeping* (1981), are in important ways linked to and defined by their emotional investment in "home."[1] However, while "housekeeping" is for most people the effort of resisting dust, disorder, and deterioration, for several women among the three generations of the Foster family—particularly the inscrutable Sylvie Fisher—housekeeping is the opportunity to commune with the absolute, to merge boundaries, to meld the human and natural worlds by accumulation of rather than resistance to nature's encroachments. As the novel's narrator and central consciousness, Ruth Stone, observes of her unorthodox aunt, "Sylvie in a house was more or less like a mermaid in a ship's cabin. She preferred it sunk in the very element it was meant to exclude" (*H*, p. 99).

Against such housekeeping efforts is the overarching force of loss, both particular and general: of identity, of family, of anchorage in the world, of life. Chance accidents, combined with deliberate choices, converge in the direction of what Mortimer's Eleanor Strathearn terms "parting," or absence. Robinson develops the correspondences between the self and home, inner and outer life, in myriad ways through a poetic language that makes each image resonate with a number of others. Thus, "housekeeping" is one of a cluster of metaphors that gather meaning during the course of the narrative, articulating Ruth's gradual comprehension of memory, time, and death.

The juxtapositions of mountains and water, movement and stasis, surface and depth are the oppositions that activate the narrative, as if to suggest the invisible boundaries that paradoxically both join and separate all people and things. The objects of the physical environment are implicated in the movement in both visible and psychic worlds toward entropy and chaos. In fact, a crucial tension within the characters and the narrative is the choice—whether deliberate or inevitable—to participate in the momentum toward chaos or to oppose it.

These contrary domains of entropy and order are bridged by recollection, for, as Ruth phrases it late in the narrative, "Memory is the sense of loss, and loss pulls us after it. God Himself was pulled after us into the vortex we made when we fell, or so the story goes" (*H*, p. 194). Ruth's retrospective narrative is the story of events that in fact happened "many years ago now" (*H*, p. 213). In retelling it, she seeks an answer to her question, "When did I become so unlike other people?" (*H*, p. 214). By the effort of remembering, Ruth attempts first to reclaim, then to undo, and only finally to accept the vanished past.

Ruth's obsession with the past can be understood through the circumstances of her family history, which is one of oddity as well as tragedy. Long before her own birth, her maternal grandfather, Edmund Foster, had impulsively left his "subterraneous" house in the Midwest to "go west," arriving at the small mountain-ringed town of Fingerbone, Idaho. There he had worked for the railroad until his death in a train accident: the train had derailed over the lake, plunging into the deep water, where it was never located. Years later, the story of that accident continues to haunt the consciousness of the town and, particularly, the Foster women.

Rather than unfolding in a chronological manner, the narrative—like that spectacular accident—advances in several dimensions at once: both forward and downward into hidden depths. In retelling her story, Ruth gives her grandfather the position of a patriarch whose demise has a ripple effect upon her own story. His death left his widow, Sylvia Foster, with three teenaged daughters, the middle one of whom was Helen, later Ruth's mother. Eventually Helen eloped and "set up housekeeping" (*H*, p. 14) with a ne'er-do-well, Reginald Stone (Ruth and Lucille's "putative" father). She returned only once to Fingerbone, to leave her two young daughters with her mother. She then drove a borrowed car off a cliff into the lake, in deliberate imitation of her father's accidental death. For the rest of her life, Ruth is haunted by her mother's suicide, her own bereavement, and the vision of her two relatives lying at the bottom of the lake.

Ruth and Lucille Stone are orphans in an entirely female world. Apart from the grandfather (who is dead before the narrative opens) and the anonymous sheriff of Fingerbone, who represents the community's distrust of Sylvie Fisher's unorthodox values, there is not a single significant male figure in *Housekeeping*. The husbands of Sylvia Foster and her two briefly married daughters are quickly dismissed as if to illustrate that erotic union is the most transient relationship of all. Instead, Robinson focuses on the nature and endurance of the bonds that link women, both across and within generations.[2] This unique characteristic sets the novel apart from most narratives of quest and discovery. Rather than occupying auxiliary roles in a story of male adventure, the women, Ruth and her aunt, Sylvie, are ultimately engaged in a profound adventure in which, bypassing the more conventional unions between male and female, they address themselves to the nature of reality itself.

Before that process begins, however, the two parentless young sisters came to share the status of "foster" children through a series of female caretakers. Cared for first by their grandmother for five years until her death, Ruth and Lucille inherited Sylvia Foster's house and the family history it has witnessed. The deaths of her close relatives in Ruth's early life have given her a special sensitivity to abandonment and loss. When her grandmother died, she equated Sylvia Foster's quiet expiration (she "eschewed awakening," p. 29) with her grandfather's and mother's watery deaths. She felt as if "the earth had opened" and her grandmother "had entered into some other element upon which our lives floated as weightless, intangible, immiscible, and inseparable as reflections in water. So she was borne to the depths, my grandmother, into the undifferentiated past . . ." (*H*, p. 41). Thus is the lake bottom a location not only in space but in time.

Of the three daughters of Sylvia and Edmund Foster, Ruth's Aunt Sylvie most resembles the mother whose name she shares; her life as a drifter is an enactment of her mother's conviction that life was "a road down which one traveled . . . and that one's destination was there from the very beginning" (*H*, p. 9). Arriving from the "Lost Hills Hotel" in Nevada, she is never entirely at home even in the house she comes to share with Ruth and Lucille. She sleeps with her clothes on, keeps a twenty-dollar bill pinned to her lapel, and in numerous ways demonstrates her reluctance to become attached to a single place. Setting up her unconventional housekeeping in her own childhood home, she hoards newspapers, bottles, and cans, and lets the detritus of everyday life accumulate within its walls. As Ruth has come to see, Sylvie "considered accumulation to be the essence of housekeeping" (*H,* p. 180).

During their joint occupancy of the Foster house, the three females reflect distinctly different orientations to the organization and comprehension of experience. Sylvie, despite her random accumulations, is attached to nothing material; she lives in a "millennial present" (*H,* p. 94) in which the very absence of rootedness leaves her open to constant new discovery. Ruth and Lucille diverge at adolescence, for Ruth feels the paradoxical "gaze of world as a distorting mirror that squashed [Lucille] plump and stretched [Ruth] narrow" (*H,* p. 99). In her effort to project a more conventional image, Lucille shifts her attention to the future; Ruth remains concentrated on the past, seeking there an antidote to her simultaneously terrifying and comforting conviction of being "invisible—incompletely and minimally existent" (*H,* p. 105).

Though both Ruth and Lucille long for their mother, they have mutually exclusive images of her. Lucille's Helen was "orderly, vigorous, and sensible, a widow . . . who was killed in an accident" (*H,* p. 109). By contrast, Ruth's Helen "tended us with a gentle indifference that made me feel she would have liked to have been even more alone—she was the abandoner, and not the one abandoned" (*H,* p. 109). Lucille, increasingly troubled by Sylvie's eccentric habits, determines to make a more secure order, severing herself from her aunt's endorsement of transience and anarchy. Ruth, in need of a way to neutralize her experience of abandonment, accepts Sylvie's chaotic "housekeeping" because her aunt fills the emotional space traumatically vacated by her mother. As she phrases it, "Lucille would busy herself forever, nudging, pushing, coaxing, as if she could supply the will I lacked, to pull myself into some seemly shape and slip across the wide frontiers into that other world, where it seemed to me then I could never wish to go. For it seemed to me that nothing I had lost, or might lose, could be found there, or, to put it another way, it seemed that something I had lost might be found in Sylvie's house" (*H,* pp. 123–24).

Through a gradual process of identification, Ruth has become a drifter like her aunt, rejecting the "common persuasion" (*H*, p. 93) favored by Lucille and the rest of Fingerbone. Her affiliation with Sylvie has slowly enabled her to come to terms with her mother's absence and the truth about the perishability of all human relationships. Throughout the narrative, images of this lost mother recur like a threnody of sorrow. Ruth can scarcely even remember that figure who bore her, yet the space created by her abandonment occupies her daughter's very being. During one of several visits to the lake (first with Lucille and later with Sylvie), Ruth has an imaginative vision of her mother's missionary sister, Molly, in heaven, sweeping the world with a net that might even bring up the bottom of Fingerbone lake, including all of its occupants from the primordial era to the present.

> [In] such a crowd my mother would hardly seem remarkable. There would be a general reclaiming of fallen buttons and misplaced spectacles, of neighbors and kin, till time and error and accident were undone, and the world became comprehensible and whole. . . . Ascension seemed at such times a natural law. If one added to it a law of completion—that everything must finally be made comprehensible—then some general rescue of the sort I imagined my aunt to have undertaken would be inevitable. . . . What are all these fragments for, if not to be knit up finally? (*H*, p. 92)

Each time Ruth visits the lake, she experiences a variation of this fantasy of resurrection and reclamation of her mother. Moreover, each journey there is a more extensive exploration of the lake's—and her own—boundaries and a deepening of comprehension that eventually transforms her. Her accumulating knowledge of both surface and perimeter of the lake is analogous to her penetration of its mystery and the secrets housed in its depths.

The lake itself, like Ruth's narrative, is composed of several overlapping levels in time and space: an older, deeper body of water whose boundaries have been hidden by the current, visible Fingerbone lake; the lake in flood, when it overflows its banks and inundates the town; and the lake sublimated into the air as droplets of water. These different states are analogous to successive states of Ruth's inner transformation as her identification with her lost mother is figuratively sublimated. Ruth—whose name recalls the faithful daughter-in-law of the Old Testament and, appropriately, signifies compassion, sorrow, grief, and remorse—

215

undertakes the perennial journey of discovery, with Sylvie as her guide.[3] "Fingerbone," suggesting an extended skeletal finger from the past point- ing the way, also resonates with the ironic title image of "housekeeping."

During early adolescence, Ruth and Lucille, bored with school, be- come truants and spend most of their days at the lake. Ruth imagines telling the hoboes about her grandfather's watery death. "Perhaps," she continues, in another image of reversal of the past,

> [W]e all awaited a resurrection. Perhaps we expected a train to leap out of the water, caboose foremost, as if in a movie run backward, and then to continue across the bridge. The passengers would arrive, sounder than they departed, accustomed to the depths, serene about their restoration to the light, disembarking at the station in Fingerbone with a calm that quieted the astonishment of friends. Say that this resurrection was general enough to include my grandmother, and Helen, my mother. (*H*, p. 96)

Once, Ruth and Lucille spend the night in the woods near the lake and feel overwhelmed by the "absolute darkness" (*H*, p. 115). Though they construct a makeshift hut, Ruth accepts that, surrounded by animals and nature, "all our human boundaries were overrun" (*H*, p. 115). With dark- ness as a "solvent" that dissolves the separations between things, Ruth feels herself merged with the external world: "I simply let the darkness in the sky become coextensive with the darkness in my skull and bowels and bones" (*H*, p. 116). Such merging of inside and outside actually began for Ruth when she and Lucille were still young children who feared the dark; their grandmother had told them to close their eyes, for then they would not see it. Ruth recalls, "That was when I noticed the corre- spondence between the space within the circle of my skull and the space around me" (*H*, p. 198). But the figure she always saw against "the lid of [her] eye or the wall of [her] room" was her mother (*H*, p. 198).

Robinson's narrative develops through antithesis and contrast. Ruth and Lucille begin as a single consciousness: "we—in recollection I feel no reluctance to speak of Lucille and myself almost as a single conscious- ness" (*H*, p. 98). Eventually (like Sula Peace and Nel Wright of Toni Morrison's *Sula*) this plural identity splits along the line of conventional and unconventional lives. The contrasts between mountains and lake, light and darkness, past and present, transience and permanence, motion and stasis recur and gather further associations during Ruth's narrative.

The terrain itself is a suggestively "female landscape" whose contours invite multiple associations.[4] Moreover, the lake of Fingerbone, simultaneously opaque and transparent, is both a mirroring surface and the plane of intersection of upper and lower worlds. Thus, reflection functions as the ambiguous locus of oppositions between surface and depth, inside and outside. Ruth describes how she and Lucille watched the trains pass in the dusk. Although they could see the passengers clearly within the lighted compartments, the passengers looking out into the darkness would see only "their own depthless images on the black glass" (*H,* p. 54).

As planes equated with both vision and reflection, "[m]irrors, like lake surfaces, glass, and the eye of another person, are thought of as reflecting, abstracting, and containing the soul of the onlooker."[5] Existentially, reflection by others is an essential aspect of the confirmation of identity; Ruth remarks that "[l]oneliness is an absolute discovery. When one looks from inside at a lighted window, or looks from above at the lake, one sees the image of oneself in a lighted room. . . . When one looks from the darkness into the light, however, one sees all the difference between here and there, this and that" (*H,* pp. 157–58).[6] This image of contrasting perceptions from light and darkness recurs as a leitmotif in the narrative.

Initially, Ruth seeks a reversal of the past that would restore her mother to her; as her experience increases, she recognizes that such inversion of the order of perishable things would be destructive rather than restorative, in part because it would deprive her of the source of her nostalgia for the idealized mother:

> It would be terrible to stand outside in the dark and watch a woman in a lighted room studying her face in a window, and to throw a stone at her, shattering the glass, and then to watch the window knit itself up again and the bright bits of lip and throat and hair piece themselves seamlessly again into that unknown, indifferent woman. . . . [L]ike reflections on water our thoughts will suffer no changing shock, no permanent displacement. . . . If they were more substantial—if they had weight and took up space—they would sink or be carried away in the general flux. But they persist, outside the brisk and ruinous energies of the world. I think it must have been my mother's plan to rupture this bright surface, to sail beneath it into very blackness, but here she was, wherever my eyes fell, and behind my eyes, whole and in fragments, a thousand images of one gesture, never dispelled but rising always, inevitably, like a drowned woman. (*H,* pp. 162–63).

Each fragment of memory reproduces itself by multiplication rather than division, like a hall of mirrors in which images repeat in infinite regress. It is this process (recalling the triple-mirror image of Joan Foster's mother in Margaret Atwood's *Lady Oracle*) that accounts for Ruth's fragmented but recurrent image of her lost mother.

As both imitations and intimations of what is real, the image of image itself occurs in other forms, signifying the discrepancy between the appearance of things and the underlying reality. Ruth refers to a number of photographs of people and places, both familiar and unknown, in family snapshots, magazine illustrations, and newspaper clippings. When she and Sylvie burn newspapers and magazines before they set fire to the house and leave Fingerbone, Ruth describes the "transfiguration" that occurs when these images are incinerated (*H*, p. 200). She has recognized earlier that "everything that falls upon the eye is apparition, a sheet dropped over the world's true workings" (*H*, p. 116).

In her desperate desire to be reunited with her mother, Ruth attaches herself to the one figure who resembles Helen, Sylvie. More and more, she feels, "Sylvie began to blur the memory of my mother, and then to displace it" (*H*, p. 53). Her aunt, whose name suggests "sylvan" with its pastoral associations, is allied with nature and the forces of renewal. Sylvie's conviction that nothing is ever lost enables Ruth to believe that, as in the cycles of the natural world, death can be "undone" (*H*, p. 124). Additionally, Sylvie is linked with several central female symbols, including the moon, water, and houses. She arrives in Fingerbone just before spring, wearing a deep green dress and a corsage of lilies of the valley (*H*, pp. 44–45). Briefly married to a sailor (her last name is Fisher), she often spends her time at the lake and returns home "with fish in her pockets" (*H*, p. 136).

Sylvie is a kind of nurturing "good mother" or godmother, replacing the "bad mother," Helen, who abandoned her daughters by taking her own life. She is further associated with the matriarchal figures of myth and fairy tale through her likeness to Hecate: wise, inscrutable, and transient. One of Hecate's roles was to facilitate reunion between Demeter and Persephone.[7] Like Margaret Atwood's inversion of elements of the classical story in *Lady Oracle* (in which, similarly, a benevolent aunt is a Hecate figure), Robinson inverts and subverts the Demeter/Persephone tale. Focusing on separation and loss rather than their initiating causes, she has the sorrowing daughter search for the mother who is lost in the underworlds of the lake and the past. Ruth's mother, Helen, whose name echoes that of the Greek beauty and daughter of Zeus by Leda, was briefly married to Reginald, whose name suggests royalty; becoming a Stone, she had literally sunk to the bottom of the lake, where her daughter tries to recover her through memory.

The house that Sylvie, Ruth, and Lucille share corroborates the unconventional lives it contains. Like Eva Peace's house in Toni Morrison's *Sula,* the Foster house is structurally haphazard; the stairs lead to a wall rather than a hall; "its fenestration was random . . . its corners were out of square" (*H*, p. 74). An emblem of its three female occupants' unorthodoxy and self-sufficiency, it is also a sacred space in which special meanings inhere. As Kathryn Rabuzzi has suggested, for women in particular home has sacramental associations. Additionally, "To the extent that home provides sanctuary and protection it serves as a kind of surrogate mother."[8]

The house reflects Sylvie's unorthodox occupancy and her connection with the cosmos: leaves, cobwebs, insects, and small animals infiltrate its corners and interstices. "[E]very time a door was opened anywhere in the house there was a sound from all the corners of lifting and alighting. . . . Thus finely did our house become attuned to the orchard and to the particularities of weather" (*H*, p. 85). Sylvie moves downstairs into her mother's former room, a location several steps lower than the rest of the house (linking her with the other "subterraneous" dwellers of the Foster family); that room, facing the orchard, is permeated in summer with the smells of earth, grass, and blossoms.

As Ruth's metaphysical perceptions grow sharper, she understands that the house and other physical structures are merely temporary containers for the eternal but insubstantial spirit. "The appearance of relative solidity in my grandmother's house was deceptive" (*H*, p. 158); rather, solid objects are "a dangerous weight on a frail structure" (*H*, p. 159). Sylvie, in her belief in "stern solvents, and most of all in air" (*H*, p. 85) and in her embrace of the transient condition, is closer to the truth of experience than the conventional people who pronounce judgment on her. Self-declared drifters like her threaten the community because they expose what others try not to see, namely that "every soul is put out of house" (*H*, p. 179), that perishability, not permanence, is the distinguishing attribute of the human condition.

Ruth, having been "turned out of house" herself (*H*, p. 154) long enough to articulate the sources of her own loneliness, eventually makes the equation between exterior forms and interior states. Only her corporeality prevents her from rejoining her lost mother and her grandfather in the lake. As she phrases it, "Let them come unhouse me of this flesh, and pry this house apart. It was no shelter now, it only kept me here alone, and I would rather be with them, if only to see them . . ." (*H*, p. 159).

In a sense, the natural history of the house recapitulates the mythology of creation. Located on Sycamore Street (the tree has classical and biblical associations), it is successively associated with four levels of materiality: earth, water, air, and fire. Not long after Sylvie arrives in Fingerbone, a spring flood caused by rain and melted snow inundates the house to a level of four inches. "The house flowed around us" (*H*, p. 64) as if the lake had infiltrated it. Because it is situated on a hill, it survives the rising waters more successfully than neighboring houses, confirming Ruth's view that her grandfather had known what he was doing despite his ignorance of carpentry. Later, Ruth makes explicit the biblical correspondence with its symbolism of destruction and renewal of the world. In the penultimate journey she and Sylvie make across the lake, she thinks of Noah. "Looking out at the lake one could believe that the Flood had never ended. If one is lost on the water, any hill is Ararat. And below is always the accumulated past, which vanishes but does not vanish, which perishes and remains" (*H*, p. 172).

The cycle of destruction and renewal is the essence of Ruth's own story as well. After her first overnight trip to the lake, she returns to the house paralyzed by profound weariness and falls asleep sitting up, musing, "So this is all death is. . . . I knew that my decay, now obvious and accelerating, should somehow be concealed for decency's sake . . ." (*H*, pp. 118–19). Her aunt understands that in such a state "'You don't just sleep. You die'" (*H*, p. 119). Moreover, Sylvie is specifically associated with darkness: evening is "her special time of day" (*H*, p. 99). As Nor Hall has observed of archetypal patterns of experience, "Initiation is an active entry into darkness. It means to 'enter into' an experience of psychic significance with one's eyes closed, mouth shut, wearing a veil—a kind of veiling that paradoxically permits seeing."[9] In Robinson's narrative, allusions to sleep, death, and darkness as well as to resurrection, transfiguration, and birth frame the sacramental dimension of Ruth's story.

On an overnight visit to the lake with Sylvie, Ruth re-experiences her original loss as prelude to a rebirth and discovery of her true place in the scheme of things. The two women travel across the lake in a borrowed boat (recalling that Ruth's mother, Helen, had accomplished her entry into the lake's depths in a borrowed car). Ruth feels a blissful sense of symbiotic union: "We are the same. [Sylvie] could as well be my mother. I crouched and slept in her very shape like an unborn child" (*H*, p. 145); soon afterwards, she crawls "under [Sylvie's] body and out between her legs" (*H*, p. 146). After docking the boat, Sylvie leaves Ruth alone near an abandoned homestead, which she suggests is occupied by feral children. The house, like Edmund Foster's original "subterraneous" house, is sunk below the surface of the earth. The several references to subterranean locations reinforce the mythical allusions, suggesting both the earth and the underworld.

During Sylvie's absence, Ruth experiences the terror of abandonment. Only later does she understand this as her aunt's way of extending her "education" (*H*, p. 202). When Sylvie returns, she sings to Ruth, rocking her like a baby; then she wraps Ruth in her own coat, mothering her with gentle solicitude. Ruth's reactions are ambivalent; as she says, "I was angry that she had left me for so long, and that she did not ask pardon or explain, and that by abandoning me she had assumed the power to bestow such a richness of grace. For in fact I wore her coat like beatitude, and her arms around me were as heartening as mercy . . ." (*H*, p. 161). In the boat, Sylvie is framed against the moonlight, its light making "a sort of nimbus" around her (*H*, p. 165). Again the language expresses sacramental rather than prosaic experience.

The return trip across the lake elaborates the symbolism of rebirth. The sky glows "like a candled egg" (*H*, p. 161); Ruth lies in the bottom of the boat "like a seed in a husk" (*H*, p. 162). She imagines herself swelling like a seed bursting from its encasement and falling to the lake's bottom, where the distinctions between death and birth, the present and the past, are blurred.

> Say that the water and I bore the rowboat down to the bottom, and I, miraculously, monstrously, drank water into all my pores until the last black cranny of my brain was a trickle, a spillet. . . . Then, presumably, would come parturition in some form, though my first birth had hardly deserved that name, and why should I hope for more from the second? The only true

birth would be a final one, which would free us from watery darkness and
the thought of watery darkness, but could such a birth be imagined? (*H,*
p. 162)

Ruth is the child newly emerging from the "watery darkness" inside
the mother's body: she sleeps beneath Sylvie's feet and later crawls back
between her legs. Before they return to the house, Sylvie and Ruth float
in the boat in the moonlight, waiting beneath the railroad bridge until
the train roars over them. They later return to Fingerbone in a boxcar of
another train, with Ruth still wearing Sylvie's coat. Thus is Ruth initiated
and delivered, with Sylvie as both mother and midwife, into the eternal
transient condition.

Through a series of imaginative extensions, Ruth recognizes the continuum that links memory, thought, desire, and feeling and that accounts
for her expectant sense that the future will reward her vigilance with
reunion with the souls of her lost loved ones. She perceives that, within
the boundaries of birth and death, all experience is transitory; each human being is cast loose from its original mooring, left alone to drift upon
the lake of experience and time, where it longs to overcome the shock of
separateness by following the parent down the vortex of the past into
annihilation of longing.

Each such recognition is both Ruth's particular way of making sense
of her personal loss and Robinson's poetic elevation of Ruth's experience
to the universal and mythic level. Thus, the severance from the mother
is both particular and generic; the original rupture of union that underscores Ruth Stone's permanent condition of loneliness is in fact congruent
with each soul's condition of transience and longing for reunion with the
original loved object. As Nor Hall phrases it, "Womb as tomb and the
other way also: all wandering is from the Mother, to the Mother, in
the Mother. The movement is in space and space is a receptacle, a vessel,
a matrix—as it were the mother or nurse of all becoming." [10]

In this sense, the afterlife envisioned in most sacred traditions is the
figurative return to the original garden of wholeness—the mother. As
Ruth articulates this correspondence, "The force behind the movement
of time is a mourning that will not be comforted. That is why the first
event is known to have been an expulsion, and the last is hoped to be a
reconciliation and return. So memory pulls us forward, so prophecy is

222

only brilliant memory—there will be a garden where all of us as one child will sleep in our mother Eve, hooped in her ribs and staved by her spine" (*H*, p. 192).

Jean Starobinski has instructively observed that "Paradise is that place where spontaneous harmony between man's body and external nature once prevailed. . . . [T]he fall is not just a migration from the inside out but the fulcral moment that dooms man to perceive, in constant pain and awareness, the points of contact or of transition between the corporeal inside and the hazardous outside."[11] All the descendants of Adam are thus "transients." As Robinson's narrator muses, even the story of Christ is animated by loss, expressing in the miracle of Resurrection the same hope for reversal of time and death that she feels: "His mother wept [when He died] and His friends could not believe the loss" (*H*, p. 194).

If the "rituals of the ordinary" (*H*, p. 16) are what one takes for granted—"act[s] of faith" (*H*, p. 16) in the comforting continuity of the familiar—then what transforms them into the extraordinary is the rift in the illusion of permanence. Ruth applies this insight to the abiding sorrow of her life, imagining that if her mother had in fact returned from the lake that day rather than choosing to drown in it so dramatically, she would not have been lost to her daughters. Rather, they eventually would have been lost to her, as they grew to adulthood.

Christine Downing has described the "great mother" Gaia in the background of Greek mythology in terms that illuminate Ruth Stone's haunting image of her lost mother. As Downing phrases it, the "mother of the beginning, the mother of infancy" is

> the mother who is there before time . . . [and] whom we come to know only as we begin to long for a mother from whom we are not separated, as in time, in consciousness, we find ourselves to be separated from the mother of the present. She is a fantasy creature behind the personal mother, construed of memory and longing, who exists only in the imagination, in myth, archetypally—who is never identical with the personal mother. Although she is there from the beginning, our discovery of her is always a return, a re-cognition.[12]

Longing for this fantasy mother-before-separation, Ruth Foster constructs a kind of ontology in which loss circles back upon itself to become reunion; desire and need become powerful enough to alter perception itself. "And here again is a foreshadowing—the world will be made whole. For to wish for a hand on one's hair is all but to feel it. So whatever we may lose, very craving gives it back to us again" (*H*, pp. 152–53).

The very theme of Ruth's reality is absence. Thus, the possibility of another separation kindles her deepest anxiety. The uncomprehending populace of Fingerbone, regarding the eccentric Sylvie as an unfit guardian for Ruth, send the sheriff to separate the two so that Ruth might have access to a more orderly life. Ruth perceives that her involuntary departure would affect Sylvie the same way Helen's death has affected Ruth: the image of the lost loved one becomes distorted by memory, so imaginatively transformed that the original image is irretrievably lost: "Sylvie did not want to lose me. She did not want me to grow gigantic and multiple, so that I seemed to fill the whole house, and she did not wish me to turn subtle and miscible, so that I could pass through the membranes that separate dream and dream. . . . But if she lost me, I would become extraordinary by my vanishing" (*H*, p. 195).

Unable to bear, either herself or for Sylvie, another recurrence of her earlier losses, Ruth creates a soothing story for herself as a spirit not bounded, as she actually is, by flesh. In the darkness of the orchard, she again invokes the biblical legend of the Flood: the lit house stands, reminiscent of the original Ark.

> Once there was a young girl strolling at night in an orchard. She came to a house she had never seen before, all alight so that through any window she could see curious ornaments and marvelous comforts. A door stood open, so she walked inside. . . . She would be transformed by the gross light into a mortal child. And when she stood at the bright window, she would find that the world was gone, the orchard was gone, her mother and grandmother and aunts were gone. Like Noah's wife on the tenth or fifteenth night of rain, she would stand in the window and realize that the world was really lost. (*H*, pp. 203–4)

In "breaking the tethers of need" (*H*, p. 204) that bind her to the world of material things, Ruth becomes most like Sylvie, whose acceptance of temporality liberates her from such impediments. Together determined to escape from the boundaries of community conventionality, they free the "soul of the house" (*H*, p. 212)—with its impress of memory, dream, and desire—from its materiality by burning it down. So completely does Ruth solidify the one union that holds her to the world that that night she and Sylvie are "almost a single person" as they reach "an end to housekeeping" (*H*, p. 209).

The two women walk in darkness to the lake and for the first time traverse it entirely by crossing the railroad bridge to the other side. Their journey signifies the crossing of a threshold into another state of being.[13] Ironically, to the community of Fingerbone the women are presumed drowned; when Ruth followed Sylvie across the bridge, "the lake claimed us" (*H*, p. 214). Through this inaccuracy, Ruth is symbolically reunited with those who actually drowned in the lake. From the light looking into the darkness, so to speak, Sylvie and Ruth are "dead" to the world (*H*, p. 217); from darkness looking into light, they are drifters, eternally committed to transience and eschewing the "ceremonies of sustenance, of nurturing" (*H*, p. 214) that periodically tug on them.

In this altered condition of being, Ruth reconsiders her experience, trying to locate the precise moment in time when she became so different from other people. She wonders whether it was her mother's leaving or her own birth—the initial separation from the mother. Like all of her kind, Ruth observes, "[O]blivion expelled me. . . . So they seal the door against our returning" (*H*, p. 215). Expulsion from the womb, like expulsion from the Garden, is the irreversible event upon which all later separations are predicated.

Ruth determines that the ultimate transformation occurred when she followed Sylvie across the railroad bridge: "[O]ne moment bulges like the belly of a lens and all the others are at the peripheries and diminished" (*H*, p. 215). Like Margaret Atwood's nameless narrator in *Surfacing*, for whom "the lake is the entrance into being"; like Joan Foster in the same author's *Lady Oracle*, who stages a mock drowning in a lake in the effort to shed her unmanageable past; and like Son, in Toni Morrison's *Tar Baby*, who crosses the water to return to the Isle des Chevaliers and a mythical immortality, Ruth is transformed by her traversal of the body of water that symbolizes both death and renewal. Together with Sylvie, she negotiates the boundary between the underworld (the lake) and the upper world bisected by the railroad bridge.

By the time Ruth undertakes that final journey across the lake, she has comprehended its mystery: the waters that destroy also purify; those who vanish in it are accorded a kind of immortality through the perennial sublimations of matter into spirit. Memory itself is the essential solvent.

Earlier Ruth has dreamed that the lake is alive with human forms (*H*, p. 41); ultimately she recognizes that

> one cannot cup one's hand and drink from the rim of any lake without remembering that mothers have drowned in it, lifting their children toward the air, though they must have known . . . that soon enough the deluge would take all the children, too. . . .
>
> I cannot taste a cup of water but I recall that the eye of the lake is my grandfather's, and that the lake's heavy, blind, encumbering waters composed my mother's limbs and weighed her garments and stopped her breath and stopped her sight. There is remembrance, and communion, altogether human and unhallowed. (*H*, pp. 193–94)[14]

Through her attachment to Sylvie—her symbolic mother and guide—and through her to the cosmos, Ruth recovers the plural voice first associated with and then severed from her mother and later her sister. It is as if the two women, first connected through their shared unorthodox housekeeping, ultimately achieve the "transfiguration" Ruth imagines for her actual mother. Mediating the boundary between two dimensions of being, they enter a timeless reality—the locus of thought and dream and myth—wherein "the perimeters of [their] wandering are nowhere" (*H*, p. 219).[15]

Ruth and Sylvie's state can only be understood through paradox: "nowhere" is everywhere.[16] From this perspective, the values of absence and presence are at last reversed. Ruth imagines her sister, Lucille, having returned to the house in Fingerbone after Ruth and Sylvie leave it, trying to ward off the apparent momentum of entropy to which her sister and aunt willingly surrendered. In this fantasy of Ruth's, Lucille snuggles her daughters in her lap as they look "at the black window to find out what their mother seems to see there, and they see their own faces and a face so like their mother's, so rapt and full of tender watching, that only Lucille could think the face was mine" (*H*, p. 218). The narrative closes with Ruth imagining Lucille's thoughts, "thronged by our absence"; no one could know how "she does not watch, does not listen, does not wait, does not hope, and always for me and Sylvie" (*H*, p. 219).

Housekeeping is in a sense the most radical of the novels discussed in this study. Its title is deeply ironic, particularly with reference to a feminist framework; "housekeeping" is revealed to be not the endless battle to maintain domestic order that has traditionally made "women's work" seem necessary but inessential, but rather the profound activity through which essence is discovered and recovered, the ordering of one's place in the cosmos. For Ruth Stone, the reenactment of memory is the necessary act to oppose psychic disorder and even destruction. Moreover, this orienting of the self, initially regressive—in that it symbolically recapitulates the daughter's loss of the original symbiosis with her mother—becomes transformative: the nurturing bond between mother and daughter expressed in the relationship between Sylvie and Ruth is the model for growth beyond the isolated self to identification with the essence of cosmic order and renewal.

The relationship between the women, originating in the mother-daughter identification, is explored with little reference to either sexuality or romantic attachment.[17] Ruth's sister Lucille's choice of the more conventional symbols of her gender is implicitly attributed to an inability to recognize the bondage of such roles. By contrast, Ruth and Sylvie are defined neither through the accoutrements of their gender nor through relationships with men but rather through a strongly nurturant and reciprocal female bond. *Housekeeping* is thus radical in its implication that the establishment of female selfhood in the cosmos need not be conceived in terms of either a solitary heroic journey or an erotic union—the terms in which most narratives of quest and discovery are cast.

Annis Pratt's description of the rarely achieved final phase of the archetypal female journey helps to clarify the nature of Ruth and Sylvie's (and Robinson's) achievement. As Pratt phrases it, "Transcendence necessitates passing through and beyond sexual politics to a new environment, a new kind of space. This visionary fiction depicts the process by which the patriarchy's most marginal heroes attain a centricity within a wholly apatriarchal space."[18] In a metaphysical sense, Mary Daly has suggested that "'withdrawal' into boundary space and time constitutes the most radical involvement/participation in the cosmic community."[19]

Thus, Ruth and Sylvie's active participation in transience can be understood as a capacity to transcend all enclosures that impede the achievement of a relational selfhood and to assert a radical freedom to create both social identity and private selfhood in terms not restrictively dependent on gender. In contrast to Penelope Mortimer's women, for whom "home" is a prison and "homelessness" a nightmare, and Morrison's Pecola Breedlove, for whom "outside" is a terrifying emptiness, Robinson's pair of protagonists embrace "outside" by making home and world congruent. In the shared space they make their own, they grasp the human task of "housekeeping" as an activity analogous to the perennial recreation of the world.

NOTES

1. Marilynne Robinson, *Housekeeping* (1981, rpt. New York: Bantam, 1982). All subsequent references, indicated by the abbreviation "*H*" and parenthetical page numbers in the text, are to this edition.

2. Nina Auerbach has traced the idea of female groups in fiction through half a dozen or so novels of the nineteenth and early twentieth centuries. If two or three women can be considered a community, then Robinson's narrative is part of this separate tributary in fiction about women. Auerbach writes, "Communities of women growing in time constitute a drama of widening cultural consciousness, finally taking shape as an evolving literary myth that sweeps across official cultural images of female submission, subservience, and fulfillment in a bounded world. As this myth takes shape as part of our imaginative inheritance, so does the fictional reality of women's autonomy: for though the communities gain substance and stature as we proceed, their isolation has had from the first the self-sustaining power to repel or incorporate the male-defined reality that excludes them." *Communities of Women: An Idea in Fiction* (Cambridge: Harvard University Press, 1978), p. 6.

3. For a valuable feminist reformulation of the archetypal journey in women's fiction, see Annis Pratt, *Archetypal Patterns in Women's Fiction* (Bloomington: Indiana University Press, 1981), esp. chapter 8, "Novels of Rebirth and Transformation," pp. 135–66.

4. See Ellen Moers, *Literary Women: The Great Writers* (Garden City, N.Y.: Doubleday, 1976), pp. 252–64.

5. Nor Hall, *The Moon and the Virgin: Reflections on the Archetypal Feminine* (New York: Harper and Row, 1980), p. 234.

6. Gaston Bachelard's analysis of spatial images as analogues for inner states provides a particularly intriguing gloss on Robinson's imagery. He writes, "[A] rather large dossier of literary documentation on the poetry of houses could be studied from the single angle of the lamp that glows in the window. . . . The lamp in the window is the house's eye and, in the kingdom of the imagination, it is never lighted out-of-doors, but is enclosed light, which can only filter to the outside." *The Poetics of Space,* trans. Maria Jolas (New York: Orion Press, 1964), pp. 33–34.

7. Hall, *The Moon and the Virgin,* pp. 64, 125.

8. Kathryn Allen Rabuzzi, *The Sacred and the Feminine: Toward a Theology of Housework* (New York: The Seabury Press, 1982), p. 62.

9. Hall, *The Moon and the Virgin,* p. 24.

10. Ibid., p. 36.

11. Jean Starobinski, "The Inside and the Outside," trans. Frederick Brown, *Hudson Review,* Vol. 28, No. 3 (Autumn 1975), pp. 344–45.

12. Christine Downing, *The Goddess: Mythological Images of the Feminine* (New York: Crossroad, 1981), p. 135.

13. J. E. Cirlot has summarized the symbolism of bridges, noting that "there are a great many cultures where the bridge symbolizes the link between what can be perceived and what is beyond perception. Even when it lacks this mystic sense, the bridge is always symbolic of a transition from one state to another—of change or the desire for change." *A Dictionary of Symbols,* 2nd ed., trans. Jack Sage (New York: Philosophical Library, 1971), p. 33.

14. Instructively, Starobinski suggests that "every anamnesis, every 'archeology,' by creating for us, outside us, a dimension of the past, marks the boundary of that 'beyond-ourselves' without which we would be gutted of interiority." "The Inside and the Outside," p. 335.

15. As Joseph Campbell expresses the mythical hero's initiatory experience into the true order of reality, "The aim is not to *see,* but to realize that one *is* . . . essence; then one is free to wander as that essence in the world. . . . The essence of oneself and the essence of the world: these two are one. Hence separateness, withdrawal, is no longer necessary. Wherever the hero may wander, whatever he may do, he is ever in the presence of his own essence—for he has the perfected eye to see. There is no separateness. . . . The individual has lost himself in the law and been reborn in identity with the whole meaning of the universe." *The Hero with a Thousand Faces,* 2nd ed. (Princeton: Princeton University Press, 1968), p. 386, emphasis in original.

16. In his study of the rhetorical place of myth in literature, Eric Gould suggests that the paradoxical presence of "absence" and the meaning encoded in "nothing" are crucial elements of myth in language. "If metaphor is built on that lack [absence]—and is the result of it—then no metaphorical language confronts non-being quite so squarely and definitively as myth. Mythicity . . . is the condition of filling the gap with signs in such a way that Being continues to conceal Nothing as a predication for further knowledge." Furthermore, "[A]ll myth reveals that man cannot get out of this paradox of language or history; even his yearning for the supernatural has this existential basis." *Mythical Intentions in Literature* (Princeton: Princeton University Press, 1981), p. 44.

17. Carroll Smith-Rosenberg's illuminating study of female friendship offers an important understanding of the complexity of relationships between women.

See "The Female World of Love and Ritual: Relationships between Women in Nineteenth-Century America," *Signs,* Vol. 1, No. 1 (Autumn 1975), pp. 1–29.

18. Pratt, *Archetypal Patterns in Women's Fiction,* p. 70.

19. Mary Daly, *Beyond God the Father: Toward a Philosophy of Women's Liberation* (Boston: Beacon Press, 1973), p. 191.

Conclusion: Boundaries of the Self

The idea of boundary, which takes its definition from our anatomy, expresses the relationship between the body and language as inter-reflexive dimensions of experience in the world. From the writers whose narratives are discussed in the preceding pages, one might construct a continuum of boundary themes, beginning with the representations of the body and extending into the more abstract expressions of being-in-the-world that emerge from both the correspondences and divergences between materiality and its representation in language.

The most literal dimension of these themes concerns corporeality: such events as incorporation of food and alterations of physical shape for which the figure of Alice in Wonderland is an apt analogue. (As Carolyn Heilbrun has suggested, Carroll's Alice "embodies the female use of male logic against itself."[1]) Margaret Atwood's Marian MacAlpin and Joan Foster literally alter in size or shape during the course of their stories. Another aspect of this shape-shifting is that of maternity, with which several of Atwood's and Mortimer's characters are preoccupied. Confinement linguistically represents a female experience that embraces both actual and figurative, private and public conditions. In the works by writers of ethnic minority cultures, the condition of confinement is more broadly experienced by characters of both genders; women may be doubly (if not triply) imprisoned by the overlapping restrictions created by gender, racism, and economic realities.

One traditional assumption about boundary in its anatomical analogues is the presumed vulnerability of the female body to penetration.

231

The negation, violation, or control of the procreative capacity through abortion, rape, sterilization, or—in the case of Atwood's "handmaids"—compulsory maternity, also presumes penetration or manipulation. In this context, blood frequently marks the point of intrusion or violation of margins of the body. Several of Penelope Mortimer's, Toni Morrison's, and Margaret Atwood's women suffer from literal wounds; Mortimer's Mrs. Armitage experiences a "haemorrhage of grief," and Maxine Kingston's woman warrior bleeds from the literally wounding words carved into her back. Menstruation appears in several of the narratives as a "polluting" condition (the value accorded it by men), but also as the affirmation of female power, as evidenced by Kingston's woman warrior during her quest journey.

Other literal alterations of the boundaries of the female body are envisioned as the extreme threats to selfhood (in addition to rape): disease and maiming. Cancer—a frequently mutilating disease that, as depicted in the two narratives discussed here, significantly affects a part of the body unique to women—and other less obviously gender-specific manifestations of maiming or wounding appear centrally in these narratives. A number of the protagonists experience the feeling of "something missing," whether an actual part of the body or some more abstract aspect of troubled selfhood for which it is the metaphorical equivalent. From the literal and figurative wounds experienced by several of Penelope Mortimer's women to the mind-body split from which most of Margaret Atwood's protagonists suffer; from the stunted or missing limbs of Toni Morrison's Eva Peace, Pauline Breedlove, and Milkman Dead to the symbolic absence of a navel that more positively suggests Pilate Dead's special powers; from the aberrant eye color that sets Leslie Silko's Tayo and other mixed-blood characters apart from the brown-eyed cultural group norm to Maxine Hong Kingston's explorations of the meaning of footbinding, cut frenums, and the writing carved into her woman warrior's back; and to Marilynne Robinson's Ruth Stone, who meditates on the accidental and deliberate events of self-destruction in her family history: together these images form a powerful cluster of representations of dismemberment and marginalization as conditions of female and/or minority ethnic reality.

Though a classical Freudian interpreter might facilely regard this persistent imagery of "something missing" as evidence of female "penis envy," the narratives themselves suggest that the experiences accord more closely with the reality of restricted circumstance in patriarchy as a consequence of gender, ethnic origin, class, or a combination of these conditions. In fact, the authors implicitly or explicitly illustrate the manner in which powerful cultural barriers are manifested in individual circumstances through internalized images of restriction, amputation, or mutilation.

Whether self-created, imposed by others, or dictated by accident, each of the representations of physical or psychic mutilation or incompleteness expresses the characters' inner distress and social or cultural plight. A character may suffer, as do Mortimer's Muriel Rowbridge, Morrison's Pecola Breedlove, Silko's Tayo, and Robinson's Ruth Stone, from a conviction of "invisibility," of not being seen; or, as do Mortimer's Mrs. Armitage and Maxine Kingston's childhood persona, of "muteness," of not being heard. In several of the narratives, mirrors figure importantly as metaphors for the importance of reflection by others as a condition of the characters' verification of their own reality or as tropes for the parallels or discrepancies between inner and outer worlds. The violated or distorted boundaries of the self body forth, as it were, the characters' difficulties or failures in achieving identities defined according to white male cultural norms.

The three narratives considered here in which men are the protagonists or central subjects—Morrison's *Song of Solomon,* Kingston's *China Men,* and Silko's *Ceremony*—demonstrate the damaging constrictions of white patriarchal values upon men as well as women of minority cultural groups. Pointedly, in each work, war and militarism figure peripherally as the most acute manifestation of the negating values of patriarchy, wherein acquisition and domination are valued over relationship and connection. Conversely, Kingston's figure of the woman warrior, besides recalling Monique Wittig's *Les Guèrriérres,* is a powerful re-vision of the traditionally male warrior image, suggesting new symbolic linkages between language, aggression, and oppression in their several forms. Women with a missing breast, the protagonists in two of the novels discussed here, might be re-considered in light of the ambiguous classical figure of the Amazon.

The body is also the template for figurative expressions of boundary conceived as enclosure (or its opposite) in temporal as well as spatial terms. Thus, rooms, walls, houses—including the more emotionally saturated meanings associated with "home"—are tropes for inner experience, as are imprisonment, escape, flight, and homelessness. Bodies of water appear in connection with drowning (or fear of it), immersion, and, figuratively, the entry into the unconscious, the return to the womb, or the engulfment of the self. Time itself is problematic in Mortimer's *Long Distance* and Robinson's *Housekeeping,* and the discontinuous nature of the past concerns several other fictive protagonists. At least three of the female characters engage in mapmaking or geography as part of the effort to make sense of their outer (and inner) worlds. The order of this study suggests a movement away from closure: literally, from indoors to outdoors; psychologically, from failure of resolution to acceptance of process; narratively, from conclusion to ambiguous endings, as the confined spaces of Mortimer's novels give way to the cosmic locations (and implications) of the narratives by Silko and Robinson.

A major expression of boundary explored in these fictions concerns the nature of relationships between people—whether filial, romantic, or affiliative. Representations of attachment, symbiosis, separation, and loss recur throughout these narratives, despite their notable differences in theme, style, and emphasis. Atwood's recurring image of Siamese twins, Mortimer's and Morrison's implicit or explicit representations of incestuous connections, the dramatization of "splitness," the loss of loved ones as both a fact of experience and a psychological threat—all reflect aspects of boundary concerns, suggesting the dialectical process through which psychological reality both mirrors and shapes private and social or cultural experience.

In Penelope Mortimer's fiction, marriage is the central fact of women's lives; the author, a generation older than the other writers considered here, whose early novels were published before the renewal of feminist consciousness, is an important recorder and critic of the assumptions of her time. In most of the other narratives, marriage is either problematic or absent, as the women struggle to understand the terms of their existence in relation to either particular men or women, the world defined by patriarchy, or both. Several of the works portray adulterous or extramarital relationships that catalyze change in the central character. Besides dramatizing conflicting loyalties, these transgressions challenge social boundaries by exposing narrow female roles or presumptions about the structure of marriage itself.

Several of these narratives focus on the way in which a female character moves beyond enclosure to regard herself or himself not as a victim but as an actor in a world in which, finally, victimization cannot be understood simply as a function of gender or ethnic origin. In virtually every narrative, the change of awareness in the protagonist depends on a moral perspective involving, to use Carol Gilligan's terms,[2] not only rights (and wrongs) but responsibilities. Significantly, two of the three writers who belong to ethnic minority groups depict the education of a male protagonist as the recognition and integration of moral values traditionally regarded, in his culture and in Western culture, as female. Morrison's Milkman Dead and Silko's Tayo are both tutored by female mentors who enable them to affirm the values of affiliation and community.

Of the explorations of relationship depicted in these narratives, one of the most persistent and powerful themes is the "maternal subtext": the bond between mother and daughter, often envisioned in terms of the classical story—or its inversion—of Demeter and Persephone. Generally, it is the mother who is lost to the daughter rather than the reverse; in more than a third of the texts considered here, the protagonist is obliged to come to terms with the death or loss of the mother, either in the past or during the current time of the narrative. The mother, as transmitter of cultural attitudes as well as the unresolved issues of her own experience as a female, influences her daughter's (or son's) acquisition of selfhood, including attitudes toward sexuality, procreation, relationship, and autonomy. Because ego boundaries between daughter and mother are often merged as a result of both psychological and social processes, the daughter must struggle to separate herself from a figure she regards as destructive before she can understand her mother's own cultural dilemma and see the "good mother" as the hidden aspect of her own parent.

The image of the lost "inner" mother is often narratively divided between two figures reflecting positive and negative attachment. Aunts and grandmothers are central figures through whom many of these characters come to understand and reconcile the rift between generations and within the self. Even in the two fictions in which the protagonists are male, female relatives function importantly as figures through whom the young men learn about (in Milkman Dead's case) the value of relationship or (in Tayo's case) the pain of its absence. The figure of the literal or figurative midwife who assists in the birth of the self—Pilate Dead and Circe in *Song of Solomon,* Maxine Hong Kingston's mother, Brave Orchid, in *The Woman Warrior,* Ts'eh in *Ceremony,* Sylvie Fisher in *House-keeping,* and Rennie Wilford herself in *Bodily Harm*—represent the capacity to generate creative change.

The influential "stepmother" figure also suggests the presence of fairy tale motifs. Indeed, in virtually all of these narratives, the authors tap and frequently recast images or themes from diverse cultural mythologies to express the complexity of female (and male) experience in (white) patriarchy: from the paradigmatic Demeter-Persephone story to the less pervasive but equally suggestive figures or images of Dorothy in Oz, Alice in Wonderland, Pandora, the pumpkin eater and his wife, the tarbaby, the Spider Woman who weaves reality, the woman warrior, the origin of evil, magic flight, and others. Mortimer, Atwood, and Robinson focus on their female protagonists' struggles for autonomy and authenticity against cultural images that define females as subordinate, dependent, and unrealized, and that in many instances are rooted in their original family relationships. The three writers of ethnic minority backgrounds express some of the same struggles, not only in terms of gender, but additionally as a function of cultural circumstances. The "community"—the social structure through which cultural values are perpetuated or challenged—is often a central presence in the narratives.

Formally, the concern with boundary manifests itself in the shape and "frames" of the narratives. Several of the texts, notably Mortimer's and Morrison's, incorporate a deliberately circular design or use framing devices, as if to underscore the condition of confinement experienced by many of their characters. Frequently, the protagonist is the narrator, who, if not initially then ultimately, takes charge of the form and emphasis of her story as she evolves from victim to creator or interpreter of her experiences. Thus she is both "inside" and "outside" the narrative, as Margaret Atwood dramatizes most fully in the meta-fictional play of Joan Foster's comic-serious odyssey in *Lady Oracle* and the more sober fable of Offred in *The Handmaid's Tale,* and as Maxine Hong Kingston achieves by interweaving personal autobiography with cultural biography. Atwood and Mortimer also employ unreliable, divided, or limited narrators to suggest the ambiguities of their characters' perspectives.

In the several narratives authored by writers of minority ethnic backgrounds, the problem of boundary extends beyond the circumstances of individual characters to the entire minority culture's relation to the dominant culture. Atwood's *The Handmaid's Tale* occupies a unique place in the group of narratives discussed here, since the handmaids of the Republic of Gilead constitute a culturally oppressed group—an apartheid of gender—analogous to nineteenth-century black slaves and other more contemporary cultural minority groups. In giving artistic form to the contexts in which dilemmas based on gender and ethnicity converge— and diverge—these writers powerfully expose the alienating and divisive values of patriarchy. Yet the few narratives that provide (however tentatively) a resolution in social as well as artistic terms imply that neither aspect of the opposing elements, whether defined across genders or cultures or both, can be omitted without incurring greater loss.

If the implicit question in many narratives written by authors from ethnic minority groups is how to preserve one's heritage without being enslaved by it, that question also describes a key issue for women in general, irrespective of ethnic origin. The problem straddles both personal and cultural circumstance, as Maxine Hong Kingston illustrates in her exploration of the mother-daughter relationship as a paradigm of conflicting cultural messages. Rennie Wilford in Atwood's *Bodily Harm* discovers that in order to do more than simply "survive" a woman must become a "subversive," not forsaking the values of her own experience but using them unapologetically to alter her relation to an imperfect world. The characters in these fictions who succeed in transcending their initial constricting circumstances learn in different ways to apply the knowledge of "outsideness" to revise the presumptions of the "inside."

One can regard the concern with "naming" in Kingston's and Morrison's works as another aspect of this pressure to appropriate or revise the dominant discourse. In their concern with the contrary dimensions of language, these writers attempt to resolve fundamental contradictions, not only in the terms of discourse, but within experience itself, whether posed as the "differentness" between genders, or between self and other, life and death, or other universal polarities. In this context, a central function of myth, according to the structuralist view proposed by Claude Lévi-Strauss, is problem-solving: the unconscious creation of "a logical model capable of overcoming a contradiction."[3] In the narratives considered here, allusions to or incorporation of myths, fairy tales, legends, and classical motifs frequently suggest attempts to mediate contradiction: to get not only "beyond language" but beyond culture to resolve the dilemmas faced by the central characters. Alternatively, paradox—the willingness to accommodate rather than resolve contradiction—indicates the characters' refusal of dualistic modes of thought themselves.

A fundamental aspect of the author's relation to her narrative, then, is the role of the storyteller, who preserves, reinterprets, and may even invert cultural stories, legends, and presumptions. In this sense, she mediates the existing boundaries between genders and/or cultures. In "reconstructing" a portion of female experience or in preserving a dimension of her cultural history that might otherwise be lost, she reinterprets it by giving voice to "invisible" or "muted" dimensions from a female point of view.

Though the writers discussed here are too small a group upon which to base generalizations, they are not isolated but representative examples of the ubiquity in fiction by contemporary women of imagery related to boundary.[4] Cheri Register, addressing the "metaphorical geography" of women's experience and the "female mythos," has framed the question of whether women are "outside a patriarchal 'real' world, inside a female sphere, or on the boundary?"[5] The answer to this question must be, paradoxically, all three. The construct of boundary reminds us that, just as experience in the world is a dialectical exchange between "inside" and "outside," so do women exist and write simultaneously inside and outside of patriarchy. Myra Jehlen has proposed that "the female territory might well be envisioned as one long border, and independence for women not as a separate country but as open access to the sea."[6]

The irreducible paradox of boundary is that it indicates the figurative line of both separation and connection between contiguous entities. That which demarcates, whether construed in an interpersonal, cultural, or geographical sense, may exclude or include, depending on the position and perception of the observer. As Robert Lifton has written in a somewhat different context, "Boundaries can be viewed as neither permanent nor by definition false, but rather as essential and yet subject to the fundamental forces for change characterizing our age. We require images of limit and restraint, if only to help us grasp what we are transcending."[7] The diverse fictions considered here—from Penelope Mortimer's envisionment of houses, homes, and marriages as constricting prisons to Marilynne Robinson's provocative revisioning of the idea of housekeeping to suggest liberation from the traditional structures of female oppression—illuminate the paradoxical cartography of female experience

through the body and beyond it: through language in its multiple manifestations of our common reality.

NOTES

1. Carolyn Heilbrun, "A Response to *Writing and Sexual Difference*," in *Critical Inquiry*, Vol. 8 (Summer 1982), pp. 806–7.

2. Carol Gilligan argues that descriptions of maturation have typically stressed achievement, mastery of successive separations, independence, and competition as normative. At the same time, affiliation, attachment, and relational values—those more characteristic of females' ethical development—have been judged as failure to master certain psychosocial and ethical stages that themselves incorporate a value bias, rather than as evidence of an equally vital and heretofore neglected dimension of moral development. See Gilligan, *In a Different Voice: Psychological Theory and Women's Development* (Cambridge: Harvard University Press, 1982).

3. Claude Lévi-Strauss, "The Structural Study of Myth," in *Myth: A Symposium*, ed. Thomas A. Sebeok (Bloomington: Indiana University Press, 1955), p. 105.

4. To suggest only a few examples of boundary motifs explored in this study that appear in other recent fiction by women: the imagery of alteration, maiming, or mutilation of the body is central in Margaret Drabble's *The Ice Age* and *The Middle Ground*, Joan Winthrop's *Underwater*, Gayl Jones's *Corrigedora* and *Eva's Man*, Judith Rossner's *Looking for Mr. Goodbar* and *Attachments*, Lisa Alther's *Kinflicks*, and Alice Walker's *Meridian*. Incest and rape, either separately or combined, figure importantly in Joan Didion's *Play It As It Lays*, Marilyn French's *The Women's Room*, Judith Rossner's *Emmeline*, and Alice Walker's *The Color Purple*. Confinement as a resonant image of maternity if not imprisonment occurs as a major image in several of Margaret Drabble's novels, including *The Millstone* and *The Waterfall*. The ambiguity of "madness" and an internally split female protagonist are dramatized in Doris Lessing's *The Golden Notebook* and *The Four-Gated City*, Sue Kaufman's *Diary of a Mad Housewife*, and Sylvia Plath's *The Bell Jar;* "madness" is additionally linked with exclusion on the basis of political or cultural minority status in Bessie Head's *A Question of Power* and Marge Piercy's *Woman on the Edge of Time*. Mary Gordon's *Final Payments* dramatizes a temporary distortion of the eating function as the expression of a disturbed daughter-mother(substitute) relationship. A number of contemporary novels explore the boundaries of the central mother–daughter relationship. See *The Lost Tradition: Mothers and Daughters in Literature*, ed. Cathy N. Davidson and E. M. Broner (New York: Frederick Ungar, 1980), for a variety of essays and an extensive bibliography on the subject.

5. Cheri Register, "Literary Criticism" (review essay), *Signs,* Vol. 6, No. 2 (Winter 1980), p. 279.

6. Myra Jehlen, "Archimedes and the Paradox of Feminist Criticism," *Signs,* Vol. 6, No. 4 (Summer 1981), p. 582.

7. Robert Jay Lifton, *Boundaries: Psychological Man in Revolution* (New York: Random House, 1969), p. xii.

Bibliography

PRIMARY TEXTS
(alphabetical by author, in order of publication)

Margaret Atwood:

Novels

The Edible Woman. 1969. Reprint. New York: Fawcett, 1976.
Surfacing. 1972. Reprint. New York: Popular Library, 1972.
Lady Oracle. 1976. Reprint. New York: Avon Books, 1978.
Life Before Man. Toronto: McClelland and Stewart, 1979.
Bodily Harm. Toronto: McClelland and Stewart, 1981.
The Handmaid's Tale. Toronto: McClelland and Stewart, 1985.

Poetry, Critical Prose, and Interviews

Power Politics. Toronto: Anansi, 1972.
Survival: A Thematic Guide to Canadian Literature. Toronto: Anansi, 1972.
Two-Headed Poems. New York: Simon and Schuster, 1978.
Interview with Graeme Gibson. In *Eleven Canadian Novelists,* edited by Graeme
    Gibson, 1–31. Toronto: Anansi, 1973.
Interview with Linda Sandler. *Malahat Review,* No. 41 (1977), 7–27.
Second Words: Selected Critical Prose. Toronto: Anansi, 1982.
Interview with Betsy Draine. In *Interviews with Contemporary Writers,* edited by
    L. S. Dembo, 358–73. Madison: University of Wisconsin Press, 1983.
Review of *The Handmaid's Tale* by Cathy N. Davidson, "A Feminist '1984': Mar-

garet Atwood Talks about Her Exciting New Novel." *Ms.* Magazine, February 1986, 24–26.

Maxine Hong Kingston

Narratives

The Woman Warrior: Memoirs of a Girlhood among Ghosts. 1976. Reprint. New York: Random House, Vintage Books, 1977.
China Men. New York: Alfred A. Knopf, 1980.

Essays and Interviews

"The Coming Book." In *The Writer and Her Work,* edited by Janet Sternberg, 181–85. New York: Norton, 1980.
"This is the Story I Heard: A Conversation with Maxine Hong Kingston and Earll Kingston" conducted by Phyllis Hoge Thompson. *Biography,* Vol. 6, No. 1 (Winter 1983), 1–12.

Toni Morrison

Novels

The Bluest Eye. 1970. Reprint. New York: Washington Square Press, 1972.
Sula. 1973. Reprint. New York: Bantam, 1975.
Song of Solomon. 1977. Reprint. New York: New American Library, 1978.
Tar Baby. New York: Alfred A. Knopf, 1981.

Interviews and Reviews

"An Interview with Toni Morrison" conducted by Nellie McKay. *Contemporary Literature,* Vol. 23, No. 4 (Winter 1983), 413–29.
"'Intimate Things in Place': A Conversation with Toni Morrison" conducted by Robert Stepto. In *The Third Woman: Minority Women Writers of the United States.* Edited by Dexter Fisher, 167–82. Boston: Houghton Mifflin, 1980.
"'The Language Must Not Sweat': A Conversation with Toni Morrison" conducted by Thomas LeClair. *The New Republic,* March 21, 1981, 25–29.
"A Novel of Exile and Home." Review of *Tar Baby* by Maureen Howard, *The New Republic,* March 21, 1981, 29–32.
"'The Seams Can't Show': An Interview with Toni Morrison" by Jane Bakerman. *Black American Literature Forum,* Vol. 12, No. 2, 56–60.

Penelope Mortimer

Johanna. London: Secker and Warburg, 1947 (as Penelope Dimont).
A Villa in Summer. New York: Harcourt Brace, 1954.

Bibliography

The Bright Prison. New York: Harcourt Brace, 1957.
Cave of Ice. New York: Harcourt Brace, 1959.
Saturday Lunch with the Brownings. New York: McGraw Hill, 1961.
The Pumpkin Eater. New York: McGraw Hill, 1962.
My Friend Says It's Bulletproof. New York: Random House, 1967.
The Home. New York: Random House, 1971.
Long Distance. New York: Doubleday, 1974.
About Time: An Aspect of Autobiography. Garden City, N.Y.: Doubleday, 1979.
The Handyman. New York: St. Martin's Press/Joan Kahn, 1985.

Marilynne Robinson

Housekeeping. 1981. Reprint. New York: Bantam, 1982.

Leslie Silko

Ceremony. 1977. Reprint. New York: New American Library, 1978.
Laguna Woman. Greenfield Center, N.Y.: Greenfield Review Press, 1974.
"Stories and Their Tellers: A Conversation with Leslie Marmon Silko" conducted by Dexter Fisher. In *The Third Woman: Minority Women Writers of the United States*, edited by Dexter Fisher, 18–23. Boston: Houghton Mifflin, 1980.

SECONDARY WORKS CITED

Abel, Elizabeth. "(E)Merging Identities: The Dynamics of Female Friendship in Contemporary Fiction by Women." *Signs,* Vol. 6, No. 3 (Spring 1981), 413–35.
———. ed. *Writing and Sexual Difference.* Chicago: University of Chicago Press, 1982.
Ahern, Emily M. "The Power and Pollution of Chinese Women." In *Women in Chinese Society,* edited by Margery Wolf and Roxane Witke, 193–214. Stanford: Stanford University Press, 1975.
Ardener, Edwin. "Belief and the Problem of Women" and "The 'Problem' Revisited." In *Perceiving Women,* edited by Shirley Ardener, 1–17, 19–25. New York: John Wiley and Sons, 1975.
Ardener, Shirley, ed. *Women and Space: Ground Rules and Social Maps.* New York: St. Martin's Press, 1981.
Auerbach, Nina. *Communities of Women: An Idea in Fiction.* Cambridge: Harvard University Press, 1978.
Bachelard, Gaston. *The Poetics of Space.* Translated by Maria Jolas. New York: Orion Press, 1964.

Bibliography

Bakan, David. *The Duality of Human Existence: Isolation and Communion in Western Man.* Boston: Beacon Press, 1966.

Balint, Enid. "On Being Empty of Oneself." *International Journal of Psycho-Analysis,* Vol. 44, No. 4, 470–80.

Baym, Nina. *Women's Fiction: A Guide to Novels by and about Women in America, 1820–1870.* Ithaca: Cornell University Press, 1978.

Becker, Ernest. *The Denial of Death.* New York: The Free Press, 1973.

Bettelheim, Bruno. *The Uses of Enchantment: The Meaning and Importance of Fairy Tales.* New York: Alfred A. Knopf, 1976.

Boskind-Lodahl, Marlene. "Cinderella's Stepsisters: A Feminist Perspective on Anorexia Nervosa and Bulimia." *Signs,* Vol. 2, No. 2 (Winter 1976), 342–56.

Bowlby, John. *Attachment and Loss.* 3 vols. New York: Basic Books, 1969, 1973, 1980.

Brown, Russell M. "Crossing Borders." *Essays on Canadian Writing,* No. 22 (Summer 1981), 154–68.

Bruch, Hilde. *Eating Disorders: Obesity, Anorexia Nervosa, and the Person Within.* New York: Basic Books, 1973.

———. *The Golden Cage: The Enigma of Anorexia Nervosa.* Reprint. New York: Random House, 1979.

Campbell, Joseph. *The Hero with a Thousand Faces.* 2nd ed. Princeton: Princeton University Press, 1968.

Chesler, Phyllis. *Women and Madness.* Reprint. New York: Avon Books, 1973.

Chodorow, Nancy. "Gender, Relation, and Difference in Psychoanalytic Perspective." In *The Future of Difference,* edited by Hester Eisenstein and Alice Jardine, 3–19. Boston: G. K. Hall, 1980.

———. *The Reproduction of Mothering: Psychoanalysis and the Sociology of Gender.* Berkeley: University of California Press, 1978.

Christ, Carol. *Diving Deep and Surfacing: Women Writers on the Spiritual Quest.* Boston: Beacon Press, 1980.

Cirlot, J. E. *A Dictionary of Symbols.* 2nd ed. Translated by Jack Sage. New York: Philosophical Library, 1971.

Cixous, Hélène. "Castration or Decapitation." Translated by Annette Kuhn. *Signs,* Vol. 7, No. 1 (Autumn 1981), 41–55

Courlander, Harold, comp. *A Treasury of Afro-American Folklore.* New York: Crown, 1976.

Daly, Mary. *Beyond God the Father: Toward a Philosophy of Women's Liberation.* Boston: Beacon Press, 1973.

Davidson, Arnold and Cathy, eds. *The Art of Margaret Atwood.* Toronto: Anansi, 1981.

———— and ————. "Margaret Atwood's *Lady Oracle:* The Artist as Escapist and Seer." *Studies in Canadian Literature,* Vol. 3, No. 2 (Summer 1978), 166–77.

Davidson, Cathy N., and E. M. Broner, eds. *The Lost Tradition: Mothers and Daughters in Literature.* New York: Frederick Ungar, 1980.

Davis, Cynthia. "Self, Society, and Myth in Toni Morrison's Fiction." *Contemporary Literature,* Vol. 23, No. 3 (Summer 1982), 323–43.

De Beauvoir, Simone. *The Second Sex.* Translated by H. M. Parshley. New York: Alfred A. Knopf, 1952.

Dinnerstein, Dorothy. *The Mermaid and the Minotaur: Sexual Arrangements and Human Malaise.* Reprint. New York: Harper and Row, 1977.

Djwa, Sandra. "The Where of Here: Margaret Atwood and a Canadian Tradition." In *The Art of Margaret Atwood: Essays in Criticism,* edited by Arnold and Cathy Davidson, 15–34. Toronto: Anansi, 1981.

Douglas, Mary. *Natural Symbols: Explorations in Cosmology.* New York: Pantheon, 1970.

————. *Purity and Danger: An Analysis of Concepts of Pollution and Taboo.* New York: Routledge and Kegan Paul, 1966.

Downing, Christine. *The Goddess: Mythological Images of the Feminine.* New York: Crossroad, 1981.

Dozier, Edward. *The Pueblo Indians of North America.* New York: Holt, Rinehart and Winston, 1970.

Fiedler, Leslie. *Freaks: Myths and Images of the Secret Self.* New York: Simon and Schuster, 1978.

Flax, Jane. "Mother–Daughter Relationships: Psychodynamics, Politics, and Philosophy." In *The Future of Difference,* edited by Hester Eisenstein and Alice Jardine, 20–40. Boston: G. K. Hall, 1980.

Forbes, Thomas Rogers. *The Midwife and the Witch.* New Haven: Yale University Press, 1966.

Freud, Sigmund. *New Introductory Lectures on Psycho-Analysis.* Translated by W. J. H. Sprott. New York: W. W. Norton, 1933.

Friedan, Betty. *The Feminine Mystique.* Reprint. New York: Dell, 1963.

Gardiner, Judith Kegan. "The Heroine as Her Author's Daughter." In *Women and Men: The Consequences of Power,* edited by Dana V. Hiller and Robin Ann Sheets, 40–48. Cincinnati: University of Cincinnati Office of Women's Studies, 1976.

Gilbert, Sandra, and Susan Gubar. *The Madwoman in the Attic: The Woman Writer and the Nineteenth-Century Literary Imagination.* New Haven: Yale University Press, 1979.

Gilligan, Carol. *In a Different Voice: Psychological Theory and Women's Development.* Cambridge: Harvard University Press, 1982.

Bibliography

Godard, Barbara. "My (m)Other, My Self: Strategies for Subversion in Atwood and Hébert." *Essays on Canadian Writing,* Vol. 26 (Summer 1983), 13–44.

Gould, Eric. *Mythical Intentions in Literature.* Princeton: Princeton University Press, 1981.

Grace, Sherrill. *Violent Duality: A Study of Margaret Atwood.* Montreal: Véhicule Press, 1980.

Grumbach, Doris. "Hail to a Distinguished Novel." Review of Penelope Mortimer's *Long Distance. The New Republic,* September 28, 1974, 23–24.

Gutman, David. "Woman and the Conception of Ego-Strength." *Merrill-Palmer Quarterly of Behavior and Development,* Vol. 11, No. 2 (1965), 229–40.

Hall, Nor. *The Moon and the Virgin: Reflections on the Archetypal Feminine.* New York: Harper and Row, 1980.

Heilbrun, Carolyn. *Reinventing Womanhood.* New York: W. W. Norton, 1979.

———. "A Response to *Writing and Sexual Difference.*" *Critical Inquiry,* Vol. 8 (Summer 1982), 805–11.

Homans, Margaret. "'Her Very Own Howl': The Ambiguities of Representation in Recent Women's Fiction." *Signs,* Vol. 9, No. 2 (Winter 1983), 186–205.

Hsu, Francis L. K. *Under the Ancestors' Shadow: Kinship, Personality, and Social Mobility in Village China.* Reprint. Garden City, N.Y.: Doubleday, 1967.

Hughes, Langston, and Arna Bontemps, eds. *The Book of Negro Folklore.* New York: Dodd, Mead, and Co., 1958.

Janeway, Elizabeth. *Powers of the Weak.* New York: Morrow, 1981.

Jehlen, Myra. "Archimedes and the Paradox of Feminist Criticism." *Signs,* Vol. 6, No. 4 (Summer 1981), 575–601.

Jelinek, Estelle, ed. Introduction to *Women's Autobiography: Essays in Criticism.* Bloomington: Indiana University Press, 1980.

Juhasz, Suzanne. "Towards a Theory of Form in Feminist Autobiography: Kate Millet's *Flying* and Maxine Hong Kingston's *The Woman Warrior.*" In *Women's Autobiography: Essays in Criticism,* edited by Estelle Jelinek, 221–37. Bloomington: Indiana University Press, 1980.

Kerenyi, Karoly. *Eleusis: Archetypal Image of Mother and Daughter.* Translated by Ralph Manheim. New York: [Bollingen Foundation, Series 65, No. 4], Pantheon, 1967.

Klotman, Phyllis R. "Dick-and-Jane and the Shirley Temple Sensibility in *The Bluest Eye.*" *Black American Literature Forum,* Vol. 13, No. 4 (Winter 1979), 123–5.

Kristeva, Julia. *About Chinese Women.* Translated by Anita Barrows. New York: Urizen Books, 1977.

———. *Powers of Horror: An Essay on Abjection.* Translated by Leon S. Roudiez. New York: Columbia University Press, 1982.

———. "Woman's Time." Translated by Alice Jardine and Marny Blake. *Signs,* Vol. 7, No. 1 (Autumn 1981), 13–35.

Laing, R. D. *The Divided Self: An Existential Study in Sanity and Madness.* Reprint. Harmondsworth, Middlesex, England: Penguin Books, 1965.

Larson, Charles R. *American Indian Fiction.* Albuquerque: University of New Mexico Press, 1978.

Lecker, Robert. "Janus through the Looking Glass: Atwood's First Three Novels." In *The Art of Margaret Atwood,* edited by Arnold and Cathy Davidson, 178–86. Toronto: Anansi, 1981.

Lester, Julius, comp. *Black Folktales.* New York: Richard W. Baron, 1969.

Lévi-Strauss, Claude. "The Structural Study of Myth." In *Myth: A Symposium,* edited by Thomas A. Sebeok, 81–106. Bloomington: Indiana University Press, 1955.

Lifton, Robert Jay. *Boundaries: Psychological Man in Revolution.* New York: Random House, 1969.

Lincoln, Kenneth. *Native American Renaissance.* Berkeley: University of California Press, 1983.

Mahler, Margaret. *Selected Papers of Margaret S. Mahler,* vol. 2: *Separation-Individuation.* New York: Jason Aronson, 1979.

———, Fred Pine, and Anni Bergman. *The Psychological Birth of the Human Infant: Symbiosis and Individuation.* New York: Basic Books, 1975.

McCombs, Judith. "Atwood's Haunted Sequences: *The Circle Game, The Journals of Susanna Moodie,* and *Power Politics.*" In *The Art of Margaret Atwood,* edited by Arnold and Cathy Davidson, 35–54. Toronto: Anansi, 1981.

McLay, Catherine. "The Dark Voyage: *The Edible Woman* as Romance." In *The Art of Margaret Atwood,* edited by Arnold and Cathy Davidson, 123–38. Toronto: Anansi, 1981.

McLuhan, Marshall. "Canada: The Borderline Case." In *The Canadian Imagination: Dimensions of a Literary Culture,* edited by David Staines, 226–48. Cambridge: Harvard University Press, 1977.

Mead, Margaret. "A Cultural Anthropologist's Approach to Maternal Deprivation." In *Woman: Body and Culture,* edited by Signe Hammer, 318–36. New York: Harper and Row, 1975.

Miller, Alice. *Prisoners of Childhood.* Translated by Ruth Ward. New York: Basic Books, 1981.

Miller, Margaret. "Threads of Identity in Maxine Hong Kingston's *The Woman Warrior.*" *Biography,* Vol. 6, No. 1 (Winter 1983), 13–33.

Moers, Ellen. *Literary Women: The Great Writers.* Garden City, N. Y.: Doubleday, 1976.

Momaday, Scott. *House Made of Dawn.* Reprint. New York: New American Library, 1969.

Bibliography

Ogunyemi, Chikwenye Okonjo. "Order and Disorder in Toni Morrison's *The Bluest Eye.*" *Critique,* Vol. 19, No. 1 (1977), 112–20.

Ortiz, Alfonso. "Ritual Drama and the Pueblo World View." In *New Perspectives on the Pueblos,* edited by Alfonso Ortiz. Albuquerque: University of New Mexico Press, 1972.

Pratt, Annis. *Archetypal Patterns in Women's Fiction.* Bloomington: Indiana University Press, 1981.

Rabuzzi, Kathryn Allen. *The Sacred and the Feminine: Toward a Theology of Housework.* New York: Seabury, 1982.

Rank, Otto. *The Myth of the Birth of the Hero and Other Essays,* edited and translated by Philip Freund. Reprint. New York: Alfred A. Knopf and Random House, 1959.

Regan, Nancy. "A Home of One's Own: Women's Bodies in Recent Women's Fiction." *Journal of Popular Culture,* Vol. 11 (Spring 1978), 772–88.

Register, Cheri. "Literary Criticism." Review Essay. *Signs,* Vol. 6, No. 2 (Winter 1980), 268–82.

Rich, Adrienne. *Of Woman Born: Motherhood as Experience and Institution.* Reprint. New York: Bantam, 1977.

Rigney, Barbara Hill. *Lilith's Daughters: Women and Religion in Contemporary Fiction.* Madison: University of Wisconsin Press, 1982.

Rose, Ellen Cronan. *The Novels of Margaret Drabble: Equivocal Figures.* Totowa, N.J.: Barnes and Noble, 1980.

Royce, Anya Peterson. *Ethnic Identity: Strategies of Diversity.* Bloomington: Indiana University Press, 1982.

Rubenstein, Roberta. "Pandora's Box and Female Survival: Margaret Atwood's *Bodily Harm. Journal of Canadian Studies/ Revue d'études canadiennes,* Vol. 20, No. 1 (Spring 1985), 120–135.

———. "The Room of the Self: Psychic Geography in Doris Lessing's Fiction." *Perspectives on Contemporary Literature,* Vol. 5 (1979), 69–78.

———. "Surfacing: Margaret Atwood's Journey to the Interior." *Modern Fiction Studies,* Vol. 22, No. 3 (Autumn 1973), 387–99.

Russ, Joanna. "What Can a Heroine Do? or Why Women Can't Write." In *Images of Women in Fiction: Feminist Perspectives,* edited by Susan Koppelman Cornillon, 3–20. Bowling Green, Ohio: Bowling Green University Press, 1972.

Salisbury, Harrison E. "On the Literary Road: American Writers in China." *New York Times Book Review,* January 20, 1985, 3, 25.

Schonfeld, William. "The Body and the Body-Image in Adolescents." In *Adolescence: Psychosocial Perspectives,* edited by Gerald Caplan and Serge Lebovici, 27–53. New York: Basic Books, 1969.

Seidenberg, Robert. "The Trauma of Eventlessness." In *Psychoanalysis and*

Women, edited by Jean Baker Miller, 350–62. Reprint. Baltimore: Penguin Books, 1973.

———, and Karen DeCrow. *Women Who Marry Houses: Panic and Protest in Agoraphobia.* New York: McGraw Hill, 1983.

Showalter, Elaine. *A Literature of Their Own: British Women Novelists from Brontë to Lessing.* Princeton: Princeton University Press, 1977.

Smith, Catherine F. "Jane Lead: Mysticism and the Woman Cloathed with the Sun." In *Shakespeare's Sisters: Feminist Essays on Women Poets,* edited by Sandra M. Gilbert and Susan Gubar, 1–18. Bloomington: Indiana University Press, 1979.

Smith-Rosenberg, Carroll. "The Female World of Love and Ritual: Relationships between Women in Nineteenth-Century America," *Signs,* Vol. 1, No. 1 (Autumn 1975), 1–29.

Sontag, Susan. *Illness as Metaphor.* New York: Farrar, Straus and Giroux, 1977.

Starobinski, Jean. "The Inside and the Outside." Translated by Frederick Brown. *The Hudson Review,* Vol. 28, No. 3 (Autumn 1975), 333–51.

Sukenick, Lynn. "Feeling and Reason in Doris Lessing's Fiction." *Doris Lessing: Critical Essays,* edited by Annis Pratt and L. S. Dembo, 98–118. Madison: University of Wisconsin Press, 1974.

Tanner, Tony. *Adultery in the Novel: Contract and Transgression.* Baltimore: Johns Hopkins University Press, 1979.

Tate, Claudia, ed. *Black Women Writers at Work.* New York: Continuum, 1983.

Thoma, Helmut. *Anorexia Nervosa.* Translated by Gillian Brydone. New York: International Universities Press, 1967.

Turner, Victor. *Dramas, Fields, and Metaphors: Symbolic Action in Human Society.* Ithaca: Cornell University Press, 1974.

Tyler, Hamilton. *Pueblo Gods and Myths.* Norman: University of Oklahoma Press, 1964.

Velie, Allan. *Four American Indian Literary Masters: Momaday, Welch, Silko, Vizenor.* Norman: University of Oklahoma Press, 1982.

Vincent, Sybil Korff. "The Mirror and the Cameo: Margaret Atwood's Comic/Gothic Novel *Lady Oracle.*" In *The Female Gothic,* edited by Juliann E. Fleenor, 153–63. Montreal: Eden Press, 1983.

Waley, Arthur, trans. *The Temple and Other Poems.* New York: Alfred A. Knopf, 1923.

Washington, Mary Helen. "Teaching *Black-Eyed Susans:* An Approach to the Study of Black Women Writers." In *All the Women Are White, All the Blacks Are Men, But Some of Us Are Brave: Black Women's Studies,* edited by Gloria T. Hull, Patricia Bell Scott, and Barbara Smith, 208–17. Old Westbury, N.Y.: The Feminist Press, 1982.

Bibliography

Weston, Jessie. *From Ritual to Romance*. Reprint. Garden City, N.Y.: Doubleday, 1957.

White, Margaret. "I want the right to be black and me." In *Black Women in White America: A Documentary History,* edited by Gerda Lerner, 607–8. New York: Pantheon, 1972.

Winnicott, D. W. *Playing and Reality*. New York: Basic Books, 1971.

Winthrop, Joan. *Underwater*. New York: G. P. Putnam's, 1974.

Wolf, Margery. *The House of Lim: A Study of a Chinese Farm Family*. New York: Appleton-Century-Crofts, 1968.

———. "Women and Suicide in China." In *Women in Chinese Society,* edited by Margery Wolf and Roxane Witke, 111–41. Stanford: Stanford University Press, 1975.

Woolf, Virginia. *A Room of One's Own*. 1929. Reprint. New York: Harcourt Brace Jovanovich, 1957.

Yamada, Mitsuye. "Invisibility Is an Unnatural Disaster: Reflections of an Asian American Woman." In *This Bridge Called My Back: Writings by Radical Women of Color,* edited by Cherríe Moraga and Gloria Anzaldúa, 35–40. Watertown, Mass.: Persephone Press, 1981.

Index

Abel, Elizabeth, 161n16
Abortion, 232; in Margaret Atwood, 71; in
  Maxine Hong Kingston, 167; in Penelope Mortimer, 28, 34, 40, 41, 43
About Time (Mortimer), 50
Adultery. *See* Infidelity
Agoraphobia, 20, 58n6, 60n20, 112; in Penelope Mortimer, 20, 30
Ahern, Emily M., 168–69
Allusions
—Biblical: Adam, 223; Ararat, 220; Ark,
  224; Christ, 223; Eden, 104, 222–23,
  225; Eve, 223; the Fall, 223; Flood, 220,
  224; Resurrection, 220, 223; Ruth, 215;
  sycamore, 220; transfiguration, 220, 226
—children's classics: *Alice in Wonderland,*
  67–68, 69, 231, 236; *The Wizard of Oz,*
  68, 69, 74, 91, 236
—classical: Amazon, 233; archetypal hero
  story, 171; Demeter and Persephone, 41,
  42, 43, 70, 90, 117n15, 175, 218, 235,
  236; fertility legend, 200, 207n16; Gaia
  (Great Mother), 223; Graie sisters, 131;
  Hecate, 70, 218; Helen, 219; initiation,
  220; nurturing/devouring goddess, 78;
  Pandora, 104, 183, 236; Psyche, 54;
  scapegoat, 150, 153, 159; sycamore, 220;
  underworld, 90, 221, 225
—fairy tale: royal parents, 88; stepmother
  figure, 193, 236
—folk tradition: blind horsemen, 159;

Bre'r Rabbit, 158; Fa Mu Lan (woman
  warrior), 171–72; tar baby, 158, 236
—oral tradition: Laguna Indian, 192, 195,
  196, 197
Alther, Lisa, 239n4
Ardener, Edwin, 7, 178
Atwood, Margaret, 8, 9, 10, 35, 63–122,
  190, 192, 193, 202, 218, 225, 231, 232,
  236, 237; on Siamese twins, 63, 64, 65,
  67, 68, 74, 112, 134; on family in Canadian fiction, 113; on Gilead, 121; on narrative structure, 100, 120n41; on political
  boundaries, 63; on power, 66; on victimization, 121n47. *See also Bodily Harm;
  The Edible Woman; The Handmaid's Tale;
  Lady Oracle; Life before Man; Surfacing;
  Two-Headed Poems*
Auerbach, Nina, 131, 228n2

Bachelard, Gaston, 4, 228n6
Bakan, David, 190–91
Balint, Alice, 61n37
Balint, Enid, 60n20
Baym, Nina, 11n6
Becker, Ernest, 49
Bettelheim, Bruno, 119n35
The Bluest Eye (Mortimer), 125, 126, 127–
  31, 132, 133, 137, 139, 142, 143, 144–
  45, 146–47, 149–51, 153, 156, 167, 173,
  203, 227–28, 232, 233

251

Index

Bodily Harm (Atwood), 35, 64, 76, 77, 87, 99, 101–7, 108, 110–11, 114, 237
Body image: distorted, 231, 239n4; in *Alice in Wonderland,* 68; in Margaret Atwood, 65, 66, 67, 69, 76, 80, 105. *See also* Boundaries: body
Boskind-Lodahl, Marlene, 119n28
Boundaries: absence of, 197, 201, 216; body, 5, 30, 33, 88, 89, 105, 106, 169, 231, 232; communal, 167, 169, 191, 225; cosmological, 225; cultural, 127, 139, 141; ego, 6–7; ethnic, 7, 125, 203; geographical, 151, 154, 234; loss of, 66, 67; matrimonial, 17, 19, 21, 24, 26, 29, 32, 39; merged, 6, 42, 43, 53, 194, 197, 199, 235 (*see also* Siamese twins); narrative, 9, 100, 164, 169, 205, 211, 236; political, 63, 65, 71, 108, 191; topographical, 215
Bounded space, 11n6, 51, 233; in Margaret Atwood, 96, 108; in Maxine Hong Kingston, 182; in Toni Morrison, 133; in Penelope Mortimer, 18, 20; in Native American culture, 191; in Leslie Silko, 194. *See also* House/home; Imprisonment
Bowlby, John, 82, 161n15
The Bright Prison (Mortimer), 17, 19, 20, 24–25, 36, 57
Broner, E. M., 239n4
Brown, Russell M., 63

Campbell, Joseph, 187n16, 229n15
Cave of Ice (Mortimer), 16, 18, 20, 33, 38, 39–44, 57
Ceremony (Silko), 190–205
Chesler, Phyllis, 31
China Men (Kingston), 180–85, 202, 233
Chodorow, Nancy, 6, 12n15, 28, 42, 61n37, 78–79, 175
Christ, Carol, 119n31
Cirlot, J. E., 229n13
Cixous, Hélène, 3
Claustrophobia, 58n6
Community: black, 126, 139–40, 149, 150–52, 155, 157, 159; cosmic, 227; ethnic, 139, 166, 168, 170, 177, 182, 203, 213, 219, 224, 225, 235; of women, 228n2

Confinement. *See* Imprisonment

Daly, Mary, 227
Davidson, Arnold, 120n41
Davidson, Cathy, 120n41
Davis, Cynthia, 160n12, 162–63n31
de Beauvoir, Simone, 34
deCrow, Karen, 20
Depression, 29, 59n18, 112
Didion, Joan, 239n4
Dinnerstein, Dorothy, 6, 59n13, 85, 175, 207n14
Divided self, 234, 239n4; in Margaret Atwood, 65, 66, 70, 71, 72, 73, 74, 76, 78, 80, 82, 87, 88, 89, 109, 232; in Toni Morrison, 126, 137, 138, 141; in Penelope Mortimer, 55; in Leslie Silko, 192, 200
Douglas, Mary, 4, 169, 177
Downing, Christine, 78, 223
Dozier, Edward, 206n11
Drabble, Margaret, 15, 239n4
Draine, Betsy, 120n41
Drowning, 225, 234; in Margaret Atwood, 66, 85, 86, 92, 113, 119n31; in Toni Morrison, 135–36; in Marilynne Robinson, 212

Eating disorders: anorexia nervosa, 79, 80, 112, 118n24, 119n28; obesity, 81, 87, 112. *See also* Eating function
Eating function: in Margaret Atwood, 81, 82; distortion of, 239n4
The Edible Woman (Atwood), 64, 67, 68, 69, 78, 79–81, 82, 85–86, 100, 114, 237
Ellison, Ralph, 160n5
Engulfment, 234; in Margaret Atwood, 66, 74, 86, 92; in Leslie Silko, 194, 197. *See also* Drowning

Faulkner, William, 193
Female friendship, 135, 161n16, 228n2, 229–30n17. *See also* Relationships
Female wound: in Margaret Atwood, 72, 112, 232; in Maxine Hong Kingston, 171, 232; in Toni Morrison, 144, 145, 232; in Penelope Mortimer, 33, 34, 35, 38, 112, 232

Index

Flax, Jane, 120n39
Floating in void, in Margaret Atwood, 85, 93, 94, 95
Forbes, Thomas Rogers, 161n18
French, Marilyn, 239n4
Freud, Sigmund, 33, 62n42
Friedan, Betty, 15, 26, 31, 57, 59n15

Gardiner, Judith Kegan, 121–22n51
Gilbert, Sandra, 4, 58n6
Gilligan, Carol, 155, 235, 239n2
Godard, Barbara, 120n41
Gordon, Mary, 239n4
Gould, Eric, 229n16
Grace, Sherrill, 117n15, 119n30
Grumbach, Doris, 62n43
Gubar, Susan, 4, 58n6
Gutman, David, 168

Hall, Nor, 220, 222
The Handmaid's Tale (Atwood), 64, 77–78, 81, 82, 84–85, 99, 101, 102, 103, 104, 107–9, 112, 113, 114, 115, 116, 232, 236, 237
The Handyman (Mortimer), 34, 38, 44, 48–49
Head, Bessie, 239n4
Heilbrun, Carolyn, 58n1, 231
Homans, Margaret, 162n22
The Home (Mortimer), 16, 18, 20, 34, 38, 39, 44–48, 49, 55, 96
House/home, 151, 233–34; in Margaret Atwood, 93, 95–96; in Maxine Hong Kingston, 168, 175; in Toni Morrison, 127, 136, 137–38, 145, 151, 228; in Penelope Mortimer, 19, 28, 31, 37, 38, 42, 44, 46, 47, 48–49, 51, 53, 54, 227, 238; in Marilynne Robinson, 211, 219–20, 221, 224, 227, 228; in Leslie Silko, 199
Housekeeping (Robinson), 211–28, 232, 233, 234
Howard, Maureen, 163n33
Hsu, Francis, 170

Imprisonment, 4, 231, 234, 239n4; in Margaret Atwood, 76, 77, 85, 90; in Toni Morrison, 125, 138–39, 145; in Penelope Mortimer, 18, 19, 20, 21, 22, 28, 31, 46, 50, 53, 54, 57

Incest, 146–48, 239n4.
Incestuous desire: in Toni Morrison, 234; in Penelope Mortimer, 46, 51, 52, 55, 234
Infidelity, 234; in Margaret Atwood, 75, 93, 112; in Toni Morrison, 138; in Penelope Mortimer, 21, 23, 24, 27, 28, 30, 33, 46
Inside/outside, 4–5, 7, 8, 12n16, 120n41, 223, 236, 237, 238; in Margaret Atwood, 76, 79, 101, 102, 105; in Marilynne Robinson, 216, 217, 225
Invisibility: in Chinese women, 185; in Toni Morrison, 164, 233; in Penelope Mortimer, 36, 164, 233; in Marilynne Robinson, 233; in Leslie Silko, 193, 197, 233

Jehlen, Myra, 238
Jelinek, Estelle, 165
Johanna (Mortimer), 17, 19, 21–22, 23, 27, 32, 59n16
Jones, Gayl, 239n4
Juhasz, Suzanne, 188n26

Kafka, Franz, 51, 188n18
Kaufman, Sue, 239n4
Kingston, Maxine Hong, 9, 10, 164–89, 202, 204, 205, 233, 235, 236, 237; on writing, 178, 186–87n12. *See also China Men, The Woman Warrior*
Klotman, Phyllis R., 160n7
Kristeva, Julia, 33, 97, 150, 187n14, 188n19

Lady Oracle (Atwood), 64, 69, 77, 81, 82, 86–91, 99, 100, 112, 113, 114, 115, 116, 218, 225, 231, 236
Laing, R. D., 55
Larson, Charles R., 206n7
Lecker, Robert, 118n27
Lessing, Doris, 23, 51, 59n14, 239n4
Lévi-Strauss, Claude, 237
Life before Man (Atwood), 64, 68–69, 73–75, 77, 82, 86, 87, 91–97, 99, 100–101, 112, 113, 114, 116, 192, 193
Lifton, Robert, 238
Lincoln, Kenneth, 207nn 12, 17, 19

253

Long Distance (Mortimer), 16, 18, 25, 50–
 56, 111, 234

Mahler, Margaret, 5–6, 61–62n38
Maiming, 144, 145, 146, 239n4. *See also*
 Mutilation
Marginalization, 232; in Chinese culture,
 177, 182, 202; in Maxine Hong Kings-
 ton, 164; in Toni Morrison, 142; in Na-
 tive American culture, 190
Maternity, 5, 97, 98, 239n4; in Margaret
 Atwood, 79, 97, 98, 99, 115, 232; in
 Maxine Hong Kingston, 166, 167; in
 Toni Morrison, 140; in Penelope Morti-
 mer, 27, 31, 42, 115. *See also* Bounda-
 ries: body; Motherhood
McCombs, Judith, 121n47
McLay, Catherine, 118n27
McLuhan, Marshall, 63
Mead, Margaret, 119n29
Midwife, 235; in Margaret Atwood, 236;
 in Maxine Hong Kingston, 173, 180,
 235; in Toni Morrison, 137, 140, 141,
 235; in Marilynne Robinson, 222, 236; in
 Leslie Silko, 236
Miller, Alice, 29, 40, 59n18
Miller, Margaret, 188n26
Mirrors: in Margaret Atwood, 67, 69, 70,
 88, 90; in Penelope Mortimer, 36, 40; in
 Marilynne Robinson, 214, 217, 218
Momaday, Scott, 206n7
Morrison, Toni, 9, 10, 125–63, 164, 167,
 173, 202, 203, 204, 208n24, 216, 219,
 225, 227–28, 232, 233, 235, 236; on
 black community, 149–52, 159; on female friendship, 161n16; on fictional
 protagonists, 163; on love, 146–47; on
 names/naming, 153–54; on narrative
 structure, 160n7, 208n24; on pariah figure, 159; on tar baby image, 158; on vision, 126. *See also The Bluest Eye; Song of
 Solomon; Sula; Tar Baby*
Mortimer, Penelope, 9, 10, 15–62, 72, 76,
 79, 96, 110, 111, 112, 113, 114, 116,
 120n45, 145, 164, 167, 202, 211, 227,
 231, 232, 233, 234, 236, 238. *See also
 About Time; The Bright Prison; Cave of
 Ice; The Handyman; The Home; Johanna;
 Long Distance; My Friend Says It's Bullet-*

*proof; The Pumpkin Eater; A Villa in
 Summer*
Mother: "angry mother," 204; "bad
 mother," 88, 89, 90, 91, 92; "good
 mother," 88, 90, 91, 204, 217, 218, 235;
 earth as mother, 199, 202; image of, 45.
 See also Relationships: lost mother,
 mother-daughter, motherhood, mother-
 son, stepmother
Mute(d)ness, 7–8, 164; in Margaret Atwood, 107; in Maxine Hong Kingston,
 164, 178, 183, 233; in Penelope Mortimer, 233
Mutilation, 232, 233, 239n4; in Margaret
 Atwood, 71, 72, 106, 107; in Maxine
 Hong Kingston, 171; in Toni Morrison,
 126, 143–44, 145–46, 148, 232
My Friend Says It's Bulletproof (Mortimer),
 17, 34–38, 44, 57, 76, 110, 233

Names/naming: in Maxine Hong Kingston, 168, 170, 237; in Toni Morrison,
 153–54, 237; in Leslie Silko, 192
Narrative structure, 236; in Margaret Atwood, 70, 81, 100, 101, 116, 120n41; in
 Maxine Hong Kingston, 165, 176, 180–
 81; in Penelope Mortimer, 25, 50, 51,
 116; in Marilynne Robinson, 212; Toni
 Morrison on, 160n7, 208n24
Native American culture: bounded space
 in, 191; marginalization in, 190; oral tradition in, 204, 205

Ogunyemi, C. O., 160–61n12
Oral tradition, 192, 195, 196, 197, 204, 205
Ortiz, Alfonso, 191, 207n17

Peterson, Anya Royce, 7
Piercy, Marge, 239n4
Plath, Sylvia, 239n4
Pollution: in Chinese culture, 168–69; in
 Toni Morrison, 150; Julia Kristeva on,
 150
Pornography, in Margaret Atwood, 105,
 106, 107
Pratt, Annis, 19, 58n3, 119n31, 187n16,
 227, 228
Psychoanalytic theory, object relations, 5,
 88

The Pumpkin Eater (Mortimer), 16, 18, 20, 25–33, 38, 44, 47, 53, 72, 79, 114, 120n45, 233

Rabuzzi, Kathryn Allen, 151, 219
Rank, Otto, 117–18n16, 187–88n17
Register, Cheri, 238
Relationships
—father-daughter: in Maxine Hong Kingston, 181; in Penelope Mortimer, 26, 28, 31, 52, 55, 62n46
—female friendship, 161n16; in Toni Morrison, 135
—incestuous, in Toni Morrison, 126. *See also* Incestuous desire
—lost father, in Margaret Atwood, 83, 114
—lost mother, 235; in Margaret Atwood, 82, 84, 91, 92, 96; in Toni Morrison, 131–32, 133; in Marilynne Robinson, 212, 214–15, 217, 218, 220, 222, 223; in Leslie Silko, 197, 199, 202
—mother-daughter, 6, 28, 41, 42, 61n37, 78–79, 89, 121–22n51, 239n4; in Margaret Atwood, 65, 81, 82, 84, 85, 86, 88, 90, 91, 93, 113, 114, 115; in Chinese culture, 170; in Maxine Hong Kingston, 166, 170, 172, 173–74, 175, 176, 179, 180, 203, 237; in Toni Morrison, 131–32, 133–34, 135, 203; in Penelope Mortimer, 39, 43, 45, 46, 48, 53, 54, 114; in Marilynne Robinson, 214, 215, 218, 221, 223, 226, 227
—mother-son: in Toni Morrison, 136, 137, 147, 148; in Penelope Mortimer, 47, 53; in Leslie Silko, 196, 202
—motherhood, in Margaret Atwood, 99
—stepmother, in Leslie Silko, 193
—symbiotic, 49, 78, 97, 98, 137; in Margaret Atwood, 65, 89, 90, 94; in Toni Morrison, 126, 134–35; in Penelope Mortimer, 29, 36, 41, 42, 43, 46, 48; in Marilynne Robinson, 221, 227; in Leslie Silko, 199
"Return to the womb" (image), 234; in Margaret Atwood, 85–86; in Toni Morrison, 135–36, 147–48; in Marilynne Robinson, 221–22
Rhys, Jean, 16
Rich, Adrienne, 41, 43, 88–89, 114

Rigney, Barbara Hill, 119n31
Robbe-Grillet, Alain, 51
Robinson, Marilynne, 9, 10, 211–28, 232, 233, 234, 236, 238. *See also Housekeeping*
Rose, Ellen Cronan, 118n25
Rossner, Judith, 239n4
Rubenstein, Roberta, 118n17
Russ, Joanna, 165

Salisbury, Harrison E., 186n4
Santayana, George, 50
Seidenberg, Robert, 20, 60n20
Siamese twins (image). *See* Atwood, Margaret
Silko, Leslie, 9, 10, 190–208; *Ceremony*, 190–205; on mixed racial heritage, 193; on relationships, 200; on war, 194
Smith, Catherine F., 3
Smith-Rosenberg, Carroll, 229–30n17
Song of Solomon (Morrison), 136–38, 140–41, 142–43, 145, 148, 151, 153–56, 203, 232, 233, 235
Sontag, Susan, 35, 106
Starobinski, Jean, 4–5, 223, 229n14
Storyteller, 238; in Margaret Atwood, 103; in Maxine Hong Kingston, 172, 174, 177, 180, 204; in Toni Morrison, 204; in Penelope Mortimer, 56; in Leslie Silko, 197, 202
Suicide, 113, 167; in Margaret Atwood, 73, 78; in Maxine Hong Kingston, 167; in Toni Morrison, 135–36; in Marilynne Robinson, 212
Sukenick, Lynn, 119–20n37
Sula (Morrison), 131, 132–33, 134–36, 137–39, 142, 145–46, 147, 151–53, 216, 219, 232
Surfacing (Atwood), 8, 64, 70–73, 76–77, 81, 82–84, 86, 89, 97–99, 100, 112, 114, 115, 116, 225
Survivor guilt, 194

Tanner, Tony, 21
Tar Baby (Morrison), 127, 130–31, 133–34, 141–42, 146, 148–49, 156–59, 203, 225
Thoma, Helmut, 118n24
Thompson, Phyllis Hoge, 186–87n12

Turner, Victor, 204, 208n23
Two-Headed Poems (Atwood), 65
Tyler, Hamilton, 199, 207n20

Velie, Allan, 207n16
Victimization, 235; Margaret Atwood on, 121
A Villa in Summer (Mortimer), 19, 22, 23–24
Vincent, Sybil Korff, 120n41
Vision: in Toni Morrison, 126, 127, 160–61n12; in Penelope Mortimer, 36

Walker, Alice, 239n4

Washington, Mary Helen, 128, 160n9
Weston, Jessie, 207n16
Winnicott, D. W., 7, 12n16, 129
Winthrop, Joan, 60n26, 239n4
Wittig, Monique, 233
Wolf, Margery, 167, 189n28
The Woman Warrior (Kingston), 165–80, 181, 182, 202, 204, 233
Woolf, Virginia, 10, 40, 61n30, 111, 173
Wound. *See* Female wound
Wright, Margaret, 125

Yamada, Mitsuye, 185n1

Note on the Author

Roberta Rubenstein is professor of literature and director of Women's Studies at American University. She is the author of *The Novelistic Vision of Doris Lessing: Breaking the Forms of Consciousness*.